D0984772

Accounting and Finance for Your Small Business

Second Edition

Accounting and Finance for Your Small Business

Second Edition

STEVEN M. BRAGG AND
E. JAMES BURTON

WILEY

John Wiley & Sons, Inc.

This book is printed on acid-free paper.♾

Copyright © 2006 by PricewaterhouseCoopers. PricewaterhouseCoopers refers to the individual member firms of the worldwide PricewaterhouseCoopers organization. All rights reserved.

Published by John Wiley & Sons, Inc., Hoboken, New Jersey.

Published simultaneously in Canada.

No part of this publication may be reproduced, stored in a retrieval system, or transmitted in any form or by any means, electronic, mechanical, photocopying, recording, scanning, or otherwise, except as permitted under Section 107 or 108 of the 1976 United States Copyright Act, without either the prior written permission of the Publisher, or authorization through payment of the appropriate per-copy fee to the Copyright Clearance Center, Inc., 222 Rosewood Drive, Danvers, MA 01923, 978-750-8400, fax 978-646-8600, or on the web at www.copyright.com. Requests to the Publisher for permission should be addressed to the Permissions Department, John Wiley & Sons, Inc., 111 River Street, Hoboken, NJ 07030, 201-748-6011, fax 201-748-6008, or online at http://www.wiley.com/go/permissions.

Limit of Liability/Disclaimer of Warranty: While the publisher and author have used their best efforts in preparing this book, they make no representations or warranties with respect to the accuracy or completeness of the contents of this book and specifically disclaim any implied warranties of merchantability or fitness for a particular purpose. No warranty may be created or extended by sales representatives or written sales materials. The advice and strategies contained herein may not be suitable for your situation. You should consult with a professional where appropriate. Neither the publisher nor author shall be liable for any loss of profit or any other commercial damages, including but not limited to special, incidental, consequential, or other damages.

For general information on our other products and services, or technical support, please contact our Customer Care Department within the United States at 800-762-2974, outside the United States at 317-572-3993 or fax 317-572-4002.

Wiley also publishes its books in a variety of electronic formats. Some content that appears in print may not be available in electronic books.

For more information about Wiley products, visit our Web site at http://*www.wiley.com*.

Library of Congress Cataloging-in-Publication Data

Bragg, Steven M. .
   Accounting and Finance for your small business / Steven M. Bragg.—2nd ed.
      p. cm.
   Rev. ed. of: Accounting and Finance for your small business / E. James Burton, Steven M. Bragg. 2001.
   Includes index.
   ISBN-13: 978-0-471-77156-2(cloth)
   ISBN-10: 0-471-77156-2 (cloth)
      1. Industrial management—Handbooks, manuals, etc. 2. Business enterprises—Finance—handbooks, manuals etc. 3. Small Business—Management. 4. New business enterprises—Management. I. Burton, E. James. Accounting and finance for your small business. II. Title.

HD31.B852 2006
658—dc22
                                                                        2005056956

Printed in the United States of America

10 9 8 7 6 5 4 3 2 1

To the Gove family,
who have run the West Newbury town library for two generations
and who taught the Bragg family to love books

About the Authors

Steven Bragg, CPA, CMA, CIA, CPIM, has been the chief financial officer or controller of four companies, as well as a consulting manager at Ernst & Young and auditor at Deloitte & Touche. He received a Master's degree in finance from Bentley College, an MBA from Babson College, and a Bachelor's degree in Economics from the University of Maine. He has been the two-time president of the Colorado Mountain Club, is an avid alpine skier and mountain biker, and is a certified master diver. Mr. Bragg resides in Centennial, Colorado. He has published the following books through John Wiley & Sons:

Accounting and Finance for Your Small Business

Accounting Best Practices

Accounting Reference Desktop

Billing and Collections Best Practices

Business Ratios and Formulas

Controller's Guide to Costing

Controller's Guide to Planning and Controlling Operations

Controller's Guide: Roles and Responsibilities for the New Controller

Controllership

Cost Accounting

Design and Maintenance of Accounting Manuals

Essentials of Payroll

Fast Close

Financial Analysis

GAAP Guide

GAAP Implementation Guide

Inventory Accounting

Inventory Best Practices

Just-in-Time Accounting

Managing Explosive Corporate Growth

Outsourcing

Payroll Accounting

Payroll Best Practices

Sales and Operations for Your Small Business

The Controller's Function

The New CFO Financial Leadership Manual

The Ultimate Accountants' Reference

Also:

Advanced Accounting Systems (Institute of Internal Auditors)

Run the Rockies (CMC Press)

Subscribe to Steve's free best practices newsletter at www.stevebragg.com

E. James Burton, Ph.D., CPA, CFE, is dean of the College of Business and a full professor of accounting at Middle Tennessee State University. He has founded, owned, managed, and sold a number of businesses in a variety of areas from service to manufacturing. He received a Bachelor of Arts degree from MacMurray College in economics/business, a Master of Business Administration degree from Murray State University in management, and a Ph.D. in accountancy from the University of Illinois at Urbana-Champaign. In addition to over 50 journal articles, he has written *Total Business Planning: A Step-by-Step Guide with Forms* that has continued through three editions and translation into Norwegian. He resides in Murfreesboro, Tennessee.

Contents

Preface

This book has been written for business owners and managers who want to refine the accounting and financial operations of their companies. It provides detailed information about how to run these operations, track cash flows, conduct analyses, analyze key financial information, create a corporate risk management strategy, and manage tax liabilities—in short, all of the key accounting and financial information required to operate a small business.

Chapter 1 reveals the interlocking system of budgets, as well as how to set up a budgeting procedure and use standard budgeting formats to ensure that revenues are properly projected and matched to related costs. This is a very important issue for those cyclical industries in which expenses may be incurred well in advance of sales receipts; it is also a highly necessary method for controlling such key expense areas as payroll and inventory.

Chapter 2 covers the budgeting techniques used for capital acquisition, such as discounted cash flows and payback analysis. We also note how to modify the capital budgeting procedure to account for high-risk expenditures, calculate the cost of capital, and stratify a set of possible capital acquisitions in terms of which is the most desirable.

Chapter 3 describes the need for a solid set of controls to ensure that the business operates in accordance with its budget. We also note a wide array of basic controls that can be adopted by most businesses not only to ensure budgetary compliance, but also to reduce the risk of asset loss.

Chapter 4 turns to the analysis of cash flows. In it we cover the creation of cash forecasts, the management of cash, and exceptions to expected cash flows, which can have a serious impact on actual cash flows. This is a critical area for the small business, which typically operates with minimal cash reserves.

Chapter 5 describes the various sources of financing that are available, including internal cash sources, such as zero working capital, and external ones, such as debt or equity financing, as well as a number of variations that are useful in specific circumstances. Because loans tend to be the chief form of financing, we also note how to obtain bank loans and key terms found in loan agreements.

Chapter 6 notes a large number of financial and operating ratios that are of considerable use in creating a system of performance measurement for all areas of a small business. We describe how to calculate and interpret each of the most common ratios.

Chapter 7 covers key areas of financial analysis that are useful in a small business, including breakeven analysis, capacity utilization, risk analysis, and business cycle forecasting. These fundamental tools allow one to fine-tune a company's operations and anticipate where problems may arise.

Chapter 8 includes coverage of a number of key areas that few small business owners want to address but that can impact their business in a negative manner. These issues include the management of tax liabilities and the creation of a risk management system that includes the selective use of insurance.

Chapter 9 covers the four main areas of reporting that are of concern to the small business owner: reports to the federal government, state government, creditors, and for internal management. We spend most space on internal management reports, because these can be used with great effectiveness if properly structured to reveal the most crucial information about ongoing operations and financial results.

The most effective way to use this book is as a reference source. We suggest that you first read the book through once, implementing the concepts section by section; it is not casual reading but rather a manual, intended for a reading-doing-reading-doing approach. Then, when you have trouble or concerns in a particular area, consult the specific chapter addressing that problem to find solutions.

Best wishes for improving, implementing, and benefiting from your decisions—and for making lots of money.

STEVEN M. BRAGG
Centennial, Colorado
July 2005

Preparing to Operate the Business

The first section of the book covers those tasks that should be accomplished prior to the start of a business or as ongoing analysis after it has been founded. It accomplishes this objective in three chapters.

Chapter 1 covers the budgeting function. The issues addressed here, such as the format of a budget, its components, and how it should be compared to actual results, are critical to the overall management of a business, and should be firmly in place before the organization is created. The budgeting function must also be regularly monitored and controlled to ensure that actual results do not stray from the plan.

Chapter 2 covers investments in large-dollar items, which are known as capital items. It covers the steps to be followed in order to investigate the need for a capital item, compare it to other capital requests, and determine what should be purchased. This is a key factor not only in the beginning of a business, but also in the renewal of key assets over time, as they gradually wear out and require replacement.

Chapter 3 describes the basic controls that should be installed, not only to ensure that the probability of fraud is reduced, but also to verify that the company is not deviating from its planned course. The full range of controls are presented, including such areas as billings, payables, fixed assets, and inventory.

Chapter 1

Budgeting for Operations

Operating budgets are used for planning, operating, and control functions. To improve your probability of success, you should engage in not only long-range but also operational budgeting/planning. The fulfillment of the planning process requires a complete set of marketing, product, capital, and financial plans as are described in this chapter.

Definition or Purpose of an Operating Budget

An operating budget is a projected and, it is hoped, realistic number picture of income and cost objectives for a period.

Usually operating budgets are constructed for a year, by months. Some people construct five-year operating budgets with varying reporting periods. Such budgets are often constructed monthly for the first two years, quarterly for the next two years, and annually or semiannually for the remaining year. However, a one-year budget that is extended quarterly so that it again projects a full year is probably adequate for most uses.

As with any plan, the ensuing actual performance can be compared with the operating budget to detect "off-target" performances and to direct attention to troubled areas. In this way, the operating budget serves both as a planning tool and a control device. All functions of the business should be included when structuring the operating budget. By including all of the operating costs, more performance measures and controls are possible. The costs incurred to increase the level of preparation detail will relate favorably to realization of cost savings through better control.

Since measurements of performance may be devised according to an operating budget, there is a natural tendency for people to "adjust" the budget process. The potential consequences should be considered: Sales managers may make overly optimistic assessments of the market, thus reducing the reliability of the cash allocations and expenses anticipated for that level of production and sales. Some manufacturing managers may "pad" a budget to build in a safety margin or premium. In a tight market or competitive sales conditions, this pad could make a product look less attractive than competing products. The concern should be to make the budget as realistic and accurate as possible because a reasonable budget based on a reasonable plan encourages reasonable performance.

Signs of Budget Ineffectiveness

Some signs that the budget or budget process is less than optimally effective are:

- *Management or supervisory inattention to the budget.* Since a budget is, or can be used as, a measurement tool, accountability and review are necessary for control. Without review, there can be little corrective action, and thus there is a loss of control. If management is not using the budget as a control tool, determine whether the problem is with the budget or with the management.
- *A lack of complete participation by all levels of management within the firm.* Budgets dictated from upper management without input from the accountable people may have negative effects on the psychology of the employees and lower management. An attitude of "It's their budget, let's see them make it!" may develop.
- *Uncorrected large variances between planned performance and budget objectives.* Large budget variances may indicate one of several weaknesses:
  - Poor estimates

- Poor feedback and lack of timely, corrective action
- Ineffective management policies concerning budget maintenance
- *Lack of participation in the operation of the business by those who actively prepare the budgets.* Without a working knowledge of the dynamics of the operations of the business, it is difficult to maintain a working knowledge of current operational status. The amount or frequency of contact with operating departments is usually directly related to the stability of processes. The greater the variability in the operations of the business, the more frequently those who prepare the budget should observe and experience the operating environment.
- *Supervisors or first-line managers do not know how their budgets were determined or what is contained within their budgets.* In such cases, department managers do not know how performance is being evaluated, how well they are performing to expectations, where they may be doing well, and where they are experiencing unplanned difficulties.

Budgets of all types are good planning tools and can also serve a very valuable control function. In order to be used for control, these systems must supplement the budget process:

- *Feedback loop.* Creating the budget itself does not cause programs to be installed to implement the budget. A feedback loop is necessary to direct attention to areas where difficulties may be encountered in meeting the business plan. Periodic budget reports should generate feedback on performance against budget. These reports should trigger action. If the budget and related performance against budget reports do not flag attention to problem areas, you are missing the opportunity for needed improvements.
- *Feedback frequency.* The feedback loop requires continuous measurement of performance to budget estimates. For feedback to work properly, it should be regular, expected, and consistently reported. Comparisons are most effective when they are done regularly, consistently, and timely. Trend analysis of budget

performance is a good early warning device. Of course, benefits of the budget reporting process must outweigh the costs. However, the ongoing evaluation process is one of the places where you should realize substantial savings.

Improvements to the Budgeting System

Some of the budgeting problems outlined in the last section can be eliminated or mitigated by implementing a sound budgeting procedure that is closely followed by the management team throughout the year. In this section we discuss a simple budgeting procedure that is useful for ensuring that the annual budget is constructed using a sufficient amount of time, and in the correct order. Later we also note the monthly schedule to be followed to ensure that the management team reviews the comparison of budget to actual results. However, these are strictly procedural matters; the management team still must be committed to following the dictates of the budget, which is largely up to the senior management team to enforce.

The budget procedure that follows is a guideline for the sequential steps a company should take to ensure that all components of the budget are completed in the correct order and reviewed by those people who will be responsible for budget results. The dates noted in the procedure are based on the assumption that a company is on a calendar year-end; for those companies with a different year-end, just shift the dates to match it.

1. *Expense update.* As of mid-November, issue to each department a listing of its expenses that are annualized based on actual expenses through October of the current year. The listing should include the personnel in each department and their current pay levels. Request a return date of 10 days in the future for this information, which should include estimated changes in expenses.
2. *Revenue update.* As of mid-November, issue to the sales manager a listing of revenue by month by business unit, through October

of the current year. Request a return date of 10 days in the future for this information.

3. *Capital expenditure update.* As of mid-November, issue a form to all department heads, requesting information about the cost and timing of capital expenditures for the upcoming year. Request a return date of 10 days in the future for this information.

4. *Automation update.* As of mid-November, issue a form to the manager of automation, requesting estimates of the timing and size of reductions in headcount in the upcoming year that are due to automation efforts. Request a return date of 10 days in the future for this information. Be sure to compare scheduled headcount reductions to the timing of capital expenditures, since they should track closely.

5. *Update the budget model.* These six tasks should be completed by the end of November:

   • Update the numbers already listed in the budget with information as it is received from the various managers. This may involve changing "hard coded" dollar amounts, or changing flex budget percentages. Be sure to keep a checklist of who has returned information, so that you can follow up with those personnel who have not returned requested information.

   • Verify that the indirect overhead allocation percentages shown on the budgeted factory overhead page are still accurate.

   • Verify that the Federal Insurance Contributions Act (FICA), State Unemployment Tax (SUTA), Federal Unemployment Tax (FUTA), medical, and workers' compensation amounts listed at the top of the staffing budget are still accurate.

   • Add job titles and pay levels to the staffing budget as needed, along with new average pay rates based on projected pay levels made by department managers.

   • Run a depreciation report for the upcoming year, add the expected depreciation for new capital expenditures, and add this amount to the budget.

   • Revise the loan detail budget based on projected borrowings through the end of the year.

6. *Review the budget.* Print out the budget and circle any budgeted expenses or revenues that are significantly different from the

annualized amounts for the current year. Go over the questionable items with the managers who are responsible for those items.

7. *Revise the budget.* Revise the budget, print it again, and review it with the president. Incorporate any additional changes. If the cash balance is excessive, you may have to manually move money from the cash line to the debt line to represent the paydown of debt.

8. *Issue the budget.* Bind the budget and issue it to the management team.

9. *Update accounting database.* Enter budget numbers into the accounting software for the upcoming year. All tasks should be completed by mid-December.[1]

Once the budget has been completed, there must be a feedback loop that sends budget variance information back to the department managers. The best feedback loop is to complete a budget to actual variance report that is sorted by the name of the responsible manager (see Figure 1.8 on page 24) as soon as the financial statements have been completed each month. The controller should take this report to all of the managers and review it with them, bringing back detailed information about each variance, as requested. Finally, there should be a meeting as soon thereafter as possible between the responsible managers and senior management to review variance problems and what each of the managers will do to resolve them. The senior managers should write down these commitments and return them to the managers in memo form; this document forms the basis for the next month's meeting, which will begin with a review of how well the managers have done to attain the targets to which they are committed. A key factor in making this system work is the rapid release of accurate financial statements, so that the department managers will have more time to respond to adverse variance information.

[1] Reprinted with permission from Bragg, Steven, *The Design and Maintenance of Accounting Manuals, 1999 Supplement* (New York: John Wiley & Sons, 1999), pp. 64–66.

Responsibility Accounting

Responsibility accounting means structuring systems and reports to highlight the accountability of specific people. The process involves assigning accountability to departments or functions in which the responsibility for performance lies.

Specific responsibility is a necessary concept of management control. Accounting encompasses at least three purposes: financial reporting, product or service cost reporting, and performance evaluation reporting. The third function of accounting, the performance measurement function, is closely related to the operational function of the business. Since many businesses now evaluate and manage employees by objectives, the need for more sophisticated performance measurement tools has increased.

In a management-by-objectives (MBO) system, the individual must have the authority necessary to carry out the responsibility he or she is asked to execute. Without the necessary authority, a person cannot, and should not, be expected to meet the responsibilities imposed.

Within this level of responsibility, a person can be evaluated only when the performance reporting system is tied to the expected level of performance. A person's actual performance is keyed to this budget expression of expected performance.

Responsibility accounting should not be restricted to any one management level but should measure expected performance throughout the hierarchy of the business. Key indicators can be built into the system to evaluate performance and to trigger reactions to unanticipated results. In this way, management at each level is called on to intervene only when it is necessary to correct problems or substandard performance. This management-by-exception system frees up significant time for managers to plan and coordinate other essential business functions.

In contrast with financial accounting, responsibility accounting does not simply group like costs but instead segments the business into distinct responsibility centers. A measurement process is established to compare results obtained against objectives established for the segment prior to the end of a plan/budget period. These objectives are part of the operating budget and comprise the targets of operation for every segment of the business.

To be effective, responsibility accounting must be tailored to each individual business. The accounting system must be adjusted to conform with the responsibility centers established. The revenue and expense categories must be designed to fit the functions or operations that management believes are important to monitor and evaluate. For example, the use of electricity by a particular machine may be significant, and excessive use may be an early warning sign of a process problem. Management would want to meter electricity consumption and have the expense reported as a line item to be measured against standard consumption rates by machine or by department.

Another function of the responsibility accounting system is to compile the individual centers' performance reports into successively aggregated collective reports to identify broader categories of responsibility. Behind these groupings is still a great deal of detailed information available for analysis.

Developing Responsibility Centers

A responsibility center has no standard size. It can be as small as a single operation or machine or as large as the entire business. The business is, after all, the responsibility center of the chief executive of the business. Typically, the business is broken down into a large number of centers or segments that, when plotted in successive layers or groupings, look like a pyramid. This pyramiding represents the hierarchy of authority and responsibility of the business. Various types of responsibility centers may be established for various purposes. The nature of the centers or segments can also vary.

If a person is charged with only the responsibility for the costs incurred in a process or operation, a *cost center* has been established. Cost centers can be line operations (i.e., painting) or staff functions (i.e., recruiting). The emphasis of a cost center is on producing goods or providing specific services in conjunction with other physical measures of performance. Usually there is no direct revenue production measurement by that center because the center does not produce the final product.

Another segment is a unit held responsible for the profit contribution it makes. This responsibility center is aptly named a *profit center*. Profit centers are often larger units than cost centers because a profit center requires the production of a complete product or service to make a contribution to the profit. (However, a salesperson could be considered a profit center.) The establishment of a profit center should be based on established managerial criteria of revenues and costs.

Other divisions can be established, such as *revenue centers* and *investment centers*. Revenue centers, for instance, are segments of the larger profit centers charged with the responsibility of producing revenue. Sales departments are a typical example. An investment center is a profit center that also has the responsibility of raising and making the necessary investment required to produce the profit. This added investment step would require the use of some rate-of-return test as an objective measure of the center's performance.

The appropriate establishment of cost centers, profit centers, and the like is a critical element of the responsibility reporting system, and as such must be performed carefully and accurately.

Establishing Costs

Another important aspect of responsibility accounting is the accumulation of costs. Accountants have labeled the standard types of costs typically encountered: fixed, variable, and semivariable. Within these classifications, some costs may be incurred at the discretion of specific levels of management whereas others are nondiscretionary at given levels of management. Sometimes costs relate to more than one center and must be allocated between them. The most effective system probably will result when responsible management has been an active participant in the determination of the allocation of costs and the maintenance of the reporting system.

One complication of accumulating costs is the problem of transfer pricing. In manufacturing businesses, a cost center's performance is a function of the added costs and the intracompany movements of raw materials, work-in-progress, finished goods, and services performed. A market price may not be available or may be too uncertain, because of fluctuations, to use as an objective measure of performance. Some compromise is often necessary to establish transfer prices among departments.

Fixed Costs.   A fixed cost is one that does not vary directly with volume. Some costs are really fixed, such as interest on debt. Other typically identified fixed costs, such as depreciation expense, may vary under some circumstances. Generally, over a broad range of operations, total fixed costs are represented as step functions because they are incurred in increments as production or the number of services increases.

This characteristic of fixed costs should not present any great difficulty. Since production or sales is predicted for a budget period, the level of fixed costs can be established from graphs such as that in Figure 1.1. Unfortunately, fixed costs, because of their apparent static behavior, are not always reviewed regularly and critically to determine reasonableness. Like all other costs, the larger the amount of individual fixed costs, the more frequently they should be reviewed. For example, insurance premiums may vary little, if at

FIGURE 1.1

Fixed Costs

Fixed Costs that Rise at Specific Volume Levels

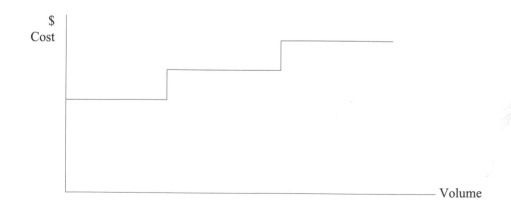

all, from year to year and may be paid without reconsideration, particularly in good times.

Figure 1.2 represents the relationship between the magnitude of a particular fixed cost and the frequency with which it should be reviewed. When making such an assessment for yourself, you should be aware of such factors as the cost of reconsideration in setting the time periods for "seldom" through "often." The process of reevaluating insurance coverage may be a significant task, requiring a major allocation of time and resources. However, the returns could be equally significant if you realize substantial savings resulting from a renegotiation of the insurance policy and rates.

Another concern with fixed costs is the method of allocation of those costs among different products or services. Fixed costs are often assigned in an arbitrary manner, creating an unrealistic profit or loss statement for each product. Otherwise, nonprofitable products are sometimes carried by an "average fixed cost" allocation, which may not accurately depict costs associated with the product. Accurate decisions are unlikely without correct information concerning a

FIGURE **1.2**

Relationship of Cost to Review Frequency

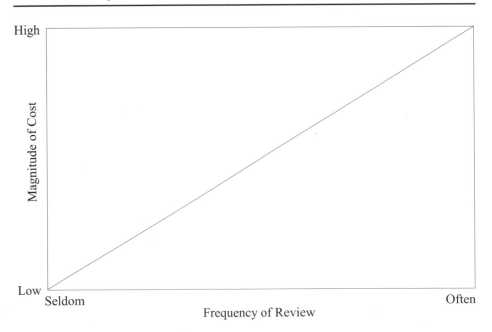

product's costs. You should undertake to allocate fixed costs properly through the preparation of an operating budget. Your accountant should have a reasonable understanding of the magnitude of the costs and of which products or services are affecting the amount. Also, you should determine how varying activity levels influence the costs you incur for different products and services.

When analyzing fixed costs, you should determine what causes that cost to be incurred and what causes it to change in amount. This analysis will help identify to which product(s) or service(s) the cost should be assigned and in what manner that allocation should be made.

For some fixed costs, this will be a very difficult process. Some administrative costs may simply not be identifiable with any one product or service. Successive allocations through your costing hierarchy may be needed to arrive finally at a "product-attributable" status.

You may treat such costs as variable and determine a rate at which to assign these costs against labor hours. In determining this burden or overhead rate, such fixed costs are divided by an estimate or projection of the anticipated direct labor hours and are allocated proportionately. However, this method may unfairly assign costs to labor-intensive products, ignoring that more fixed costs should perhaps be allocated to products with large capital or fixed investments. Furthermore, this assignment could underrecover fixed costs by misestimating projected direct labor hours. Or, equally likely, an overrecovery of fixed costs could occur.

You should take a realistic approach in the allocation of these costs. If a direct hour allocation is realistic, then use it. If fixed costs can be identified to particular product(s) or service(s), it is appropriate to do so.

Variable Costs. In order to be properly classified as variable, a cost should meet two distinct criteria:

1. No cost should be incurred until an activity begins.
2. A direct relationship should exist between the amount of the cost and the level of activity.

An example of a purely variable cost is a sales commission. As sales increase or decrease, the amount of commission varies in direct relationship to the level of sales.

The relationship between the cost and the level of production may be a straight-line relationship, or the cost rate may increase as the level of output increases. When plotted, this increasing cost relationship will appear as a curvilinear (or curved shape) graph.

Although this relationship is common to variable costs, Figure 1.3 is not the usual way it is shown. The more usual case is the straight-line relationship. Often setup costs are spread over production, in which case there is a curvilinear relationship; but that is not the same case. In the setup cost allocation, a fixed cost is spread over varying units of output, decreasing as the length of the production run increases. The earlier example is an increasing cost per unit as the number of units produced increases.

Typically, costs such as direct labor, scrap costs, packaging, and shipping are treated as variable costs. However, direct labor and other costs may not be purely variable. For example, the assumption

FIGURE 1.3

Actual Relationship between Variable Cost and Level of Production

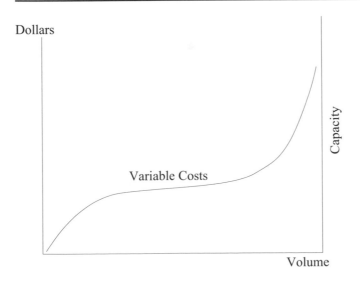

that direct labor varies directly with the number of units produced relies on the divisibility assumption. But labor is not infinitely divisible. If an employee can produce 1,600 units in a standard eight-hour workday but only 1,200 units are required, unless that employee can be used in another operation, he or she has been used at a 75 percent utilization level. Either this idle-time labor can be used effectively in other places or 25 percent of these (unutilized) efforts are assigned to fewer units produced. In most cases, direct labor and direct materials are treated as variable costs for budget purposes even if they are not perfectly divisible.

If you have established labor standards for your operations, these can be used for budgeting purposes. By accumulating data and establishing labor standards, you can begin to target costs. The difficulty is establishing objective labor-hour targets for the planning period. Reliance solely on historical data may bias projections, ignore the effects of the learning curve on efficiency, and avoid consideration of past inefficiencies.

For planning purposes, remember that the graph of these fixed and variable costs appears reversed *when they are assigned on a per-unit basis*. When variable costs are assigned on a per-unit basis, they are constant and fixed per unit. When fixed costs are assigned on a per-unit basis, they vary as production levels change.

Mixed Costs.   Mixed costs are those that behave as if they have fixed and variable components. Many items of cost fall into this category. Some people treat mixed costs as fixed costs. If you do so, you must assume an average or projected level of output and allocate the cost over that level. This may over- or underrecover that component of fixed cost. Some might say that it is not important because the over- or underrecovery will be insignificant.

If a consistent bias toward underrecovery of the fixed component of one mixed cost exists, underrecovery of the fixed component of every mixed cost, allocated on the basis of that misestimated output level, may exist. If you use these biased data to make capital investment decisions, marketing and pricing decisions, and expansion or contraction decisions, you may experience serious problems.

It is sometimes difficult to determine what portion of a mixed cost is fixed and what portion is variable. Fortunately, this allocation usually can be established from historical data. As an example, data for the consumption of electricity in one department were tabulated for the previous six months (see Figure 1.4).

Plotting this consumption (see Figure 1.5), with the Y axis being kilowatt hours (kWh) consumed and the X axis being the units produced, the Y intercept is 5,000 kWh. This indicates that for zero production, the department still consumes 5,000 kWh of electricity each month, the fixed component of cost.

The variable component can then be determined by using the formula:

$$Y = MX + B$$

Because B, the Y intercept, is 5,000:

$$Y = MX + 5,000$$

Substituting any set of values from the table into the equation:

$$7,500 = M(400) + 5,000$$

and solving for (M), $M = 6.25$. Therefore, each unit of production has a variable component of 6.25 kWh in electrical consumption. By applying the electric rate to each component of electrical usage, the fixed- and variable-cost components of the mixed cost are determined.

Historical Data. One major concern of using historical data as a basis for future prediction is that the firm may be perpetuating past inefficiencies. However, historical data may be the best or even the only data available. When using historical data, you should be sure that:

- Historical data accurately state the past. An examination must be made of the conditions under which data were collected and what is and is not contained in the data.
- Historical data are relevant to what the firm is trying to predict. To the extent current conditions are not the same as past

FIGURE **1.4**

Consumption of Power Table

	kWh Used	Units Produced
Jan	7,500	400
Feb	8,000	480
Mar	8,250	520
Apr	8,750	600
May	9,500	720
June	8,750	600

FIGURE **1.5**

Consumption of Power Graph

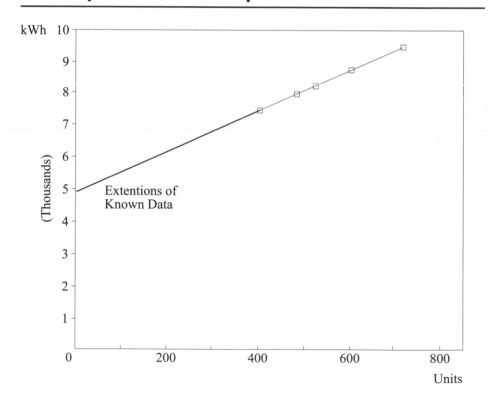

conditions, historical data become more difficult to use in projecting the future.

- The use of the data encourages performance that improves on the past performance.
- The effects of inflation are properly considered.

Further *practical points* in the use of historical data include:

- Avoid using historical data more than 12 months old in periods of high inflation or deflation.
- Be consistently objective. Do not bias the data by summarily rejecting data that seem to be out of line. There may be a reason for unusual numbers.
- Be creative; try not to be bound by traditional thinking. Some of the relationships between costs and activities may not seem direct and quantifiable. This could be the result of delayed billings or nontraditional billings.
- Consider and try using moving averages for data that tend to be nonlinear or scattered.
- Use extrapolation to project data for future estimated production or service levels.
- Never use tools past the point that common sense tells you is meaningful.

Projecting Revenues

Often firms want a forecast of earnings for the entire enterprise to compare with the operating budgets. This forecast of revenues should be reconciled with the operating budget.

The basis of all revenue projections is a sales forecast. Many companies start the operating budget process by first generating this sales forecast. The sales forecast is exploded with lead and lag times added so that departmental schedules are created. This departmental scheduling of activities is then used to create the operating budget. For example, Fruit Crate Manufacturing Co., Inc., has a maximum production capacity of 1,000 crates per week and expects this sales forecast:

	July	Aug
Type A crate	2,000	3,000

To produce a type A crate, the firm's process breaks down into three steps: sawing, curing or drying, and assembly. The sawing and curing is done in batches of 1,000 crates, and the rate of production is:

FIGURE 1.6

Exploded Production Schedule

Production Schedules
1,000-Crate Batches

MAY			JUNE			JULY			AUGUST		
S					A						
	D	D	D								
	S					A					
		D	D	D							
		S				A					
			D	D	D						
			S				A				
				D	D	D					
				S				A			
					D	D	D				

Sawing	1,000 crates/1 week
Drying	1,000 crates/3 weeks
Assembly	1,000 crates/1 week

Since all sales are shipped on the first of each month, the exploded production schedule shown in Figure 1.6 is used for budgeting.

Armed with this operating schedule, the company can plan its equipment, labor, and materials scheduling, and a budget of expenses can be generated. For example, in May, two weeks of sawing and one week of drying must be budgeted; in June, three weeks of sawing, eight weeks of drying, and two weeks of assembly; and so forth.

As manufacturing and related costs are pushed back in time, the receipt of payments (cash flows) is pushed forward in time. If Fruit Crate Manufacturing Co., Inc., offers a 2/10, N/30 payment schedule (2 percent discount if paid within 10 days of invoice, the net amount due within 30 days), it will ship on July 1, having incurred expenses in May and June, but not expect payment until July 10 or August 1. The timing of cash flows, the revenue portion, and the expense portion of the plan must be coordinated to ensure that adequate funds are on hand (cashflow budget) to meet expected operations. For this example, there is a negative cash flow for at least two and a half months.

Budget Tracking and Maintenance

So far, this chapter has emphasized establishing responsibility and developing a budget and accounting system that conforms to an allocation of responsibility. The cardinal principle behind this system is that those who are to be measured by the system understand how it works and agree that the objectives are attainable *through their efforts.*

The first requirement should be an integration of your objectives, goals, and tactics to the managerial level involved. One method for integration is to have each manager participate in establishing and maintaining the objectives and goals. The test of reasonableness should apply. That is, there should be a reasonable likelihood of obtaining the objective in order to motivate compliance.

An element that often impedes effective budgeting and attainability is the inability to identify controllable and uncontrollable costs or expenses. Controllable costs should be identified and targeted. If elements of uncontrollable costs are included in a responsibility-based budget, they may have a negative motivation factor. Practically, all revenue and expense factors are controllable by some manager at some point. However, expenses such as property taxes may influence profits, yet be beyond the control of an operations manager. Items such as administrative overhead allocation are uncontrollable within departments of the firm. As a general rule, these items should be assigned and accounted for separately, so as not to indicate responsibility of the manager (e.g., heating, lighting, janitorial).

The final element in the budget tracking plan is variance analysis and reporting. Variance reporting can take many forms, but the most common is to compare monthly actuals to monthly projections with year-to-date comparisons as well. Often the report will contain space for an explanation of the variance from budget. The report can be generated in many forms, including by product, by operation or group, by labor, and by materials. A typical report could look like the one shown in Figure 1.7.

The report shown in Figure 1.7 compares budgeted to actual costs by account category, such as repair supplies or insurance. Although this format is good for determining trends in certain cost categories, it does not assist in targeting which managers are responsible for specific costs. An example of a report that includes this information is shown in Figure 1.8. In this example, we have used the same expense line items but also added a column that lists the name of the manager who is responsible for each expense. Further, we have sorted the report by the names of those managers. This sorting has two purposes:

1. It divides the report into separate pages for each manager, so that each one can easily group together the expenses for which he or she is responsible.
2. Sorting the report by manager allows you to summarize variances for each person, so that senior managers can determine which managers are doing the best job of keeping their costs

Figure 1.7

Budgeted versus Annual Costs

	Month			Year-to-Date			Explanations
	Budget	Actual	% Var	Budget	Actual	% Var	
A. Controllable							
Direct Labor							
Operating Supplies							
Repair Labor							
Repair Supplies							
Heat, Light, Power							
Subtotal							
B. Raw Materials							
Subtotal							
C. Overhead							
Supervisory Salaries							
Corporate Overhead							
Taxes							
Insurance							
Depreciation Expense							
Subtotal							
Total							

FIGURE 1.8

Comparison of Budget to Actual, Sorted by Responsibility

Expense Description Variance	Responsible Manager	Month			Year-to-Date		
		Budget	Actual	% Variance	Budget	Actual	%
Direct Labor	D. Hendricks	25,400	23,000	-9%	177,800	161,000	-9%
Repair Labor	D. Hendricks	8,000	7,250	-9%	56,000	50,750	-9%
Supervisory Salaries	D. Hendricks	7,250	7,000	-3%	50,750	49,000	-3%
Totals		40,650	37,250	-8%	284,550	260,750	-8%
Operating Supplies	R. Olbermann	1,450	1,500	3%	10,150	10,500	3%
Repair Supplies	R. Olbermann	3,300	3,500	6%	23,100	24,500	6%
Depreciation Expense	R. Olbermann	500	520	4%	3,500	3,640	4%
Totals		5,250	5,520	5%	36,750	38,640	5%
Heat, Light, Power	T. Abrams	3,200	1,700	-47%	22,400	11,900	-47%
Raw Materials	T. Abrams	89,450	79,500	-11%	626,150	556,500	-11%
Corporate Overhead	T. Abrams	55,000	56,000	2%	385,000	392,000	2%
Taxes	T. Abrams	11,500	10,250	-11%	80,500	71,750	-11%
Insurance	T. Abrams	27,050	26,000	-4%	189,350	182,000	-4%
Totals		186,200	173,450	-7%	1,303,400	1,214,150	-7%

within designated goals, which can be of assistance when determining the size of manager bonuses.

In Figure 1.8, the report reveals that the only manager who is consistently failing to achieve actual costs that are less than the budget is R. Olbermann, whose cumulative variance performance is 5 percent worse than the budget.

When the management team reviews revenue and expense variances, it does not have time to review what may be hundreds of individual accounts. Instead, it has sufficient time to analyze only a small proportion of the largest variances. Accordingly, the accounting staff can issue a summarized version of Figure 1.8 that lists only line items for which variances exceed a certain monthly or year-to-date dollar amount or percentage. The remaining accounts can still be issued as an addendum to the variance report. This slight format change will focus management's attention on the few largest variances that are most in need of correction.

This form of reporting consistently shows management the variations from budget, with an explanation of causes and circumstances. It thus meets the second and third objectives of a budget: to keep score and direct attention.

The System of Interlocking Budgets[2]

A properly designed budget is a complex web of spreadsheets that accounts for the activities of virtually all areas within a company. As noted in Figure 1.9, the budget begins in two places, with both the revenue budget and the research and development (R&D) budget. The revenue budget contains the revenue figures that the company believes it can achieve for each upcoming reporting period. These estimates come partially from sales staff members, who are responsible for estimates of sales levels for existing products within their current territories. Estimates for the sales of new products that have not yet been released and for existing products in new markets will

---

[2] Adapted with permission from Steven M. Bragg, *Ultimate Accountants' Reference* (Hoboken, NJ: John Wiley & Sons, 2005), pp. 340–348.

come from a combination of sales and marketing staff members, who will use their experience with related product sales to derive estimates. The greatest fallacy in any budget is to impose a revenue budget from the top management level without any input from the sales staff; this can result in a company-wide budget that is geared toward a sales level that is most unlikely to be reached.

A revenue budget requires prior consideration of a number of issues. For example, a general market share target will drive several other items within the budget, since greater market share may come at the cost of lower unit prices or higher credit costs. Another issue is the compensation strategy for the sales staff, since a shift to higher or lower commissions for specific products or regions will be a strong incentive for sales staff members to alter their selling behavior, resulting in some changes in estimated sales levels. Yet another consideration is which sales territories are to be entered during the budget period; those with high target populations may yield very high sales per hour of sales effort, while the reverse will be true if the remaining untapped regions have smaller target populations. It is also necessary to review the price points that will be offered during the budget period, especially in relation to the pricing strategies that are anticipated from competitors. If there is a strategy to increase market share as well as to raise unit prices, then the budget may fail due to conflicting activities. Another major factor is the terms of sale, which can be extended, along with easy credit, to attract more marginal customers; conversely, they can be retracted in order to reduce credit costs and focus company resources on a few key customers. A final point is that the budget should address any changes in the type of customer to whom sales will be made. If an entirely new type of customer will be added to the range of sales targets during the budget period, then the revenue budget should reflect a gradual ramp-up that will be required for sales staff members to work through the sales cycle of the new customers.

Once all of these factors have been combined to create a preliminary revenue budget, the sales staff members should also compare the budgeted sales level per person to the actual sales level that has been experienced in the recent past to see if the company has the existing capability to make the budgeted sales. If not, the revenue budget should be ramped up to reflect the time it will take

FIGURE 1.9

The System of Budgets

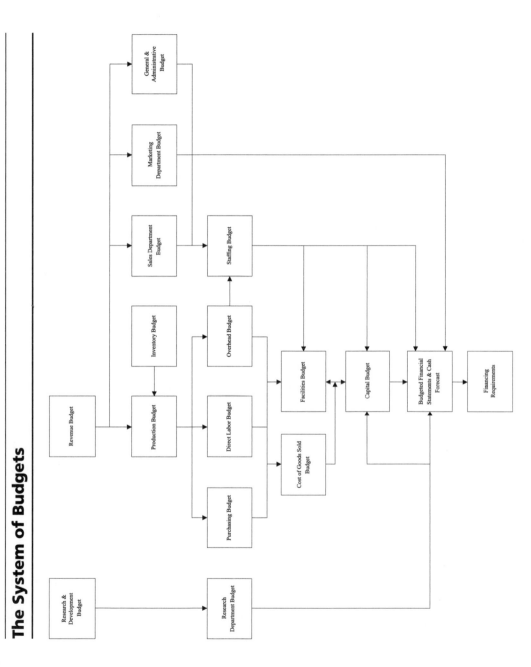

to hire and train additional salespeople. The same cross-check can be conducted for the amount of sales budgeted per customer, to see if historical experience validates the sales levels noted in the new budget.

Another budget that initiates other activities within the system of budgets is the R&D budget. Unlike most other budgets, this is not related to the sales level at all, but instead is a discretionary budget based on the company's strategy to derive new or improved products. The decision to fund a certain amount of project-related activity in this area will drive a departmental staffing and capital budget that is, for the most part, completely unrelated to the activity conducted by the rest of the company. However, there can be a feedback loop between this budget and the cash budget, since financing limitations may require management to prune some projects from this area. If so, the management team must work with the R&D manager to determine the correct mix of projects with both short-range and long-range payoffs that will still be funded.

The production budget is driven largely by the sales estimates contained within the revenue budget. However, it is also driven by the inventory-level assumptions in the inventory budget. The inventory budget contains estimates by the materials management supervisor regarding the inventory levels that will be required for the upcoming budget period. For example, a new goal may be to reduce the level of finished goods inventory from 10 turns per year to 15. If so, some of the products required by the revenue budget can be bled off from the existing finished goods inventory stock, requiring smaller production requirements during the budget period. Alternatively, if there is a strong focus on improving the level of customer service, then it may be necessary to keep more finished goods in stock, which will require more production than is strictly called for by the revenue budget. This concept can also be extended to work-in-process (WIP) inventory, where the installation of advanced production planning systems, such as manufacturing resources planning or just-in-time, can be used to reduce the level of required inventory. All of these assumptions should be clearly delineated in the inventory budget, so that the management team is clear about what systemic changes will be required in order to effect altered inventory turnover levels.

Given this input from the inventory budget, the production budget is used to derive the unit quantity of required products that must be manufactured in order to meet revenue targets for each budget period. This involves a number of interrelated factors, such as the availability of sufficient capacity for production needs. Of particular concern should be the amount of capacity at the bottleneck operation. It is important to budget a sufficient quantity of funding to ensure that this operation includes enough equipment to meet the targeted production goals. If the bottleneck operation involves skilled labor, rather than equipment, then the human resources department should be consulted regarding its ability to bring in the necessary personnel in time to improve the bottleneck capacity in a timely manner.

The expense items included in the production budget should be driven by a set of subsidiary budgets: the purchasing, direct labor, and overhead budgets. These budgets can simply be included in the production budget, but they typically involve such a large proportion of company costs that it is best to lay them out separately in greater detail in separate budgets. Specifics on these budgets follow.

- *Purchasing budget.* The purchasing budget is driven by several factors, first of which is the bill of materials that comprises the products that are planned for production during the budget period. These bills must be accurate, or else the purchasing budget can include seriously incorrect information. In addition, there should be a plan for controlling material costs, perhaps through the use of concentrated buying through few suppliers or perhaps through the use of long-term contracts. If materials are highly subject to market pressures, comprise a large proportion of total product costs, and have a history of sharp price swings, then a best-case and worst-case costing scenario should be added to the budget, so that managers can review the impact of costing issues in this area. It is also worthwhile to budget for a raw material scrap and obsolescence expense; there should be a history of costs in these areas that can be extrapolated based on projected purchasing volumes.
- *Direct labor budget.* Do not make the mistake of budgeting for direct labor as a fully variable cost. The production volume from

day to day tends to be relatively fixed, and requires a set number of direct labor personnel on a continuing basis to operate production equipment and manually assemble products. Thus, direct labor should be shown in the budget as a fixed cost of production, within certain production volume parameters.

Also, this budget should describe staffing levels by type of direct labor position; this is driven by labor routings, which are documents that describe the exact type and quantity of staffing needed to produce a product. When multiplied by the unit volumes located in the production budget, the labor routing results in an expected level of staffing by direct labor position. This information is most useful for the human resources department, which is responsible for staffing the positions.

The direct labor budget should also account for any contractually mandated changes in hourly rates, which may be itemized in a union agreement. Such an agreement may also have restrictions on layoffs, which should be accounted for in the budget if this will keep labor levels from dropping in proportion with budgeted reductions in production levels. Thus, the presence of a union contract can result in a much more complex direct labor budget than would normally be the case.

Any drastic increases in the budgeted level of direct labor personnel will likely result in some initial declines in labor efficiency, since it takes time for new employees to learn their tasks. If this is the case, the budget should reflect a low level of initial efficiency that will result in greater initial direct labor costs, with a ramp-up over time to higher levels.

- *Overhead budget.* The overhead budget can be a simple one to create if there are no significant changes in production volume from the preceding year, because this budget involves a large quantity of static costs that will not vary much over time. Included in this category are machine maintenance; utilities; supervisory salaries; wages for the materials management, production scheduling, and quality assurance personnel; facilities maintenance; and depreciation expenses. Under the no-change scenario, the most likely budgetary alterations will be to machinery or facilities maintenance, which are dependent on the condition and level of usage of company property.

If there is a significant change in the expected level of production volume, or if new production lines are to be added, then you should examine this budget in great detail, for the underlying production volumes may cause a ripple effect that results in wholesale changes to many areas of the overhead budget. Of particular concern is the number of overhead-related personnel who must be either laid off or added when capacity levels reach certain critical points, such as the addition or subtraction of extra work shifts. Costs also tend to rise substantially when a facility is operating at very close to 100 percent capacity, which calls for an inordinate amount of effort to maintain on an ongoing basis.

The purchasing, direct labor, and overhead budgets can then be summarized into a cost-of-goods-sold budget. This budget should incorporate, as a single line item, the total amount of revenue, so that all manufacturing costs can be deducted from it to yield a gross profit margin on the same document. This budget is referred to constantly during the budget creation process, since it tells management if its budgeting assumptions are yielding an acceptable gross margin result. Since it is a summary-level budget for the production side of the budgeting process, this is also a good place to itemize any production-related statistics, such as the average hourly cost of direct labor, inventory turnover rates, and the amount of revenue dollars per production person.

Thus far, we have reviewed the series of budgets that descend in turn from the revenue budget and then through the production budget. However, other expenses unrelated to production are categories in a separate set of budgets. The first is the sales department budget, which includes the expenses that the sales staff members must incur in order to achieve the revenue budget, such as travel and entertainment, as well as sales training. Of particular concern in this budget is the amount of budgeted headcount that is required to meet the sales target. It is essential that the actual sales per salesperson from the most recent completed year of operations be compared to the same calculation in the budget to ensure that there is a sufficiently large budget available for an adequate number of sales personnel. Often companies make the false assumption that the existing sales staff can make heroic efforts to wildly exceed previous-year sales efforts. Furthermore, the budget must account for a sufficient time period in which new sales personnel can be trained and form an adequate base of customer contacts to create a meaningful stream of revenue for the company. In some industries, this learning curve may be only a few days, but it can be the better part of a year if considerable technical knowledge is required to make a sale. If the latter situation is the case, it is likely that the procurement and retention of qualified sales staff is the key element of success for a company, which makes the sales department budget one of the most important elements of the entire budget.

The marketing budget is also closely tied to the revenue budget, for it contains all of the funding required to roll out new products, merchandise them properly, advertise for them, test new products, and so on. A key issue here is to ensure that the marketing budget is fully funded to support any increases in sales noted in the revenue budget. It may be necessary to increase this budget by a disproportionate amount if you are trying to create a new brand, issue a new product, or distribute an existing product in a new market. These costs can easily exceed any associated revenues for some time.

Another nonproduction budget that is integral to the success of the corporation is the general and administrative budget, which contains the cost of the corporate management staff, plus all accounting, finance, and human resources personnel. Since this is a cost center, the general inclination is to reduce these costs to the bare minimum. However, there must be a significant investment in technology in order to achieve reductions in the manual labor usually required to process transactions; thus, there must be some provision in the capital budget for this area.

There is a feedback loop between the staffing and direct labor budgets and the general and administrative budget, because the human resources department must staff itself based on the amount of hiring or layoffs anticipated elsewhere in the company. Similarly, a major change in the revenue volume will alter the budget for the accounting department, since many of the activities in this area are driven by the volume of sales transactions. Thus, the general and administrative budget generally requires a number of iterations in response to changes in many other parts of the budget.

Although salaries and wages should be listed in each of the departmental budgets, it is useful to list the total headcount for each position through all budget periods in a separate staffing budget. By doing so, the human resources staff members can tell when specific positions must be filled, so that they can time their recruiting efforts most appropriately. This budget also provides good information for the person responsible for the facilities budget, since he or she can use it to determine the timing and amount of square footage requirements for office space. Rather than being a stand-alone budget, the staffing budget tends to be one whose formulas are closely intertwined with those of all other departmental budgets. A change in headcount information on this budget will translate automatically into a change in the salaries expense on other budgets. It is also a good place to store the average pay rates, overtime percentages, and average benefit costs for all positions. By centralizing this cost information, the human resources department can update budget information more easily. Since salary-related costs tend to comprise the highest proportion of costs in a company (excluding materials costs), this budget tends to be heavily used.

The facilities budget is based on the level of activity that is estimated in many of the budgets just described. For this reason, it is one of the last budgets to be completed. This budget is closely linked to the capital budget, since expenditures for additional facilities will require more maintenance expenses in the facilities budget. This budget typically contains expense line items for building insurance, maintenance, repairs, janitorial services, utilities, and the salaries of the maintenance personnel employed in this function. When constructing this budget, it is crucial to estimate the need for any upcoming major repairs to facilities, since these can greatly amplify the total budgeted expense.

Another budget that includes input from virtually all areas of a company is the capital budget. This budget should comprise either a summary listing of all main fixed asset categories for which purchases are anticipated or else a detailed listing of the same information; the latter case is recommended only if there are comparatively few items to be purchased. The capital budget is of great importance to the calculation of corporate financing requirements, since it can involve the expenditure of sums far beyond those that are normally encountered through daily cash flows. It is also necessary to ensure that capital items are scheduled for procurement sufficiently far in advance of related projects that they will be fully installed and operational before the scheduled first activity date of the project. For example, a budget should not itemize revenue from a printing press for the same month in which the press is scheduled to be purchased, because it may take months to set up the press.

The end result of all the budgets just described is a set of financial statements that reflects the impact of the upcoming budget on the company. At a minimum, these statements should include the income statement and cash flow statement, since these are the best evidence of fiscal health during the budget period. The balance sheet is less necessary, since the key factors on which it reports are related to cash, and that information is already contained within the cash flow statement. These reports should be directly linked to all the other budgets, so that any changes to the budgets will immediately appear in the financial statements. The management team will closely examine these statements and make numerous adjustments to the budgets in order to arrive at a satisfactory financial result.

The budget-linked financial statements are also a good place to store related operational and financial ratios, so that the management team can review this information and revise the budgets in order to alter the ratios to match benchmarking or industry standards that may have been set as goals. Typical measurements in this area can include revenue and income per person, inventory turnover ratios, and gross margin percentages. This type of information is also useful for lenders, who may have required minimum financial performance results as part of loan agreements, such as a minimum current ratio or debt-to-equity ratio.

The cash forecast is of exceptional importance, for it tells company managers if the proposed budget model will be feasible. If cash projections result in major cash needs that cannot be met by any possible financing, then the model must be changed. The assumptions that go into the cash forecast should be based on strictly historical fact, rather than the wishes of managers. This stricture is particularly important in the case of cash receipts from accounts receivable. If the assumptions are changed in the model to reflect an advanced rate of cash receipts that exceeds anything that the company has ever experienced, it is very unlikely that it will be achieved during the budget period. Instead, it is better to use proven collection periods as assumptions and alter other parts of the budget to ensure that cash flows remain positive.

The last document in the system of budgets is the discussion of financing alternatives. This is not strictly a budget, although it will contain a single line item, derived from the cash forecast, that itemizes funding needs during each period itemized in the budget. In all other respects, it is simply a discussion of financing alternatives, which can be quite varied. Alternatives may involve a mix of debt, supplier financing, preferred stock, common stock, or some other, more innovative approach. The document should contain a discussion of the cost of each form of financing, the ability of the company to obtain it, and when it can be obtained. Managers may find that there are so few financing alternatives available, or that the cost of financing is so high, that the entire budget must be restructured in order to avoid the negative cash flow that calls for the financing. There may also be a need for feedback from this document into the budgeted financial statements in order to account for the cost of obtaining the funding and any related interest costs.

Need for Budget Updating

Flexible or variable budgets should be kept current so that targets are realistic and accurately reflect deviations from expected costs. Budgets, however, may lose their effectiveness as a measuring and control device if they are adjusted for every small change in operating costs. There is no rule of thumb for triggering a budget adjustment. However, budgets should be adjusted for changes in product mix, major changes in cost levels, and schedule variations that significantly alter cost relationships.

On a departmental level, budget performance reflects actual departmental cost behavior, and budget gains or savings directly result in improvements in profits. The budget becomes an individual department's profit and loss expectation based on responsibility accounting.

One area in which potential problems may not be recognized is deferred maintenance. When increased output or profit is being emphasized, periodic maintenance is often deferred to "keep the wheels turning." This may be shortsighted, resulting instead in deferred costs when breakdowns occur.

Summary

The operating budget is a tool that can be integrated into overall operations. It can give an indication about the delays between cash outlays for manufacturing and sales receipts. This delay can be quantified in the budget and thereby permit you to plan for carrying or acquiring additional cash for predictable periods.

As with any good planning tool, the operating plan and related budget points up the opportunity for capital expenditures or the need for tightening capital investments. Because sales predictions are the driving force behind budget numbers, you will plan sales forces, marketing objectives, advertising budgets, sales quotas, credit policies, and many other factors as parts of operational budgeting/planning.

Finally, manpower planning and allocation can be computed from the production schedule and direct labor rates. The formula is simply a direct allocation of hours per operation per product times the number of units of product scheduled for production, summed over all operations. For example, in the Fruit Crate case:

- The total labor hours per crate was .158 hours in May.
- In May, the firm scheduled 2,300 crates (equivalent) for production, which represents 363.4 direct labor hours.
- There were 176 hours (gross) per worker available in the month. The firm planned for 81 percent utilization in hours as a result of breaks, sickness, leave, and fatigue.

- The firm calculates 142.6 hours per man per month effective work time.
- By dividing 363.4 by 142.6, the firm arrives at 2.5 direct laborers necessary to produce the crates.

Using such an analysis, the firm can also break out, by operation, the number of employees needed for each task.

As a control device, an operating plan or budget can provide needed information and direct attention where variances have occurred.

Chapter 2

Investing in Long-Term Assets and Capital Budgeting

Most capital investment decisions should be made in two parts: first, the investment decision; then, the financing decision. You should first decide what facilities, equipment, or other capital assets you will acquire, when to acquire them, and what to do with them. Then you should decide where and how to get the money. This chapter will consider only the investment decision; the financing issues are left to Chapter 5.

The term *capital budgeting* may be defined as planning for an expenditure or outlay of cash resources and a return from the anticipated flow of future cash benefits. The necessary elements to be considered for this decision are:

- Expected costs and their timing
- The flow of anticipated benefits
- The time over which those funds will flow
- The risk involved in the realization of those benefits

Each of these elements has distinct characteristics associated with a company's management philosophy. Tools have been developed that use the numbers generated by management to help answer questions and to make reasoned decisions among competing business opportunities for the use of scarce investment dollars. In this chapter, we look at the capital budgeting process as part of a cycle, not as an isolated exercise. We begin with an idea for a new product and proceed through to the discontinuance of that product and into the next generation.

Definitions

Before attempting an explanation of the capital budgeting process, we need to be familiar with several terms. The common financial terms used in this chapter are:

Present value. The present value of an item is the value *today* of an amount you expect to receive or to pay at some future date. For example, if you expect to receive $100 one year from today, and you can get 12 percent for your money, that stream of income has a *present* value of $89.29 because $89.29 invested today at 12 percent return *will be* $100.00 one year from today.

Annuity (regular or ordinary). The receipt or payment of a series of equal payments made at the end of each of a number of fixed periods. The receipt of $100 on December 31 of each year for 10 years is an ordinary annuity. (An "annuity due" means payments are received at the beginning of each period rather than at the end.)

Payback period. The payback period indicates how long it takes for you to get your money back. In other words, it is the time necessary for net cash inflows to amortize an original investment. Interest or the time value of money often is not considered in simple payback calculations. However, a more appropriate form of payback calculation, called the discounted payback period, does consider the time value. In discounted payback, the present value of the inflows is considered in determining how long it takes to get the investment back.

Net present value (NPV). The present value of inflows of cash minus the present value of the outflows of cash. This is normally after-tax cash flows.

Present value index. The net present value divided by original investment. (This index is useful only for positive net present values.)

Internal rate of return (IRR). The discount (interest) rate, which when used in calculating NPV results in NPV being zero. This is sometimes called the true rate of return.

Overview and Use of Capital Budgeting

Budgets, a frequently used tool, have been around for a long time. Operating budgets seem to be the most common. Although seldom used to their potential, operating budgets are ordinarily among the first budgets attempted. The numbers for these budgets are not difficult to obtain, and most managers will give at least some credence to their usefulness. Operating budgets are discussed in detail in Chapter 1.

Cash budgets are not greatly different from operating budgets in their preparation and use. In cash budgeting, attention is focused on the receipt and expenditure of cash. However, cash budgets often are limited to use by fewer people within a business and often are not formalized until required by shortages of cash or the high cost of maintaining cash reserves. In periods of better financial conditions, the inefficiency of having too much cash often is overlooked. As a result, cash budgets sometimes fall into disuse during periods of prosperity.

Capital budgeting, however, does not fare well with many businesspeople. This is due in part to the difficulties of preparing a capital budget. Estimates of cash flows must be pushed farther into the future and unfamiliar terms, such as *weighted average cost of capital* and *internal rate of return,* creep into the terminology. The calculations associated with these terms are often unfamiliar; many businesspeople have learned to operate with no formal capital budget. However, used properly, a capital budgeting process can help to reduce the risk of making the wrong decision.

Capital budgeting is useful as a decision tool. Accountants, and some of your staff and some managers, probably have been trained to make the calculations necessary for determinations of present values, internal rates of return, and payback periods. These calculations are fairly simple and can be done using the forms provided in the appendix to this chapter. Some inexpensive calculators can do most of the calculations with ease. The critical work is the gathering of the information necessary to make the capital budgeting process more understandable and useful to the business.

Life Cycles

Products and projects, like people, have life cycles, as shown in Figure 2.1. They all go through similar stages: conception, birth, growth, maturity, decline, and ultimately death. Each stage requires a certain degree of attention. The applicability of capital budgeting concepts to new projects or new products extends beyond application to new ventures. It can be used to consider the replacement of existing product lines and even to cost reductions in existing lines in the current or future periods.

FIGURE 2.1

Project Life Cycle

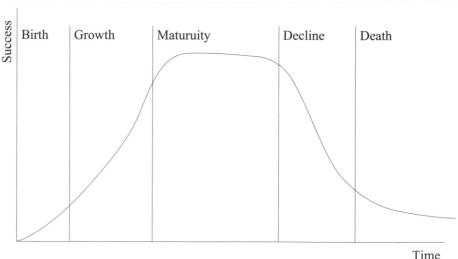

Capital Budgeting Sequence

Four basic sets of actions occur in a capital budgeting plan: proposal solicitation or generation, evaluation, implementation, and follow-up. We shall examine each in some detail.

Proposal Solicitation or Generation

1. The first step in proposal generation is evaluation of your present status. Many factors should be considered when making an evaluation of status. It is particularly important to pay attention to your position with respect to the availability of management talent, technological talent, financial and market positions, sources of labor, and the availability of markets for your product.

   Example: Assume you manufacture heavy cast-iron cylinders for which "the market" is located in southeastern sunbelt states. Therefore, one particularly important factor is the cost of transportation of the product to the ultimate user. At least two alternatives are available: Locate the plant in the area where the product is consumed or acquire manufacturing facilities on low-cost transportation networks, such as rail or water.

   Another option may be to redesign the product. For example, assume you find that you can manufacture the cylinders out of aluminum with the installation of a tooled steel sleeve instead of the cast-iron cylinder. The product now requires different raw materials, different processing and handling, and different packaging and shipping. The new product may change your marketing plans, and a proposal for capital expenditures may result.

2. The questions that you should answer are standard business planning questions: "What do we do best?" and "Where are we going?" These require an evaluation of your business plan. The objectives formulated as a result of these questions may point out potential projects requiring capital expenditures.

   Decisions relative to capital expenditures may be made at various levels within the organization depending on their size and significance. Rules for decision making should be consistently applied at whatever level of management you have established.

3. Cost reduction programs may be a rich source of capital budgeting projects. Cost reduction programs generally carry with them less risk than any other form of project, because they have obvious cost justifications. Potential payback periods and returns on investments can be calculated readily because the programs are intended to improve the cost efficiency of existing projects. Such programs, if adopted, help make employees feel that they are a part of the decision-making process, because a large part of these proposals usually are generated from line employees.

4. Ideas from employees and customers are also often low-risk sources for increased profitability. Marketing or sales personnel meet with customers on a regular basis. They should be able to determine current market needs and may assess demands not being met. Often these opportunities can be exploited with little additional cost to you. By taking advantage of unmet market needs head-on, competition can be avoided and you may successfully expand your market presence. To encourage new ideas and market opportunities, you may use either or both of these avenues: (a) Encourage entrepreneurship by allowing self-interest to work for you. Monetary incentive programs for sales staff and other employees are extremely effective in generating growth-producing ideas. (b) Survey customer needs on a regular basis to learn of potential growth possibilities.

5. Competitors are often a good source of potential growth-producing ideas. Sometimes it is beneficial to let competitors pioneer certain new products. Letting them take the risks often eliminates these products from your consideration as a result of their lack of profitability or outright product failure. Of course, this gives the competitor a head start on successful ventures.

6. Product matrix analysis sometimes will disclose holes in the market.

7. Often new ideas are available through purchase from independent research and development (R&D) firms or may be generated by your own R&D efforts.

8. Trade shows, conventions, seminars, and publications are good sources of potential ideas. In this case, you are not paying for

the development of ideas but instead are picking other people's brains.

9. You may decide on vertical growth—being your own supplier or marketer. Supplying yourself with components, services, or raw materials is a source of potential profit. Setting up your own distribution network outlets can be profitable as well. For example, some utilities have diversified into fields such as coal production and transportation in order to guarantee a source of supply and to reduce the risk associated with fuel cost variations. In this way, vertical integration provides them with additional revenue-producing sources of unregulated profit. Some natural gas utilities sell gas appliances. Being "the gas company" gives them an entrée for marketing the appliances. Customers trust a company that provides gas to know which are the best gas appliances.

10. You may want to grow horizontally through product diversification or buying of competitors.

11. You can expand the use of current technologies. Constantly ask: "What can we do with what we know or what we do best?" How adaptable is the current technology to meet new product innovation or new processes? The opportunity here is to have growth-producing ideas with minimal risks. If you have learned to utilize your technologies efficiently, further endeavors with known technologies generally carry less risk than ventures into new and yet untried technologies.

12. Expand the use of your existing equipment. In-place equipment may not be fully utilized. Increased utilization through subcontracting and selling of time on equipment or process capabilities will better utilize existing capital resources with little additional risk. More use of the fixed-cost base increases efficiency and at the same time produces additional cash flows.

Evaluation of Proposals

After proposals have been generated, you must evaluate competing proposals in a consistent manner to determine which proposals merit further consideration. There are basically four steps in the evaluation process.

1. The most critical step is a qualitative evaluation: Is this proposal consistent with the strategic plan of the business? If not, no future consideration is necessary. If yes, further analysis is indicated. A lot of time, effort, and money can be wasted on things that do not fit the direction you are determined to go in.

2. Define the evaluation process. Set up a system that will be applied consistently for all proposals.
   - Estimate costs accurately and in the same way for all proposals.
   - Estimate the benefits consistently.
   - Use the same time constraints.
   - Use the same method for calculating the net benefits.

3. Qualify your information sources. When gathering information, you must evaluate the reliability and accuracy of the source of the information. For example:
   - Engineers often underestimate the time (and costs) necessary.
   - Salespeople frequently overestimate potential sales.
     You should ask:
   - Who is providing the information?
   - How accurate were their last predictions?
   - How often have I relied on this source before?
   - Do my competitors use this same source?

4. Install the process. To install the process properly, all affected persons must understand how to use it.
   - Develop capital purchase evaluation forms to be used throughout the organization.
   - Explain the forms and the evaluation methods to all affected persons.
   - Use the system consistently to evaluate proposals.
   - Provide prompt responses to applicants as to why their proposals were or were not accepted.

Implementation of a Proposal

In the implementation phase, effective project management requires a firm line of control. First, define responsibility. You need to know who will be responsible at various stages in the proposal's implementation to ensure accountability and control. It is important to consider the time and the talent of the individuals involved and to match their abilities to the needs and responsibilities of each key position in the implementation process. Few things affect the failure or success of a product more than the match or mismatch of key personnel at critical steps in project implementation.

Next, establish checkpoints by setting goals and objectives for milestones at successive stages in the process. Review your decisions regularly, *before* the next costly step is taken and when progress can be compared with established standards. You may choose to terminate a proposal at some point short of completion if it appears that the project is exceeding cost projections or failing to meet benefit expectations.

It may be necessary to change the budget. This may seem a radical idea. However, if budgets are managed properly, changing a budget is nothing more than considering better data as they flow into the system. Budget changing should not become a self-fulfilling prophecy. Budgets are planning tools, and, as such, comparisons between actual performance and projected performance often will show how well or poorly your project is proceeding. Updating budgets for better control is useful in order to improve the quality of decision making for the project.

When budgets are used for control, regular feedback of information is needed. The establishment of reports is another critical element in the implementation phase. The amount of reporting is a function of balancing the risk of ignorance against the cost of reporting. When reports are generated on a regular basis, you can ensure maintenance of adequate control of the project.

Follow-up

Neglect near the concluding stages of a project can result in unnecessary delays, increased risk, and higher costs for the discontinuation or normal termination of a product's life cycle. In the follow-up step, you should review the assumptions under which the original project was accepted, determine how well those assumptions have been met, review the evaluation systems that were in place, and, finally, evaluate the implementation of the project. It is at this point that an overall review of a project will show you how well it was planned, how well the budget projected reality, and the necessary areas where improvement in the system will help better evaluate future proposals.

There is really no doubt that all projects eventually will find themselves in the decline phase of Figure 2.1. Predicting when this will occur and planning appropriate actions for when it does can be time- and money-saving.

An important part of the follow-up step is the prediction of discontinuance or normal termination dates for the project. This allows for the timely introduction of proposals for the replacement project. Capital budgeting is cyclical, allowing you to control growth on a continuous basis. The follow-up stage naturally reverts back to proposal generation as each project approaches termination.

Producing Numbers to Get Dollars, the Use of Forms, and the Capital Budgeting Model

Risk/Return Relationship

High-risk ventures should have expectations of high returns; low-risk ventures will be expected to have a lower rate of return. Both must be made attractive to investors.

Figure 2.2 demonstrates the relationship between the risk and return expected for a new line, extending a current line, and the modification or change of a product line or cost reduction programs. From this relationship, a function can be derived to estimate the discount rate. The discount rate, or the necessary return for a project, is equal to the cost of capital plus the risk premium:

$$\text{Required return} = \text{Cost of capital} + \text{Risk}$$

The most important criterion in the calculation of a capital budgeting model is the required return. This number can be obtained by subjective estimation or by analytical methods that offer a means of estimating risk. But risk is mostly a perception in the mind of investors.

When considering the cost of capital to be used for the generation of net present value numbers, you should be concerned

FIGURE 2.2

Risk Return Relationship

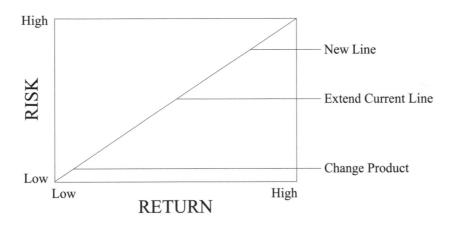

more with the incremental cost of capital for the project than with the overall cost of obtaining funds. It is the incremental cost of capital—the cost of financing this deal (internally or externally)— with which you are concerned when determining whether a project is cost justified. Nonetheless, it is also useful to know the company's overall cost of capital, since each incremental funding decision will impact it. The next section describes how to calculate the cost of capital.

Components of the Cost of Capital[1]

The components of the cost of capital are debt, preferred stock, and common stock. The least expensive of the three forms of funding is debt, followed by preferred stock and then common stock. Here we show how to calculate the cost of each of these three components of capital and then how to combine them into the weighted cost of capital.

When calculating the cost of debt, the key issue is that the interest expense is tax deductible. This means that the tax paid by

[1] This section is adapted with permission from Chapter 16 of Steven M. Bragg, *Financial Analysis* (Hoboken, NJ: John Wiley & Sons, 2000).

the company is reduced by the tax rate multiplied by the interest expense. This concept is shown in the next example, where we assume that $1,000,000 of debt has a basic interest rate of 9.5 percent and the corporate tax rate is 35 percent.

Calculating the Interest Cost of Debt, Net of Taxes

$$\frac{(\text{Interest expense}) \times (1 - \text{tax rate})}{\text{Amount of debt}} = \text{Net after-tax interest expense}$$

Or,

$$\frac{\$95,000 \times (1 - .35)}{\$1,000,000} = \text{Net after-tax interest expense}$$

$$\frac{\$61,750}{\$1,000,000} = 6.175\%$$

The example clearly shows that the impact of taxes on the cost of debt significantly reduces the overall debt cost, thereby making this a most desirable form of funding.

Preferred stock stands at a midway point between debt and common stock. The main feature shared by all kinds of preferred stock is that, under the tax laws, interest payments are treated as dividends instead of interest expense, which means that these payments are not tax deductible. This is a key issue, for it greatly increases the cost of funds for any company using this funding source. By way of comparison, if a company has a choice between issuing debt or preferred stock at the same rate, the difference in cost will be the tax savings on the debt. In the next example, a company issues $1,000,000 of debt and $1,000,000 of preferred stock, both at 9 percent interest rates, with an assumed 35 percent tax rate.

$$\text{Debt cost} = \text{Principal} \times (\text{interest rate} \times (1 - \text{tax rate}))$$
$$\text{Debt cost} = \$1,000,000 \times (9\% \times (1 - .35))$$
$$\underline{\$58,500} = \$1,000,000 \times (9\% \times .65)$$

If the same information is used to calculate the cost of payments using preferred stock, we have this result:

$$\text{Preferred stock interest cost} = \text{Principal} \times \text{interest rate}$$
$$\text{Preferred stock interest cost} = \$1,000,000 \times 9\%$$
$$\underline{\$90,000} = \$1,000,000 \times 9\%$$

This example shows that the differential caused by the applicability of taxes to debt payments makes preferred stock a much more expensive alternative.

The most difficult cost of funding to calculate by far is common stock, because there is no preset payment from which to derive a cost. One way to determine its cost is the capital asset pricing model (CAPM). This model derives the cost of common stock by determining the relative risk of holding the stock of a specific company as compared to a mix of all stocks in the market. This risk is composed of three elements. The first is the return that any investor can expect from a risk-free investment, which usually is defined as the return on a U.S. government security. The second element is the return from a set of securities considered to have an average level of risk. This can be the average return on a large "market basket" of stocks, such as the Standard & Poor's 500, the Dow Jones Industrials, or some other large cluster of stocks. The final element is a company's beta, which defines the amount by which a specific stock's returns vary from the returns of stocks with an average risk level. This information is provided by several of the major investment services, such as Value Line. A beta of 1.0 means that a specific stock is exactly as risky as the average stock, while a beta of 0.8 would represent a lower level of risk and a beta of 1.4 would be higher. When combined, this information yields the baseline return to be expected on any investment (the risk-free return), plus an added return that is based on the level of risk that an investor is assuming by purchasing a specific stock.

The calculation of the equity cost of capital using the CAPM methodology is relatively simple, once all components of the equation are available. For example, if the risk-free cost of capital is 5 percent, the return on the Dow Jones Industrials is 12 percent, and ABC Company's beta is 1.5, the cost of equity for ABC Company would be:

Cost of equity capital = Risk-free return + Beta (Average stock return − risk-free return)
Cost of equity capital = 5% + 1.5 (12% − 5%)
Cost of equity capital = 5% + 1.5 × 7%
Cost of equity capital = 5% + 10.5%
Cost of equity capital = <u>15.5%</u>

Although the example uses a rather high beta that increases the cost of the stock, it is evident that, far from being an inexpensive form of funding, common stock is actually the *most* expensive, given the size of returns that investors demand in exchange for putting their money at risk with a company.

Now that we have derived the costs of debt, preferred stock, and common stock, it is time to assemble all three costs into a weighted cost of capital. This section is structured in an example format, showing the method by which the weighted cost of capital of the Canary Corporation is calculated.

The chief financial officer of the Canary Corporation, Mr. Birdsong, is interested in determining the company's weighted cost of capital, to be used to ensure that projects have a sufficient return on investment, which will keep the company from going to seed. There are two debt offerings on the books. The first is $1,000,000 that was sold below par value, which garnered $980,000 in cash proceeds. The company must pay interest of 8.5 percent on this debt. The second is for $3,000,000 and was sold at par, but included legal fees of $25,000. The interest rate on this debt is 10 percent. There is also $2,500,000 of preferred stock on the books, which requires annual interest (or dividend) payments amounting to 9 percent of the amount contributed to the company by investors. Finally, there is $4,000,000 of common stock on the books. The risk-free rate of interest, as defined by the return on current U.S. government securities, is 6 percent, while the return expected from a typical market basket of related stocks is 12 percent. The company's beta is 1.2, and it currently pays income taxes at a marginal rate of 35 percent. What is the Canary Company's weighted cost of capital?

The method we will use is to separate the percentage cost of each form of funding and then calculate the weighted cost of capital, based on the amount of funding and percentage cost of each of the above forms of funding. We begin with the first debt item, which was $1,000,000 of debt that was sold for $20,000 less than par value, at 8.5 percent debt. The marginal income tax rate is 35 percent. The calculation is:

Net after-tax interest percent =

$$\frac{((\text{Interest expense}) \times (1 - \text{tax rate})) \times \text{Amount of debt}}{(\text{Amount of debt}) - (\text{Discount on sale of debt})}$$

$$\text{Net after-tax interest percent} = \frac{((8.5\%) \times (1 - .35)) \times \$1,000,000}{\$1,000,000 - \$20,000}$$

Net after-tax interest percent = <u>5.638%</u>

We employ the same method for the second debt instrument, for which there is $3,000,000 of debt that was sold at par. Legal fees of $25,000 are incurred to place the debt, which pays 10 percent interest. The marginal income tax rate remains at 35 percent. The calculation is:

Net after-tax interest percent =

$$\frac{((\text{Interest expense}) \times (1 - \text{tax rate})) \times \text{Amount of debt}}{(\text{Amount of debt}) - (\text{Discount on sale of debt})}$$

$$\text{Net after-tax interest percent} = \frac{((10\%) \times (1 - .35)) \times \$3,000,000}{\$3,000,000 - \$25,000}$$

Net after-tax interest percent = <u>7.091%</u>

Having completed the interest expense for the two debt offerings, we move on to the cost of the preferred stock. As noted, there is $2,500,000 of preferred stock on the books, with an interest rate of 9 percent. The marginal corporate income tax does not apply, since the interest payments are treated like dividends and are not deductible. The calculation is the simplest of all, for the answer is 9 percent, since there is no income tax to confuse the issue.

To arrive at the cost of equity capital, we take from the example a return on risk-free securities of 6 percent, a return of 12 percent that is expected from a typical market basket of related stocks, and a beta of 1.2. We then plug this information into the formula to arrive at the cost of equity capital.

Cost of equity capital = Risk-free return + Beta (Average stock return − risk-free return)
Cost of equity capital = 6% + 1.2 (12% − 6%)
Cost of equity capital = <u>13.2%</u>

Now that we know the cost of each type of funding, it is a simple matter to construct a table listing the amount of each type of funding and its related cost, which we can quickly sum to arrive at a weighted cost of capital. The weighted cost of capital is 9.75 percent.

Weighted Cost of Capital Calculation

Type of Funding	Amount of Funding	Percentage Cost	Dollar Cost
Debt number 1	$980,000	5.638%	$55,252
Debt number 2	2,975,000	7.091%	210,957
Preferred stock	2,500,000	9.000%	225,000
Common stock	4,000,000	13.200%	528,000
Totals	$10,455,000	9.75%	$1,019,209

Producing Better Numbers for Dollars

Most capital budgeting models use after-tax cash flows as their basis. Figure 2.3 is a capital budgeting cash flow schedule, which will be used to help organize the numbers necessary for the capital budgeting model. Some helpful hints for getting the appropriate numbers into the columns of this schedule are provided (see Figure 2.3). The numbers correspond to the columns.

Filling Out the Capital Budgeting Worksheet

1. Column 1 is used to list the estimated net annual cash inflows and outflows.

   Misestimating or underestimating in early years is more damaging than incorrect estimates of amounts in the distant future as

FIGURE 2.3

Capital Budgeting Cash Flow Worksheet

	1	2	3	4	5	6
Year	Annual Operating Cash Flow	Adjustments	Depreciation	Net Before Tax 1 + 2 + 3	Tax	After Tax 1 + 2 − 5
0						
1						
2						
3						
4						
5						
6						
7						
8						
9						
10						

a result of the discount factor. Thus, greater significance is placed on cash flows in the beginning periods. The initial outflow usually will be in year zero, which means as of Day 1 of the project period. Therefore, the discount factor is 1.0000 because that is current dollars. (Remember that for most discounting tables, all cash flows are assumed to occur at the end of each year. Although this may be an unrealistic assumption in that carrying costs may be incurred throughout the year, these carrying costs can be calculated and added to the net cash outflows to predict more accurately the total first year cost.)

The initial investment includes not only the usual items, such as plant and equipment, but also investments in inventory, accounts receivable, training, product introduction, and the expenses for administrative changes and accounting. The next section provides a more detailed list of cash flow items to check in the capital budgeting proposals.

For new products, annual inflows that stay level without fluctuations should usually be suspect because the actual patterns seldom occur this way.

2. In column 2, cash adjustments should include such items as buildups of accounts receivable and inventories. This allows recognition of the actual cash flows in appropriate years. For example, a new product line may build up $500,000 in inventories in the first year, which may not be recovered in cash inflow until the end of the product's life cycle. Taxes and the treatment of expenses and income for tax purposes must be considered and adjusted for in the model. For example, increases in receivables and inventories are examples of adjustments that affect current tax liabilities and must be considered in the calculation of estimated taxes. Inventories require cash in the year purchased but have tax effects when used or sold. Receivables may be taxable in the year sales are made, even though not collected until later periods.

Also, the effect of investment tax credits and other project-related tax deductions should be included for the period in which the cash impact occurs.

3. Depreciation is included solely for the purpose of considering its effect on taxes. The model uses only cash flows and the items affecting cash flows. Depreciation expense is a noncash item in the current period. If depreciation has already been "expensed" in the operating cash flows of column 1, then an adjustment is necessary to ensure that it is not double counted. In the model, the full cost of the investment is made in period 0. Showing the allocation of that cost again through depreciation will count it twice.

4. Column 4 calculates the taxable portion of the inflows. Care must be taken to determine the appropriate tax consequences, as the goal of the model is to determine after-tax cash flows.

5. Column 5 is used for the calculation of tax, which must be subtracted from cash flows.

6. Column 6 is the after-tax cash flow to be used in the various capital budgeting models for the evaluation of the proposals.

Ten Cash Flow Items to Check on Capital Budget Proposals

This list of 10 cash flow items to be considered in evaluating a capital budget proposal is not intended to be exhaustive. However, these items should be carefully scrutinized for every proposal so that you can make a complete evaluation of appropriate costs.

1. Plant and equipment items
2. Installation and debugging of equipment and systems
3. Inventories including consideration of:
   - Raw materials
   - Work-in-process
   - Finished goods
   - Spare parts
4. Market research and product introduction
5. Training
6. System changes necessitated by engineering changes and product redesign
7. Accounts receivable
8. Accounts payable
9. Taxes, to include:
   - Income
   - Investment tax credits
   - Property tax
   - Credits
10. Cash and requirements for cash working capital

Inflation and Cash Flow Estimates

When estimating cash flows, inflation should be anticipated and taken into account. Often there is a tendency to assume that the price for the product and the associated costs will remain constant throughout the life of the project. Occasionally this assumption is made unwittingly, and future cash flows are estimated simply on the basis of existing prices.

If anticipated inflation is embodied in the required return criteria, it is important that it also be reflected in the estimated cash flows from the product over the life of the project. To reflect cash flows properly in later periods, consider adjusting both the expected sales price and the expected costs by reasonable inflation numbers.

You may assume that if all proposals are evaluated without consideration of inflation, the decision matrix will be unchanged. This is not necessarily the case. As in the case for the generation of internal rates of return, inflation will change future cash flows relative to the year in which they occur by the inflation rate specific to that product or industry. Therefore, by not anticipating inflation and assigning values for particular future time periods, the decision model may be biased by not taking into account the different effects on cash inflows and outflows as a result of different rates of inflation. As a result, the project selection may not be optimal.

Discounted Cash Flow

Because the primary concern is discounted cash flow, we should begin our discussion with the required rate of return. This rate is called by many names, including hurdle rate, cost of capital, interest rate, and discount rate.

Actually, hurdle rate is probably best. It implies a barrier, in terms of the return on investment, which the proposal must clear in order to be considered. The other names arise from the mistaken idea that the cost of capital or interest, which is the cost of some of the capital, is the criterion for judging the investment. A weighted average cost of capital has been suggested; for small businesses, it may not be difficult to calculate because of the limited sources of capital employed. However, neither the marginal cost of capital nor the weighted average cost of capital alone take into account other factors that should be considered in deciding on a required return or hurdle rate to be used, such as:

- The relative risk of this proposal to other proposals
- Other opportunities

- Return on other investments already made
- The company's loan limit

There is no magic formula for the evaluation of all the relative factors used in arriving at a correct rate. However, you are encouraged to consider:

- How much return do you usually get?
- How much return can you reasonably expect to receive?
- How much does it cost you to borrow?
- How much should you penalize the proposal for the risk involved?

For many businesses, a simple formula for normal risk projects might be: discount rate = New York bank prime interest rate + 3 points (borrowing premium) + 4 to 6 points risk premium. This is, of course, a very rough rule of thumb and should be used with all appropriate caution.

Capital Budgeting Evaluation Worksheet

Once the cash flows have been determined from the capital budgeting cash flow worksheet (Figure 2.3), they are listed on the capital budgeting evaluation worksheet (Figure 2.4). Included at the bottom of the capital budgeting evaluation worksheet is an illustrative present value table for 15 years, at rates varying from 10 percent to 40 percent. It is best to keep this table together with the capital budgeting worksheet so that later referral to the worksheet will not result in questions concerning the origin of the numbers used in the calculation. The use of the evaluation worksheet is straightforward. The cash flows are taken from the cash flow worksheet and are listed in column 2. In column 3, the first trial percentage rate is listed to generate the present value of income flow. Column 4 is read directly from the present value table for the first trial interest rate. Those numbers are filled into the form from the matrix. Column 5 is the multiplication of the cash flow from column 2 by the present value factor from column 4. Column 6 is used for a second trial percentage. Once again the process is repeated

FIGURE 2.4

Capital Budgeting Evaluation Worksheet and Present Value Table

1 Year	2 Raw Cash Flow	3 Trial % No. 1	4 PV of $1 from Table	5 PV of Cash Flow (2 × 4)	6 Trial % No. 2	7 PV of $1 from Table	8 PV of Cash Flow (2 × 7)
1	$			$			$
2	$	xxx		$	xxx		$
3	$	xxx		$	xxx		$
4	$	xxx		$	xxx		$
5	$	xxx		$	xxx		$
6	$	xxx		$	xxx		$
7	$	xxx		$	xxx		$
8	$	xxx		$	xxx		$
9	$	xxx		$	xxx		$
10	$	xxx		$	xxx		$
11	$	xxx		$	xxx		$
12	$	xxx		$	xxx		$
13	$	xxx		$	xxx		$
14	$	xxx		$	xxx		$
15	$	xxx		$	xxx		$
		Total				Total	$

(*continued*)

FIGURE 2.4 *(continued)*

								Rate								
Year	**.10%**	**.12%**	**.14%**	**.16%**	**.18%**	**.20%**	**.22%**	**.24%**	**.27%**	**.28%**	**.30%**	**.32%**	**.34%**	**.36%**	**.38%**	**.40%**
1	.9091	.8929	.8772	.8621	.8475	.8333	.8197	.8065	.7937	.7812	.7692	.7576	.7463	.7353	.7246	.7143
2	.8264	.7972	.7695	.7432	.7182	.6944	.6719	.6504	.6299	.6104	.5917	.5739	.5569	.5407	.5251	.5102
3	.7513	.7118	.6750	.6407	.6086	.5787	.5507	.5245	.4999	.4768	.4552	.4348	.4156	.3975	.3805	.3644
4	.6830	.6355	.5921	.5523	.5158	.4823	.4514	.4230	.3968	.3725	.3501	.3294	.3102	.2923	.2757	.2603
5	.6209	.5674	.5194	.4761	.4371	.4019	.3700	.3411	.3149	.2910	.2693	.2495	.2315	.2149	.1998	.1859
6	.5645	.5066	.4556	.4104	.3704	.3349	.3033	.2751	.2499	.2274	.2072	.1890	.1727	.1580	.1448	.1328
7	.5132	.4523	.3996	.3538	.3139	.2791	.2486	.2218	.1983	.1776	.1594	.1432	.1289	.1162	.1049	.0949
8	.4665	.4039	.3506	.3050	.2660	.2326	.2038	.1789	.1574	.1388	.1226	.1085	.0962	.0854	.0760	.0678
9	.4241	.3606	.3075	.2630	.2255	.1938	.1670	.1443	.1249	.1084	.0943	.0822	.0718	.0628	.0551	.0484
10	.3855	.3220	.2697	.2267	.1911	.1615	.1369	.1164	.0992	.0847	.0725	.0623	.0536	.0462	.0399	.0346
11	.3505	.2875	.2366	.1954	.1619	.1346	.1122	.0938	.0787	.0662	.0558	.0472	.0400	.0340	.0289	.0247
12	.3136	.2567	.2076	.1685	.1372	.1122	.0920	.0757	.0625	.0517	.0429	.0357	.0298	.0250	.0210	.0176
13	.2897	.2292	.1821	.1452	.1163	.0935	.0754	.0610	.0496	.0404	.0330	.0271	.0223	.0184	.0152	.0126
14	.2633	.2046	.1597	.1252	.0985	.0779	.0618	.0492	.0393	.0316	.0254	.0205	.0166	.0135	.0110	.0090
15	.2394	.1827	.1401	.1079	.0835	.0649	.0507	.0397	.0312	.0247	.0195	.0155	.0124	.0099	.0080	.0064

and the present value rates are included in column 7 for the second percentage selected. Column 8 is again calculated by the multiplication of the cash flows from column 2 and, this time, the present value numbers in column 7. In this manner, two trials can be made to evaluate the present values of a single cash flow estimate over two different discount rates. Using these worksheets, the cash flows for various proposals may be compared. Examples are included in the appendix to this chapter.

Improving the Estimates

In most cases, the unfortunate truth is that things normally can get only a little bit better but a whole lot worse than expected. Therefore, if the distribution of possible outcomes is considered, it probably would be skewed to the left, in that there is a greater number of unfortunate outcomes than fortunate ones (see Figure 2.5).

The possibility of improvement is also limited by the production capabilities. Therefore, the limiting factor on the right side may be plant capacity. Since capacity is normally added in significant increments as opposed to one or two units at a time, there is no continuum of outcome possibilities. Instead, production capacities occur

FIGURE 2.5

Distribution of Outcomes

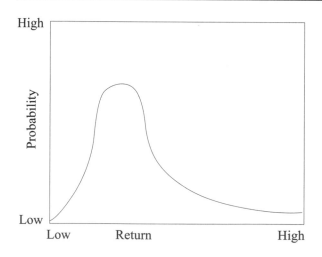

in steps. Without getting into the problem of analyzing additional production quantities, consider the problem of improving the estimates from the standpoint of fixed or limited capacity.

The problem encountered in capital budgeting, as in all other planning, is that a "most likely" figure is normally offered. However, other alternatives should be considered. This situation is not uncommon: "most likely" sales estimate is $300,000; "best case" (limited by capacity) is $400,000; "worst case" sales estimate is $100,000. One way to use this information is to multiply each by some estimated probability. For example, the probable outcome for "most likely" may be estimated as 5 chances out of 10; "best" is 2 chances out of 10; and "worst" is 3 chances out of 10. To calculate the expected outcome, we start by multiplying the "most likely" sales estimate by 5 and repeat this process for each outcome. So:

$$
\begin{array}{r}
\$3,000 \times 5 = \$1,500,000 \\
\$400,000 \times 2 = 800,000 \\
\$100,000 \times 3 = \underline{300,000} \\
\underline{10} \quad \underline{\$2,600,000}
\end{array}
$$

Sum up the probabilities of 5, 3, and 2 for a total of 10. Finally, divide the sum of the multiplications by the sum of the probabilities. The expected value is: $2,600,000/10 = $260,000.

The resulting expected value amount of $260,000 is less than the most likely figure of $300,000 and reflects the fact that the curve is skewed to the left. While $300,000 is still most likely, a conservative estimate of $260,000 is also reasonable.

Although not impressive statistically, this approach does make use of more information; this fact usually would justify its inclusion in cash flow projections. Understand that each of the figures—the sales figures and the probabilities associated with each of the three cases—is an estimate. In making these estimates, you should take care to ask a lot of what-if questions.

When trying to evaluate what is behind the numbers, it is also extremely important to evaluate the information sources. As mentioned previously, engineers may tend to underestimate time to complete projects and thereby underestimate costs. Marketing and sales personnel may overestimate sales and sales potentials. Ask: "How good are the forecasts of the market, the economic conditions and the expectation of future cash flows?" Often it is necessary to question where the numbers came from, who generated them, on what assumptions they were based, and what data were used. It is helpful to know the sources of data, the age of the data, and the method of generation.

Often these sources are used:

- Government publications, which give useful information on the trends in the economy, consumer spending, and other market information
- Private company publications such as Chase Econometric, Dow Jones, and the like
- Trade publications
- Newspapers

Experience in the industry usually helps provide an understanding about the availability and reliability of certain information and data sources.

A major task in capital budgeting is estimating future cash flows. The quality of the final budget and plan is really only as good as the accuracy of the estimates. You should have efficient procedures set up to collect the information necessary for capital budgeting decisions. Try to standardize this information as much as possible for all investment proposals; otherwise, proposals cannot be compared objectively. One of the more difficult capital budgeting problems to evaluate concerns projects associated with environmental protection or safety. It is difficult in those projects to quantify the net cash flows because in most cases the benefit to you is more in the nature of a cost avoidance.

The reason the expected benefits from a particular project are expressed in terms of cash flows rather than in terms of income is that cash is central to all your decisions. You invest cash now in the hopes of receiving cash returns of a greater amount in the future. Only cash receipts can be reinvested or paid to stockholders in the form of dividends. Thus cash, not income, is what is important in capital budgeting.

Miscellaneous Considerations

Another aspect of estimating future cash flows is that the information must be provided on an incremental basis so that the difference between your cash flows may be analyzed with and without the project. This is important in that, if you are contemplating a new product that is likely to compete with existing products, it is not appropriate to express cash flows in terms of estimated sales of the new product without consideration of the effect the new product may have on existing products. You must consider that there probably will be some cannibalization of existing products.

Another assumption often made is that the risk or quality of all investment proposals under consideration is the same as the risk of existing investment projects. Therefore, the acceptance of any proposal or group of investment proposals does not change the relative business risk of the firm. This is not necessarily true; each proposal should be looked at individually relative to its riskiness.

Depreciation

Ordinarily, after-tax cash flows are used for capital budgeting calculations. Usually depreciation at the maximum allowable method is used for tax purposes. Remember, however, that if depreciation is subtracted other than for calculating taxable income, you are double counting. This occurs because you have already "expensed" (treated the cost as a cash outflow) the investment in year zero. The only reason for being interested in depreciation is for the calculation of expected tax.

Lease-Purchase

The internal rate of return cannot be used for making a decision to lease or purchase a piece of equipment, because a true lease requires no investment. The rate of return, therefore, would be infinite. It is, however, often more profitable to buy. Leasing usually is done because of a lack of or an attempt to conserve cash. It is a method of financing and therefore is a part of the second-stage financing decision mentioned at the beginning of this chapter.

Interest

Interest costs on borrowed money should not be included in the calculation of cash flows because the method of financing should not determine the decision as to whether the project is a good deal. Besides, the cash flows will be multiplied by the discount rate, which already includes interest as part of the cost of capital considerations.

Uncertainty

Uncertainty should be included in the discount rate. When trying to quantify uncertainty, you should question the sources of the information: "How old is the information?" and "How reliable is the information?" Always search for alternative sources of information.

There is rarely only one way to accomplish a project. Find other methods and evaluate them. Be suspicious if it appears there is only one way to do the project. Your people may be reluctant to consider alternatives. Ask such questions as: "Are there less expensive ways? Are there less risky ways? Are there ways that retain more options?"

Product Discontinuance

One of the often-overlooked uses of the capital budgeting process is for the determination of product discontinuance. In a highly diversified business, in which large numbers of similar or related products are manufactured, reevaluation of existing product lines should be undertaken on a regular basis using capital budgeting techniques. This is useful to determine whether existing products are optimally utilizing the company's resources.

Checklist of Data

A 10-step checklist of the data required to make a decision about maintaining or eliminating a product follows.

1. An estimate of the variable expenses directly applicable to the production of specific products, including the costs of production and marketing

2. An indication of the number of units of the product sold during past periods, net of sales returns
3. Total sales revenues generated by each product within each time period
4. Estimates of sales revenues for competitive products and the price per unit, units sold, and market share of each competitor
5. Current and past pricing structures for all products including price discount policies and the distribution of order quantities
6. Inventory turnover ratio for each period of time
7. A projection of future sales for each product carried
8. Estimation of the total overhead costs devoted to each product
9. The trend line of product returns and warranty claims
10. Forecasted changes in the cost of components required to build each product

This checklist can be used to detect whether a product needs help or should be considered for elimination. The discontinuation of products can result in increased profits through the elimination of marginally profitable or high-cost products and by reducing overdiversification in a business's product mix. Elimination of over-diversification can increase production and marketing efficiencies by concentrating your efforts and resource utilization.

It should be noted, however, that the indications of candidacy for elimination of a product is not simply a go/no-go test established from quantification of the checklist items. Sometimes healthy products should be eliminated if an analysis shows that your overall goals are better met by product elimination and concentration of efforts. An evaluation of the contributions products make to your objectives often reveals that the assets dedicated to production of a particular product, if expended on the production of a more profitable item, will create greater returns.

Warning Signals Indicating Product Difficulties

- A decline in absolute sales volume
- Sales volume decreasing as a percentage of the firm's total sales
- A decrease in market share
- Sales volumes not up to projected amounts

- Unfavorable future market potential of products
- Return on investment below minimally acceptable levels
- Variable cost in excess of actual revenues
- Costs, as a percentage of sales, consistently increasing
- An increasingly greater percentage of managerial and executive oversight necessary for the product
- Repeated price reductions necessary to maintain current or projected sales levels
- Increased promotional budgets necessary to maintain sales
- Increasing product returns

For most of these indicators, a simple graph on a month-by-month basis can quickly show trends. The graph then becomes a simple budget-tracking device.

The key to a successful elimination program is the availability of timely and pertinent information. This is true of all major business decisions. Accounting sources provide the requisite raw data on which you may decide which products to discontinue, which to retain, and which to expand or contract in your business plan.

Bailout

"What happens if things go sour?" is a question that few people want to think about. Although the answers do not always yield clear-cut decisions, they do provide input to the go/no-go decision. Furthermore, the use of the bailout consideration forces some planning.

To consider bailout, start by asking questions. For example: "What can we bail out with if the project must be shut down after two years?" Then look at cash flows (discounted, of course) through that period, including salvage. Because a likely reason to bail out may be lack of sales, lowered sales estimates should be substituted for original estimates. All this can be done in the same format previously used to estimate net present value.

An important value of the bailout consideration is that it reminds you that things do not always go as planned. Many people are eternally optimistic and will resist looking at "the dark side."

But such considerations can result in much more protection for the remainder of your business should projections not come to pass.

Summary

The seven necessary steps in the evaluation of capital budgeting decisions include:

1. *Use a discounted payback screen.* A screen is in essence nothing more than a go/no-go test. Think of the device used to screen gravel for size: At each successive stage, a keep or reject decision is made and the process continues. Ultimately the process narrows down the alternatives so that an educated choice can be made.

2. *Use net present value index.* A little more conservative than the net present value in its assumptions, the index therefore will act as a more critical go/no-go decision. The index is the net present value divided by the going-in cost. As an example, if for an initial investment of $300,000 the net present value is $150,000, the NPV index would be .5. For an initial investment of $600,000 and a net present value of $200,000, the NPV index would be .33. If you looked just at the NPV, the $600,000 investment would appear to be the better option, as its NPV is $200,000 instead of $150,000. However, for an investment of $300,000, the NPV index of .5 indicates a better return than does the .33 for the larger investment. Thus the NPV index may give a relative go/no-go test and a better indication than a NPV-only test.

3. *Use break-even in examining alternatives.* Often break-even analysis is helpful in assessing risks as a result of misestimations in sales levels. The break-even analysis, although a very simple test, shows how varying sales forecasts will affect the period over which we can expect to break even.

4. *Ask what-if questions and apply some calculations using the bailout consideration.* Bailout is simply an attempt to determine the minimum amount for breakeven on operations.

5. *Relate the size of the decision to the decision maker.* This is merely a reminder that the level in management at which the decision

ultimately should be made relates to the significance of that project to your overall objectives.

6. *Keep records.* It is difficult to learn from mistakes if no records exist. Feedback is necessary for improvements. It is a good idea for records to be kept from the inception. In order to use this information fully, records should be indexed and retained for future analysis or review. Often estimates generated for other projects can be very useful in evaluating future projects.

7. *Plan for retirement—not just yours, but the end of each project.* Periodic discontinuance is part of the process. Remember that as each product is discontinued, another product should be ready to take its place to ensure that your growth and prosperity continue. Planning is a cyclical process, and the element of discontinuance should herald the introduction of new products.

Appendix: Examples and Comparison of Calculations

The facts are:

A project with an initial cost of $55,000 will return:

	Inflows	Depreciation
Year 1	$5,000	$5,000
Year 2	25,000	10,000
Year 3	35,000	10,000
Year 4	15,000	10,000
Year 5	20,000	10,000
Year 6	15,000	-0-

The tax rate is 20 percent.

Internal Rate of Return Calculation:

	18%	20%
Present value of inflows	$58,572.00	$55,480.00
Present value of outflows	55,000.00	55,000.00
Net present value	$3,572.00	$480.00

Based on the table, the IRR (the discount rate, which causes the NPV to be zero) is very close to 20 percent.

To determine the project's net present value, we load the specified cash inflows and depreciation into the Capital Budgeting Cash Flow Worksheet, which we then combine with present value rates from the Present Value Table to arrive at the results shown on the Capital Budgeting Cash Flow Worksheet.

Capital Budgeting Cash Flow Worksheet

	1	2	3	4	5	6
Year	Annual Operating Cash Flow	Adjustments	Depreciation	Net Before Tax 1 + 2 + 3	Tax	After Tax 1 + 2 − 5
0	<55,000>	0	0	<55,000>	0	<55,000>
1	5,000	0	5,000	0	0	5,000
2	25,000	0	10,000	15,000	3,000	22,000
3	35,000	0	10,000	25,000	5,000	30,000
4	15,000	0	10,000	5,000	1,000	14,000
5	20,000	0	10,000	10,000	2,000	18,000
6	15,000	0	10,000	5,000	1,000	14,000

Capital Budgeting Evaluation Worksheet

1	2	3	4	5	6	7	8
Year	Raw Cash Flow	Trial % No. 1	PV of $1 from Table	PV of Cash Flow (2 × 4)	Trial % No. 2	PV of $1 from Table	PV of Cash Flow (2 × 7)
1	$5,000	18%	.8475	$4,238	20%	.8333	$4,167
2	$22,000	xxx	.7182	$15,801	xxx	.6944	$15,277
3	$30,000	xxx	.6086	$18,258	xxx	.5787	$17,361
4	$14,000	xxx	.5158	$7,221	xxx	.4823	$6,752
5	$18,000	xxx	.4371	$7,868	xxx	.4019	$7,234
6	$14,000	xxx	.3704	$5,186	xxx	.3349	$4,689
			Total	58,572		Total	$55,480

Present Value Table

Rate

Year	.10%	.12%	.14%	.16%	.18%	.20%	.22%	.24%	.27%	.28%	.30%	.32%	.34%	.36%	.38%	.40%
1	.9091	.8929	.8772	.8621	.8475	.8333	.8197	.8065	.7937	.7812	.7692	.7576	.7463	.7353	.7246	.7143
2	.8264	.7972	.7695	.7432	.7182	.6944	.6719	.6504	.6299	.6104	.5917	.5739	.5569	.5407	.5251	.5102
3	.7513	.7118	.6750	.6407	.6086	.5787	.5507	.5245	.4999	.4768	.4552	.4348	.4156	.3975	.3805	.3644
4	.6830	.6355	.5921	.5523	.5158	.4823	.4514	.4230	.3968	.3725	.3501	.3294	.3102	.2923	.2757	.2603
5	.6209	.5674	.5194	.4761	.4371	.4019	.3700	.3411	.3149	.2910	.2693	.2495	.2315	.2149	.1998	.1859
6	.5645	.5066	.4556	.4104	.3704	.3349	.3033	.2751	.2499	.2274	.2072	.1890	.1727	.1580	.1448	.1328
7	.5132	.4523	.3996	.3538	.3139	.2791	.2486	.2218	.1983	.1776	.1594	.1432	.1289	.1162	.1049	.0949
8	.4665	.4039	.3506	.3050	.2660	.2326	.2038	.1789	.1574	.1388	.1226	.1085	.0962	.0854	.0760	.0678
9	.4241	.3606	.3075	.2630	.2255	.1938	.1670	.1443	.1249	.1084	.0943	.0822	.0718	.0628	.0551	.0484
10	.3855	.3220	.2697	.2267	.1911	.1615	.1369	.1164	.0992	.0847	.0725	.0623	.0536	.0462	.0399	.0346
11	.3505	.2875	.2366	.1954	.1619	.1346	.1122	.0938	.0787	.0662	.0558	.0472	.0400	.0340	.0289	.0247
12	.3136	.2567	.2076	.1685	.1372	.1122	.0920	.0757	.0625	.0517	.0429	.0357	.0298	.0250	.0210	.0176
13	.2897	.2292	.1821	.1452	.1163	.0935	.0754	.0610	.0496	.0404	.0330	.0271	.0223	.0184	.0152	.0126
14	.2633	.2046	.1597	.1252	.0985	.0779	.0618	.0492	.0393	.0316	.0254	.0205	.0166	.0135	.0110	.0090
15	.2394	.1827	.1401	.1079	.0835	.0649	.0507	.0397	.0312	.0247	.0195	.0155	.0124	.0099	.0080	.0064

Comparison of the Internal Rate of Return Method and the Net Present Value Method

When comparing two mutually exclusive proposals using both the net present value method and the internal rate of return method, you will find cases where one project is preferable to the other using one method, and the reverse is true using the other method. It is important to understand how and why this happens. The result is obtained because the two projects will have differing cash flows in different periods. Therefore, the compounding effect of the discount rate and the time value of money will produce different results.

Case 1

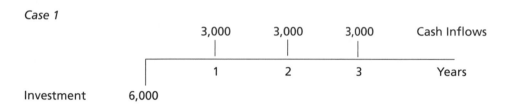

The NPV at 15 percent discount rate is $849.68.
The IRR is 23.5 percent.
The project returns $9,000 total and an undiscounted break-even in 2 years.

Case 2

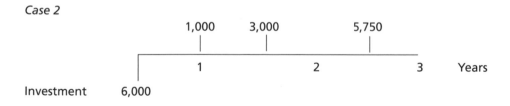

The NPV at 15 percent discount rate is $918.71.
The IRR is 22 percent.
The project returns $9,750 total and a break-even in 2 years and 4 months.
Which project is a better investment?
This example shows how similar cash flows in different periods will affect your decision-making process. Thus reliance on any one

method, without understanding how it works may result in a distorted decision-making process.

Some people prefer the NPV method as superior to the IRR, because the IRR method implies reinvestment rates that will differ depending on the cash flow stream for each investment proposal under consideration. With the NPV method, however, the implied reinvestment rate, namely the required rate of return or hurdle rate, is the same for each proposal. In essence, this reinvestment rate presents the minimum return on opportunities available to you. You must employ judgment in evaluating what each model generates as a decision. Factors other than the rate of return may alter the choice of one proposal or the other. For instance, long-term tax planning may favor one cash flow projection over the other in order to optimize long-term tax liabilities. Therefore, evaluate the expected cash flows and their timing.

Capital budgeting in the ongoing system of planning, evaluation, and execution of the business is itself a process. It starts with a determination of where you are, then where you want to be, then how you intend to get there. Even if you do not institute capital budgeting as an ongoing process, simply going through the exercise of setting up a process is a valuable endeavor of self-examination. It gets people to think through how prudent investments in capital-intensive projects may help the business grow, diversify, or replace existing plant and equipment.

Capital budgeting is a four-step process of (1) proposal solicitation or generation, (2) evaluation, (3) implementation, and (4) follow-up. In the evaluation step, various alternative proposals have various related returns associated with the investment. With this expected return is a probable risk of loss of all or part of the invested funds. In any endeavor, the decision must be based on balancing the return against the associated risk. The problem, of course, is that no certainty, even in the estimates of risk and return, exists. In order to minimize the risk, you should consider the method by which estimates, projections, and other numbers are generated.

You should be cautious when only one solution is proposed because there is seldom a problem without several possible solutions. When preparing a capital budgeting plan, develop contingency plans and scenarios after asking many what-if questions. As part of your contingency planning, do not put your head in the sand. Consider the dark side of the project: "What if it goes sour?" For such a proposition, you should be ready for bailout as a planned withdrawal; you should not be forced into mindless panic if a project faces immediate failure.

Chapter 3

Basic Control Systems[1]

In Chapters 1 and 2, we discussed the need for proper operational and capital budgeting to ensure that a company meets its goals. However, these plans can go seriously awry if the company does not also have a solid set of basic controls to keep its funds and assets from going astray. In this chapter we review the need for control systems, specify the types of fraudulent activities that make the use of controls particularly important, and itemize many controls that can be installed in a small business.

As controls frequently have a cost associated with them, it is also possible to take them out of an accounting system in order to save money; we discuss the process of spotting these controls and evaluating their usefulness prior to removing them.

The Need for Control Systems

The most common situation in which a control point is needed is when an innocent error is made in the processing of a transaction. For example, an accounts payable clerk neglects to compare the price on a supplier's invoice to the price listed on the authorizing purchase order, which results in the company paying more than it should. Similarly, the warehouse staff decides to accept a supplier

---

[1] Adapted with permission from Chapter 28 of Steven M. Bragg, *The Ultimate Accountant's Reference* (Hoboken, NJ: John Wiley & Sons, 2005).

shipment, despite a lack of approving purchasing documentation, resulting in the company being obligated to pay for something that it does not need. These types of actions may occur based on poor employee training, inattention, or the combination of a special set of circumstances that were unforeseen when the accounting processes were constructed originally. There can be an extraordinary number of reasons why a transactional error arises, which can result in errors that are not caught, and which in turn lead to the loss of corporate assets.

Controls act as review points at those places in a process where transactional errors have a habit of arising. A process flow expert who reviews a flowchart that describes a process will recognize the potential for some errors immediately, simply based on his or her knowledge of where errors in similar processes have a habit of arising. Other errors will be specific to a certain industry—for example, the casino industry deals with enormous quantities of cash and thus has a potential for much higher monetary loss through its cash-handling processes than do similar processes in other industries. Also, highly specific circumstances within a company may generate errors in unlikely places. For example, a manufacturing company that employs mostly foreign workers who do not speak English will experience extra errors in any processes where these people are required to fill out paperwork, simply due to a reduced level of comprehension of what they are writing. Consequently, the typical process can be laced with areas in which a company has the potential for loss of assets.

Many potential areas of asset loss will involve such minor or infrequent errors that accountants can safely ignore them and avoid constructing any offsetting controls. Others have the potential for very high risk of loss and so are shored up with not only one control point, but a whole series of multilayered cross-checks that are designed to keep all but the most unusual problems from arising or being spotted at once.

The need for controls also is driven by the impact of their cost and interference in the smooth functioning of a process. If a control requires the hiring of an extra person, then a careful analysis of the resulting risk mitigation is likely to occur. Similarly, if a highly efficient process is about to have a large and labor-intensive control point plunked down in the middle of it, quite likely an alternative approach should be found that provides a similar level of control but from outside the process.

The controls installed can be of the *preventive* variety, which are designed to spot problems as they are occurring (i.e., online pricing verification for the customer order data entry staff), or of the *detective* variety, which spot problems after they occur, so that the accounting staff can research the associated problems and fix them after the fact (i.e., a bank reconciliation). The former type of control is the best, since it prevents errors from ever being completed; the second type of control results in much more labor by the accounting staff to research each error and correct it. Consequently, the type of control point installed should be evaluated based on its cost of subsequent error correction.

All of these factors—perceived risk, cost, and efficiency—will have an impact on a company's need for control systems and the preventive or detective type of each control that is contemplated.

Types of Fraud

The vast majority of transactional problems that controls guard against are innocent errors caused by employee errors. These tend to be easy to spot and correct, when the proper control points are in place. However, the most feared potential loss of assets is not through these mistakes but through deliberate fraud on the part of employees, since these transactions are deliberately masked, making it much more difficult to spot them. Discussion of the eight most common types of frauds that are perpetrated follows.

- *Cash and investment theft.* The theft of cash is the most publicized type of fraud, and yet the amount stolen is usually quite small, when compared to the byzantine layers of controls typically installed to prevent such an occurrence. The real problem in this area is the theft of investments, when someone sidesteps existing controls to clean out a company's entire investment account. Accordingly, the accountant should spend the most time designing controls over the movement of invested funds.

- *Expense account abuse.* Employees can use fake expense receipts, apply for reimbursement of unapproved items, or apply multiple times for reimbursement through their expense reports. Many of these items are so small that they are barely worth the cost of detecting, while others, such as the duplicate billing to the company of airline tickets, can add up to very large amounts. Controls in this area tend to be costly and time-consuming.

- *Financial reporting misrepresentation.* Although no assets appear to be stolen, the deliberate falsification of financial information is still fraud, because it impacts a company's stock price by misleading investors about financial results. Controls in this area should involve internal audits to ensure that processes are set up correctly, as well as full audits (not reviews or compilations) by external auditors.

- *Fixed assets theft.* Although the term *fixed assets* implies that every asset is big enough to be immovable, many items—particularly computers—can be easily stolen and then resold by employees. In many instances, there is simply no way to prevent the loss of assets without the use of security guards and surveillance equipment. Given that many organizations do not want to go that far, the most common control is the purchase of insurance with a minimal deductible, so that losses can be readily reimbursed.

- *Inventory and supplies theft.* The easiest theft for an employee is to remove inventory or supplies from a storage shelf and walk away with them. Inventory controls can be enhanced through the use of fencing and limited access to the warehouse, but employees still can hand inventory out through the shipping and receiving gates. The level of controls installed in this area will depend on the existing level of pilferage and the value of inventory and supplies.

- *Nonpayment of advances.* The employees who need advances, either on their pay or for travel, are typically those who have few financial resources. Consequently, they may not pay back advances unless specifically requested to do so. This requires detailed tracking of all outstanding advances.

- *Purchases for personal use.* Employees with access to company credit cards can make purchases of items that are diverted to their homes. Controls are needed that require detailed records of all credit card purchases, rather than relying on a cursory scan and approval of an incoming credit card statement.

- *Supplier kickbacks.* Members of the purchasing staff can arrange with suppliers to source purchases through them in exchange for kickback payments directly to the purchasing staff. This usually results in a company paying more than the market rate for those items. This is a difficult type of fraud to detect, since it requires an ongoing review of prices paid as compared to a survey of market rates.

Fraud problems are heightened in some organizations, because the environment is such that fraud is easier to commit. For example, a rigorous emphasis on increasing profits by top management may lead to false financial reporting in order to "make the numbers." Problems also can arise if the management team: is unwilling to pay for controls or for a sufficient number of supervisory personnel; is dominated by one or two people who can override existing controls; or has high turnover, so that new managers have a poor grasp of existing controls. Fraud is also common when the organizational structure is very complex or the company is growing quite rapidly; both situations tend to result in fewer controls, which create opportunities to remove assets. Consequently, fraud is much more likely if there are unrealistic growth objectives, if there are problems within the management ranks, or if controls are not keeping pace with changes in the organizational structure.

Key Controls

Thousands of possible controls can be used to ensure that a company maintains proper control over its assets. The following list represents the 14 most common controls found in most smaller organizations. These can be supplemented by additional controls in cases where the potential for loss of assets is considered to be exceptionally high, with the reverse being true in other instances.

1. *Cash.* The handling of cash is considered to be rife with control issues, resulting in perhaps an excessive use of controls.

Although many potential controls are listed here, you should attempt to create a mix of controls that balances their cost against incremental gains in the level of control achieved.

• *Compare check register to actual check number sequence.* The computer's list of checks printed should exactly match the checks that actually have been used. If not, this can be evidence that someone has removed a check from the check stock in hopes that it will not be noticed. This irregularity is most common for laser check stock, since these checks are stored as separate sheets and so can be more easily pilfered than continuous rolls of check stock.

• *Conduct spot audits of petty cash.* It is possible to misrepresent the contents of a petty cash box through the use of miscellaneous receipts and IOU vouchers. By making unscheduled audits, you sometimes can spot these irregularities.

• *Control check stock.* The check stock cannot be stored in the supply closet along with the pencils and paper, because anyone can remove a check from the stack and then is only a forged signature away from stealing funds from the company. Instead, the check stock should be locked in a secure cabinet, to which only authorized personnel have access.

• *Control signature plates.* If anyone can access the company's signature plates, then it is possible not only to forge checks, but also to stamp authorized signatures on all sorts of legal documents. Accordingly, these plates should always be kept in the company safe.

• *Deposit all checks daily.* If checks are kept on hand for several days, there is an increased likelihood that someone will gain access to them and cash them into his or her own account. Consequently, bank deposits should be made every day.

• *Divert incoming cash to a lockbox.* If cash or checks from customers never reach a company, a host of control problems related to the potential misuse of that cash goes away. To do this, set up a lockbox that is controlled by the company's bank, and ask customers to send their payments to the lockbox address.

• *Limit petty cash reserves.* If there is little money in a petty cash box, then there is less incentive for anyone to steal the box. If a large amount of cash volume flows through the box, a useful alternative is procurement cards.

• *Reconcile petty cash.* There tends to be a high incidence of fraud related to petty cash boxes, since money can be removed from them more easily. To reduce the incidence of these occurrences, initiate unscheduled petty cash box reconciliations, which may catch perpetrators before they have covered their actions with a false paper trail. This control can be strengthened by targeting those petty cash boxes that have experienced unusually high levels of cash replenishment requests.

• *Require that petty cash vouchers be filled out in ink.* Anyone maintaining a petty cash box can easily alter a voucher previously submitted as part of a legitimate transaction and remove cash from the petty cash box to match the altered voucher. To avoid this, require that all vouchers be completed in ink. To be extra careful, you can even require users to write the amount of any cash transactions on vouchers in words instead of numbers (e.g., "fifty-two dollars" instead of "52.00"), since numbers can be more easily modified.

• *Perform bank reconciliations.* This is one of the most important controls anywhere in a company, for it reveals all possible cash inflows and outflows. Carefully compare the bank statement's list of checks cashed to the company's internal records to ensure that checks have not been altered once they leave the company or that the books have not been altered to disguise the amount of the checks. Also compare the bank's deposit records to the books to see if there are discrepancies that may be caused by someone taking checks or cash out of the batched bank deposits. Further, compare the records of all company bank accounts to see if any check kiting is taking place. In addition, it is absolutely fundamental that the bank reconciliation be completed by someone who is completed unassociated with the accounts payable, accounts receivable, or cash receipts functions, so that there is no way for anyone to conceal their wrongdoings by altering the bank reconciliation. Finally, it is now possible to call up online bank records through the Internet, so that a reconciliation can be conducted every day.

This is a useful approach, since irregularities can be spotted and corrected much more quickly.

• *Separate responsibility for the cash receipt and cash disbursement functions.* It is easy for a person with access to both the cash receipt and disbursement functions to commit fraud by altering the amount of incoming receipts and then pocketing the difference. To avoid this, each function should be handled by different people within the organization.

• *Stamp incoming checks with "deposit to account number . . ."* Employees with access to customer checks may try to cash them, as might anyone with access to the mail once it has left the company. This can be made more difficult by stamping the back of the check with "deposit to account number xxxxx," so that they would have to deface this stamp in order to cash the check.

2. *Investments.* The shifting of investment funds is the area in which a person has the best chance for stealing large quantities of company funds or of placing them in inappropriate investments that have a high risk of loss. The next controls are designed to contain these risks.

• *Impose investment limits.* When investing its excess funds, a company should have a policy that requires it to invest only certain amounts in particular investment categories or vehicles. For example, only the first $100,000 of funds are insured through a bank account, so excess funding beyond this amount can be shifted elsewhere. As another example, the company owner may feel that there is too much risk in junk bond investments and so will place a general prohibition on this type of investment.

• *Require authorizations to shift funds among accounts.* A person who is attempting to fraudulently shift funds out of a company's accounts must have approval authorization on file with one of the company's investment banks to transfer money out to a noncompany account. This type of authorization can be strictly controlled through signatory agreements with the banks. It is also possible to impose strict controls over the transfer of funds *between* company accounts, since a person may uncover a loophole in the control system whereby a particular bank has not been warned *not* to allow fund transfers outside of a preset range of company accounts and then shift all funds to that account and thence to an outside account.

3. *Accounts Receivable.* Controls are needed in the accounts receivable area to ensure that employees do not take payments from customers and then hide the malfeasance by altering customer receivable records. Here are the most common controls.

• *Compare checks received to applications made against accounts receivable.* It is possible for an accounts receivable clerk with the dual responsibility of cash application to cash a check to his or her personal account and then hide evidence of the stolen funds by continually applying subsequent cash received against the oldest accounts receivable. You can spot this by conducting an occasional comparison of checks listed on the deposit slip for a given day to the accounts against which the funds were credited.

• *Confirm receivables balances.* To check whether an employee is falsely applying cash from customers to different accounts in order to hide the loss of some cash that he or she has extracted from the company, periodically send out confirmation forms to customers to verify what they say they have paid to the company.

• *Match invoiced quantities to the shipping log.* It is useful to spot-check the quantities invoiced to the quantities listed on the shipping log. By doing so, you can detect fraud in the billing department caused by invoicing for too many units, with the accounting staff pocketing the difference when it arrives. This is a rare form of fraud, since it generally requires collaboration between the billing and cash receipts staff. The control is needed only where the fraud risk clearly exists.

• *Require approval of bad debt expenses.* A manager should approve any bad debt write-offs from the accounts receivable listing. Otherwise, it is possible for someone to receive a check from a customer, cash it into his or her own account, and write off the corresponding account receivable as a bad debt. This control can be greatly enhanced by splitting the cash receipts function away from the collections function, so that collusion would be required to make this type of fraud work.

• *Require approval of credits.* It is possible for someone in the accounts receivable area to grant a credit to a customer in exchange for a kickback from the customer. You can prevent this by using approval forms for all credits granted, as well as a periodic comparison of credits granted to related approval forms. It is acceptable to allow the accounting staff to grant very small credits in order to clean up miscellaneous amounts on the accounts receivable listing, but these should be watched periodically to see if particular customers are accumulating large numbers of small credits.

• *Verify invoice pricing.* The billing department can commit fraud by issuing fake invoices to customers at improperly high prices and then pocketing the difference between the regular and inflated prices when the customer check arrives. Having someone compare the pricing on invoices to a standard price list before invoices are mailed can spot this issue. This form of fraud is possible only when there is a risk of collaboration between the billing and cash receipts staff, so the control is only needed when the fraud risk is present.

4. *Inventory.* A company's inventory can be so large and complex that extensive controls are needed simply to give it any degree of accuracy at all. Consequently, virtually all of the next controls are recommended to achieve a high level of inventory record accuracy:

• *Conduct inventory audits.* If no one ever checks the accuracy of the inventory, gradually it will vary from the book inventory, as an accumulation of errors builds up over time. To counteract this problem, you can schedule either a complete recount of the inventory from time to time or else an ongoing cycle count of small portions of the inventory each day. Whichever method is used, it is important to conduct research in regard to why errors are occurring, and attempt to fix the underlying problems.

• *Control access to bill of material and inventory records.* The security levels assigned to the files containing bill of material and inventory records should allow access to only a very small number of well-trained employees. By limiting access, you minimize the risk of inadvertent or deliberate changes to these valuable records. The security system should also store the keystrokes and user access codes for anyone who has accessed these records, in case evidence is needed to prove that fraudulent activities have occurred.

• *Pick from stock based on bills of material.* An excellent control over material costs is to require the use of bills of material for each item manufactured and then require that parts be picked from the raw materials stock for the production of these items based on the quantities listed in the bills of material. A reviewer then can hone in on those warehouse issuances that were *not* authorized through a bill of material, since there is no objective reason why these issuances should have taken place.

• *Require approval to sign out inventory beyond amounts on pick list.* If a standard pick list is used to take raw materials from the warehouse for production purposes, it should be the standard authorization for inventory removal. If production staff members require any additional inventory, they should go to the warehouse gate and request it, and the resulting distribution should be logged out of the warehouse. Furthermore, any inventory that is left over after production is completed should be sent back to the warehouse and logged in. By using this approach, the cost accountant can tell if there are errors in the bills of material that are used to create pick lists, since any extra inventory requisitions or warehouse returns probably represent errors in the bills.

• *Restrict warehouse access to designated personnel.* Without access restrictions, the company warehouse is like a large store with no prices—just take all you want. This does not necessarily mean that employees are taking items from stock for personal use, but they may be removing excessive inventory quantities for production purposes, which leads to a cluttered production floor. Also, this leaves the purchasing staff with the almost impossible chore of trying to determine what is in stock and what needs to be bought for immediate manufacturing needs. Consequently, a mandatory control over inventory is to fence it in and closely restrict access to it.

• *Review inventory for obsolete items.* The single largest cause of inventory valuation errors is the presence of large amounts of obsolete inventory. To avoid this problem, periodically print a report that lists which inventory items have *not* be used recently, including the extended cost of these items. A more accurate variation is to print a report itemizing all inventory items for which there are no current production requirements (possible only if a material requirements planning system is in place). Alternatively, you can use a report that compares the amount of inventory on hand to annual historical usage of each item. With this information available, you should then schedule regular meetings with the materials manager to determine what inventory items should be scrapped, sold off, or returned to suppliers.

5. *Prepaid Expenses.* The largest problem with prepaid expenses is that they tend to turn into a holding area for payments that should have been converted into expenses at some point in the past. There is also a potential for advances to be parked in this area that should have been collected. The next controls address these problems:

• *Reconcile all prepaid expense accounts as part of the month-end closing process.* By conducting a careful review of all prepaid accounts once a month, it becomes readily apparent which prepaid items should now be converted to an expense. The result of this review should be a spreadsheet that itemizes the nature of each prepaid item in each account. Since this can be a time-consuming process involving some investigative work, it is best to review prepaid expense accounts shortly before the end of the month, so that a thorough review can be conducted without being cut short by the time pressures imposed by the usual closing process.

• *Require approval of all advance payments to employees.* The simplest way to reduce the burden of tracking employee advances is not to make them in the first place. The best approach is to require management approval of any advances, no matter how small they may be.

6. *Fixed Assets.* The purchase and sale of fixed assets require special controls to ensure that proper authorization has been obtained to conduct either transaction and also to ensure that the funds associated with fixed assets are properly accounted for. All of

the next controls should be implemented to ensure that these goals are achieved.

• *Compare capital investment projections to actual results.* Managers have been known to make overly optimistic projections in order to make favorable cases for asset acquisitions. This issue can be mitigated by conducting regular reviews of the results of asset acquisitions in comparison to initial predictions and then tracing these findings back to the initiating managers. This approach can also be used at various milestones during the asset construction to ensure that costs incurred match original projections.

• *Ensure that fixed asset purchases have appropriate prior authorization.* A company with a capital-intensive infrastructure may find that its most important controls are over the authorization of funds for new or replacement capital projects. Depending on the potential amount of funding involved, these controls may include a complete net present value (NPV) review of the cash flows associated with each prospective investment as well as multilayered approvals that reach all the way up to the company owner or board of directors. A truly comprehensive control system will also include a postcompletion review that compares the original cash flow estimates to those actually achieved, not only to see if a better estimation process can be used in the future but also to see if any deliberate misrepresentation of estimates was initially made.

• *Verify that fixed-asset disposals are properly authorized.* A company does not want to have a fire sale of its assets taking place without any member of the management team knowing about it. Consequently, the sale of assets should be properly authorized prior to any sale transaction being initiated, if only to ensure that the eventual price paid by the buyer is verified as being a reasonable one.

• *Verify that cash receipts from asset sales are properly handled.* Employees may sell a company's assets, pocket the proceeds, and report to the company that the asset actually was scrapped. This control issue can be reduced by requiring that a bill of sale or receipt from a scrapping company accompany the file for every asset that has been disposed of.

7. *Accounts Payable.* This is one of the most common areas in which the misuse of assets will arise, as well as the one where transactional errors are most likely to occur. Nonetheless, an excessive use of controls in this area can result in a significant downgrading in the performance of the accounts payable staff, so a judiciously applied blend of controls should be used.

• *Audit credit card statements.* When employees are issued company credit cards, there will be some risk that the cards will be used for noncompany expenses. To avoid this, you can spot-check a few line items on every credit card statement, if not conduct a complete review of every statement received. For those employees who have a history of making inappropriate purchases but for whom a credit card is still supplied, it is also possible to review their purchases online (depending on what services are offered by the supplying bank) on the same day that purchases are made and alter credit limits at the same time, thereby keeping tighter control over credit card usage.

• *Compare payments made to the receiving log.* With the exception of payments for services or recurring payments, all payments made through the accounts payable system should have a corresponding record of receipt in the receiving log. If not, there should be grounds for investigation into why a payment was made. This can be a difficult control to implement if there is not an automated three-way matching system already in place, since otherwise a great deal of manual cross-checking will be needed.

• *Require approval of all invoices that lack an associated purchase order.* If the purchasing department has not given its approval to an invoice, then the accounting staff must send it to the supervisor of the department to whom it will be charged, so that this person can review and approve it.

8. *Current Liabilities.* The general area of current liabilities is one in which items can inadvertently build up over time when they should be charged to expense. The next controls impose close monitoring over the most common current liability accounts.

• *Include an accrual review in the closing procedure for bonuses, commissions, property taxes, royalties, sick time, vacation time, unpaid wages, and warranty claims.* There are many possible expenses for which an accrual is needed, given their size and repetitive nature. This control is designed to force a continual review of every possible current liability as part of the standard monthly closing procedure, so that no key accruals are missed.

• *Review accrual accounts for un-reversed entries.* Some accruals, such as unpaid wage accruals and commission accruals, are supposed to be reversed in the following period, when the actual expense is incurred. However, if an accountant forgets to set up a journal entry for automatic reversal in the next period properly, a company will find itself having recorded too large an expense. A simple control point is to include in the period-end closing procedure a review of all accounts in which accrual entries are made, to ensure that all reversals have been completed.

• *Create standard entries for reversing journal entries.* As a continuation of the last control point, an easy way to avoid problems with accrual journal entries that are supposed to be reversed is to create boilerplate journal entry formats in the accounting system that are preconfigured to be reversed automatically in the next period. As long as these standard formats are used, there will never be an unreversed journal entry.

• *Create a standard checklist of recurring supplier invoices to include in the month-end cutoff.* A number of invoices arrive after month-end that are related to services and for which an accrual should be made. The easiest way to be assured of making these accruals is to create a list of recurring invoices, with their approximate amounts, and use it as a check-off list during the closing process. If the invoice has not yet arrived, then accrue for the standard amount shown on the list.

9. *Notes Payable.* The acquisition of new debt is usually a major event that is closely watched by the company owner, and so requires few controls. Nonetheless, the next control point is recommended as a general corporate policy.

• *Require supervisory approval of all borrowings and repayments.* As was the case with the preceding control point, high-level supervisory approval is required for all debt instruments—except this time it is for final approval of each debt commitment. If the debt to be acquired is extremely large, it may be useful to have a policy requiring approval by the company owner or board of directors, just to be sure that there is full agreement at all levels of the organization regarding the nature of the debt commitment. To be a more useful control, this signing requirement should be communicated to the lender, so that it does not inadvertently accept a debt agreement that has not been signed by the proper person.

10. *Revenues.* The key controls concern related to revenues is that all shipments be invoiced in a timely manner. A controls failure in this area can lead to a major revenue shortfall and threaten overall company liquidity.

    • *Compare all billings to the shipping log.* There should be a continual comparison of billings to the shipment log, not only to ensure that everything shipped is billed but also to guard against illicit shipments that involve collusion between outside parties and the shipping staff. Someone who is handing out products at the shipping dock rarely will be obliging enough to record this transaction in the shipping log, so the additional step of carefully comparing finished goods inventory levels to physical inventory counts and reviewing all transactions for each item must be used to determine where inventory shrinkage appears to be occurring.

    • *Compare customer-requested delivery dates to actual shipment dates.* If customer order information is loaded into the accounting computer system, run a comparison of the dates on which customers have requested delivery to the dates on which orders were actually shipped. If there is an ongoing tendency to make shipments substantially early, there may be a problem with trying to create revenue by making early shipments. Of particular interest is when there is a surge of early shipments in months when revenues would otherwise have been low, indicating a clear intention to increase revenues by avoiding customer-mandated shipment dates. It may be possible to program the computer system to not allow the recording of deliveries if the entered delivery date is prior to the customer-requested delivery date, thereby effectively blocking early revenue recognition.

    • *Compare invoice dates to the recurring revenue database.* In cases where a company obtains a recurring revenue stream by billing customers periodically for maintenance or subscription services, there can be a temptation to create early billings in order to record revenue somewhat sooner. For example, a billing on a 12-month subscription could be issued after 11 months, thereby accelerating revenue recognition by one month. This issue can be spotted by comparing the total of recurring billings in a month to the total amount of recurring revenue for that period as compiled from the corporate database of customers with recurring revenue. Alternatively, you can compare the recurring billing dates for a small sample of customers to the dates on which invoices actually were issued.

• *Investigate all journal entries increasing the size of revenue.* Any time a journal entry is used to increase a sales account, this should be a "red flag" indicating the potential presence of revenues that were not created through a normal sales journal transaction. These transactions can be legitimate cases of incremental revenue recognition associated with prepaid services but can also be barter swap transactions or fake transactions whose sole purpose is to increase revenues. It is especially important to review all sales transactions where the offsetting debit to the sales credit is *not* accounts receivable or cash. This is a prime indicator of unusual transactions that may not really qualify as sales. For example, a gain on an asset sale or an extraordinary gain may be incorrectly credited to a sales account to mislead the reader of a company's financial statements that its operating revenues have increased.

• *Issue financial statements within one day of the period-end.* By eliminating the gap between the end of the reporting period and the issuance of financial statements, it is impossible for anyone to create additional invoices for goods shipping subsequent to the period-end, thereby automatically eliminating any cutoff problems.

11. *Cost of Goods Sold.* There are many ways in which a company can lose control over its costs in the cost of goods sold area, since it involves many personnel and the largest proportion of company costs. The application of the next suggested controls to a production environment will rely heavily on the perceived gain

that will be experienced from using them versus the extent to which they will interfere with the smooth functioning of the production department.

• *Audit inventory material costs.* Inventory costs usually are assigned either through a standard costing procedure or as part of some inventory layering concept, such as last in, first out or first in, first out. In the case of standard costs, you should regularly compare assigned costs to the actual cost of materials purchased to see if any standard costs should be updated to bring them more in line with actual costs incurred. If it is company policy to update standard costs only infrequently, then you should verify that the variance between actual and standard costs is being written off to the cost of goods sold.

• *Compare the cost of all completed jobs to budgeted costs.* A company can suffer from major drops in its gross margin if it does not keep an eagle eye on the costs incurred to complete jobs. To do so, the cost accountant should compare a complete list of all costs incurred for a job to the initial budget or quote and determine exactly which actual costs are higher than expected. This review should result in a list of problems that caused the cost overruns, which in turn can be addressed by the management team so that they do not arise again. This process should also be performed while jobs are in process (especially if the jobs are of long duration), so that problems can be found and fixed before job completion.

• *Pick from stock based on bills of material.* An excellent control over material costs is to require the use of bills of material for each item manufactured and then to require that parts be picked from the raw materials stock for the production of these items based on the quantities listed in the bills of material. By doing so, a reviewer can hone in on those warehouse issuances that were *not* authorized through a bill of material, since there is no objective reason why these issuances should have taken place.

12. *Travel and Entertainment Expenses.* Employee expense reports can involve dozens of line items of requested expense reimbursements, a few of which may conflict with a company's stated reimbursement policies. In order to ensure that these gray-area

expense line items are caught, many accountants apply a disproportionate amount of clerical time to the minute examination of expense reports. The need for this level of control will depend on the accountant's perception of the amount of expenses that will be reduced through its use. In reality, some lesser form of control, such as expense report audits, are generally sufficient to keep expense reports "honest."

• *Audit expense reports at random.* Employees may be more inclined to pass through expense items on their expense reports if they do not think that the company is reviewing their expenses. This issue can be resolved fairly inexpensively by conducting a few random audits of expense reports and following up with offending employees regarding any unauthorized expense submissions. Word of these activities will get around, resulting in better employee self-monitoring of their expense reports. Also, if there is evidence of repeat offenders, random audits can be made less random by requiring recurring audits for specific employees.

• *Issue policies concerning allowable expenses.* Employees may submit inappropriate expenses for reimbursement simply because they have not been told that the expenses are inappropriate. This problem can be resolved by issuing a detailed set of policies and procedures regarding travel. The concept can be made more available to employees by posting the information on a corporate intranet site. Also, if an online expense report submission system is in place, these rules can be incorporated directly into the underlying software, so that the system will warn employees regarding inappropriate reimbursement submissions.

13. *Payroll Expenses.* The controls used for payroll cover two areas: the avoidance of excessive amounts of pay to employees and the avoidance of fraud related to the creation of paychecks for nonexistent employees. Both types of controls are addressed here.

• *Require approval of all overtime hours worked by hourly personnel.* One of the simplest forms of fraud is to come back to the company after hours and clock out at a later time, or have another employee do it on one's behalf, thereby creating false overtime hours. This issue can be resolved by requiring supervisory approval of all overtime hours worked. A more advanced approach is to use a computerized time clock that categorizes each employee by a specific work period, so that any hours worked after his or her standard time period will be flagged automatically by the computer for supervisory approval. Such a system may not even allow an employee to clock out after a specific time of day without a supervisory code first being entered into the computer.

• *Require approval of all pay changes.* Pay changes can be made quite easily through the payroll system if there is collusion between a payroll clerk and any other employee. This problem can be spotted through regular comparisons of pay rates *paid* to the approved pay rates *stored* in employee folders. It is best to require the approval of a high-level manager for all pay changes, which should include that person's signature on a standard pay change form. It is also useful to audit the deductions taken from employee paychecks, since these can be altered downward to effectively yield an increased rate of pay. This audit should include a review of the amount and timing of garnishment payments, to ensure that these deductions are being made as required by court orders.

14. *General.* A few continuing payments to suppliers are based on long-term contracts. Most of the next controls are associated with having a complete knowledge of the terms of these contracts, so that a company does not make incorrect payment amounts.

• *Monitor when contracts are due for renewal.* A company may find itself temporarily paying much higher prices to a supplier if it inadvertently lets expire a long-term contract containing advantageous price terms. To avoid this difficulty, a good control is to set up a master file of all contracts that includes contract expiration dates, so that there will be fair warning of when contract renegotiations must be initiated.

• *Require approval for various levels of contractually based monetary commitment.* There should be a company policy that itemizes the levels of monetary commitment at which additional levels of management approval are required. Although this step may not help the company to disavow signed contracts, it is a useful

prevention tool for keeping managers from signing off on contracts that represent large or long-term monetary commitments.
• *Obtain bonds for employees in financially sensitive positions.* If there is some residual risk that, despite all the foregoing controls, corporate assets still will be lost due to the activities of employees, it is useful to obtain bonds on either specific employees or for entire departments, so that the company can be reimbursed in the event of fraudulent activities.

These recommended controls encompass only the most common problem areas. They should be supplemented by reviewing the process flows used by a company to see if there is a need for additional (or fewer) controls, depending on how the processes are structured. Controls will vary considerably by industry, as well; for example, the casino industry imposes multilayered controls over cash collection, since it is a cash business. Thus, these controls should be considered only the foundation for a comprehensive set of controls that must be tailored to each company's specific needs.

When to Eliminate Controls

Despite the lengthy list of controls noted in the last section, there are times when you can safely take controls away. By doing so, frequently you can eliminate extra clerical costs or at least streamline the various accounting processes. Five steps should be used to see if a control is eligible for removal.

1. *Flowchart the process.* The first step is to create a picture of every step in the entire process in which a control fits by creating a flowchart. This flowchart is needed in order to determine where other controls are located in the process flow. With a knowledge of redundant control points or evidence that there are no other controls available, you then can make a rational decision regarding the need for a specific control.
2. *Determine the cost of a control point.* Having used a flowchart to find controls that may no longer be needed, we must then determine their cost. This can be a complex calculation, for it

may not involve just a certain amount of labor, material, or overhead costs that will be reduced. The control may be situated in the midst of a bottleneck operation, so that the presence of the control is directly decreasing the capacity of the process, thereby resulting in reduced profits. In this instance, the incremental drop in profits must be added to the incremental cost of operating the control in order to determine its total cost.

3. *Determine the criticality of the control.* If a control point is merely a supporting one that backs up another control, then taking it away may not have a significant impact on the ability of the company to retain control over its assets. However, if its removal can be counteracted only by a number of weaker controls, it may be better to keep it in operation.

4. *Calculate the control's cost/benefit.* Points 2 and 3 can be compared to see if a control point's cost is outweighed by its criticality or if the current mix of controls will allow it to be eliminated with no significant change in risk, while stopping the incurrence of its cost.

5. *Verify the use of controls targeted for elimination.* Even when there is a clear-cut case for the elimination of a control point, it is useful to notify everyone who is involved with the process in which it is embedded, in order to ascertain if it is being used for some other purpose. For example, a control that measures the cycle time of a manufacturing machine may no longer be needed as a control point, but may be an excellent source of information for someone who is tracking the percentage utilization of the equipment. In these cases, it is best to determine the value of the control to its alternate user before eliminating it. It may be necessary to work around the alternate use before the control point can be removed.

This control evaluation process should be repeated whenever there is a significant change to a process flow. Even if there has not been a clear change for some time, it is likely that a large number of small changes have been made to a process, whose cumulative impact will necessitate a controls review. The period of time between these reviews will vary by industry; some have seen little process change in many years, while others are constantly shifting their business models, which inherently requires changes to their supporting processes.

If there are any significant changes to a business model, such as the addition of any kind of technology, entry into new markets, or the addition of new product lines, a complete review of all associated process flows should be conducted both prior to and immediately after the changes, so that unneeded controls can be removed promptly or weak controls enhanced.

Summary

The main focus of this chapter has been on the specific control points that can be attached to an accounting system, both to reduce the risk of loss and assist in attaining budgeted goals. The selection of these controls should be contingent on an evaluation of the risks to which an accounting system is subject as well as the cost of each control point and its impact on the overall efficiency of each accounting process. In a larger organization, the continuing examination, selection, and installation of control points can easily become a full-time job for a highly trained process expert. Smaller organizations that cannot afford the services of such a person will likely call on the in-house accounting staff to provide such control reviews, which should be conducted on a fixed schedule in order to ensure that ongoing incremental changes to processes are adequately supported by the correct controls.

Section II

Operating the Business

S ection I was largely devoted to tasks that can and should be accomplished prior to the start of the business (or of the fiscal period for an ongoing business). It focused on planning what you want and intend to make happen.

The two chapters of Section II discuss those areas you must manage when the business period is under way:

- Cash flow concerns
- Financing

Obviously, these also require planning. But they are, to a greater degree, day-to-day management functions.

Day-to-day management should be based on the overall planning and control discussed in Section I, but changes to the plan may be necessitated by unanticipated occurrences. Therefore, the concepts presented in the next chapters offer a system for adjusting the implementation of the plan in response to new information without changing the basic and underlying desired accomplishments.

Chapter 4

Cash Flow Concerns

Managing working capital is an important function of the business. Contained within working capital are four major elements that you must plan for and consider in order to maintain viability:

1. Cash
2. Accounts receivable
3. Accounts payable
4. Inventory

This chapter discusses the management of cash, accounts receivable, and accounts payable.

Cash

Cash is the most liquid of all assets and serves many purposes within the business.

- *Transactions.* Cash is used as a medium for transactional payments. Regardless of the form or nature of the payments, in the final analysis there is normally a transfer of cash.
- *Investment.* Whether made by outside individuals, businesses, banks, or the business investing in itself (reinvestment of excess cash), the transactions ultimately involve cash.

- *Security.* A reasonable level of cash in a liquid account is a measure of security to the business. Depending on the nature and size of the business, the amount of cash necessary may be significant.

When considering the investment of cash, most investors consider four factors in determining whether to invest and, if so, how much:

1. *Yield.* Yield is in itself composed of two elements: growth and dividends. The *growth* of a business is represented in the market by the market price of its stock or an increase in its valuation, indicating an increase in the equity worth. For example, if your stock is increasing in value in the market at a rate of 12 to 15 percent per year, this could be an adequate expected return, sufficient to attract investors even without cash dividends. If your stock is valued at a relatively constant $10 per share in the market but pays an average annual *dividend* of $1.20 to $1.50, it too is yielding 12 to 15 percent on the investment. In the small or closely held business, the yield often is taken out in the form of higher compensation or "perks" by the owners.

2. *Risk.* This element of investing is intangible. Different investors— for example, institutional investors and individual ones looking at the same business—will make different assessments of risk. A constant growth business and a steady earnings business, although both have the same return, may be seen as having different risks. If your business demonstrates steady growth and reinvestment of excess earning, bankers may view it as less risky than a business that earns a steady amount and "throws off dividends" to its owners.

3. *Liquidity.* Here the investor is concerned with how quickly the investment can be converted to cash. Liquidity is essentially a timing issue; risk and return will affect liquidity. Real estate may be more risky and have higher returns than Treasury bills, but an investor who wants a liquid asset will prefer T-bills because they can be traded with little or no delay. Real estate may tie up investors' funds for months while they try to find a buyer, or they may have to discount the price in order to convert the asset quickly.

4. *Transactional costs.* Whatever gross yield an investment shows, transactional costs have to be deducted. For the preceding example, the steadily growing business shows a gross yield of 12 to 15 percent per year, but the investor realizes no gain until he or she sells the stock and pays brokerage fees and appropriate taxes. In the steady dividend business, the investor realizes the yield periodically through direct payments with no transactional costs except taxes. The transactional costs associated with a real estate sale can be quite significant. Brokerage fees may amount to 6 percent or more. Attorney's fees, recordings, documentary stamps, title search, title insurance, and other factors may amount to an appreciable portion of the gain.

Cash becomes of critical concern when there is too little to meet the immediate needs of the business. However, it is equally important to consider cash when there is an ample supply available. Many people ignore the significance of a surplus of cash. Many businesses leave excess cash idle in non-interest-bearing accounts. Optimal cash management requires the investment of idle cash in profitable endeavors. It is easier to earn an income on cash than any other commodity you have. Since it is liquid, cash may be managed or converted without the delay that inhibits the liquidity of other assets.

What to Do with Excess Cash

There are many profitable means available to invest excess cash. Some of the more convenient opportunities will be discussed here.

Interest Accounts

Cash flows into and out of the business on a daily basis. Unfortunately for most businesses, large and small, the inflows and outflows are neither steady nor all predictable within an acceptable degree of certainty. The business may be cash-rich or poor at different times during the month.

Because of this uncertainty, you must always have adequate

cash on hand or in liquid accounts to meet the demands as they are returned for payment. You should be equally concerned that no idle excess cash is sitting in a non–interest-bearing checking account. If the buffer of cash is excessive, you are losing the opportunity to earn on that money.

Investigate the options available at your bank for earning interest on checking or for keeping cash in an interest-bearing account, with provisions for automatic transfers when checking balances are below a certain level.

Another option is the deposit of cash in money market accounts. This is a liquid, higher-yield form of savings account. Often these accounts may be used in conjunction with a form of checking, with restrictions as to minimum balances in the accounts and as to the maximum number of transactions per period.

Idle cash represents an opportunity easy to capture; the returns can be worth the effort expended in finding a solution.

Treasury Securities

U.S. Treasury obligations constitute the largest segment of the money market. The principal securities issued are bills, tax anticipation bills, notes, and bonds. Treasury bills are auctioned weekly by the Treasury Department, with maturities of 91 days and 182 days. In addition, nine-month and one-year bills are sold periodically. Treasury bills carry no coupon but are sold on a discount basis. These securities are extremely popular with companies, large or small, as short-term investments. In part because of the large amount outstanding, the market is very active and the transaction costs involved in the sale of Treasury bills in the secondary market are small. Very often, in some of the more sophisticated financial models, Treasury bills are considered risk-free, interest-bearing notes.

Agency Securities

Obligations of various agencies of the federal government are guaranteed by the agency issuing the security and not usually by the Treasury. The principal agencies issuing securities are the Federal

Housing Administration and the Government National Mortgage Association. These obligations are not guaranteed by the Treasury; however, there is an implied backing of the government. It would be hard to imagine the federal Treasury allowing an agency to fail. Major government-sponsored agencies that issue securities include the federal home loan banks, federal land banks, and the Federal National Mortgage Association. The securities provided by these agencies return a modest yield advantage over treasury securities of the same maturity. These securities have a high degree of marketability and are sold in the secondary market through the same security dealers as the Treasury securities.

Banker's Acceptances

Banker's acceptances are drafts accepted by banks and used in financing foreign and domestic trade. The creditworthiness of banker's acceptances is judged relative to the bank accepting the draft rather than the drawer. Acceptances generally have maturities of less than 180 days and are of very high quality. They are traded in an over-the-counter market dominated by a few dealers. The rates on banker's acceptances tend to be slightly higher than rates on Treasury bills of similar maturity.

Commercial Paper

Commercial paper consists of short-term unsecured promissory notes issued by finance companies and certain industrial concerns. Commercial paper can be purchased either directly or through dealers. Among the companies selling commercial paper on this basis are CIT Financial Corporation, Ford Motor Credit Company, and General Motors Acceptance Corporation.

Negotiable Certificates of Deposit

Negotiable time certificates of deposit (CDs) are time-certain investments. The CD is evidence of the deposit of funds at a commercial bank for a specified period of time and at a specified rate of interest. Money market banks quote rates on CDs that are changed periodically in keeping with changes in other money market rates. Yields on CDs are greater than on T-bills but are about the same as on banker's acceptances and commercial paper.

Cash Flows

Before dealing with the problem of insufficient cash, we should consider the sources of cash inflow. There are four sources of cash inflow to the business:

1. New investment
2. New debt
3. Sale of fixed assets
4. Operating revenues (including collection of accounts receivable)

Each of these sources has important limitations on it. The only source that can be relied on in an ongoing way is operating profits. That is what makes profit planning such an important activity for any business. When the business experiences continued profitable operations, *accompanied by a positive cash inflow,* it can grow most efficiently.

Inflows

The inflows, or the receipt of payment from customers for product or services, is the lifeblood of any business. The obvious rule with inflows is to get customers to pay as promptly as possible. For example, many doctors and lawyers now demand payment on receipt of service for routine office visits.

It is obvious that the efficiency of cash management improves with the acceleration of customers' payments. The fast food industry illustrates how, by sticking strictly to a credit card and cash-only business, an extremely low current ratio can be maintained. In contrast to cash payments, payments by check have an inherent delay associated with the time it takes for a check to clear the bank. During this period, the funds are not available for use by the business. The objective should be to reduce the delay in receiving payment and the clearing time necessary for the transfers of funds. In addition to federal legislation concerning maximum times for banks to clear checks, several methods have been developed to decrease the float (i.e., the speed of realizing actual cash receipt).

- *Concentration banking.* If your business is large enough to have broad market coverage, you may consider using banks at various locations within your market areas to speed the clearance of checks. Using banks in areas where sales occur allows for the processing of local checks. These generally clear faster, and funds can be more quickly concentrated for wire transfer to a central bank.
- *Lockboxes.* Businesses may use a lockbox system for collections. To do so, rent a post office box, centrally located in a market, and authorize your bank to open the box and directly credit payments to your account. This procedure has advantages and disadvantages. The obvious disadvantage is the loss of control over the physical receipt of funds and the direct monitoring of clients' payment habits. You do not have the ability to process receipts before the bank gets them. This elimination of handling saves you time, but the bank does charge a fee for the service.
- *Elimination of unnecessary accounts.* Having an account in each local bank where you do business or have some operations creates goodwill and a sense of presence. However, by maintaining many separate and diverse accounts, you are dispersing money that could be used more effectively if it was concentrated. By concentrating cash, you probably can reduce cash reserves and still function efficiently.
- *Zero-balance accounts.* If a company wants to retain a number of checking accounts, it is wastefully keeping cash in each of those accounts that is earning either zero or very little interest income. A better approach is to keep it in a single, central account that earns the highest possible rate of interest, because the company has concentrated its funds in one place and now can access higher-earning investments that require a higher minimum investment. To make this cash centralization system work while still retaining several checking accounts, a company can use a zero-balance account. This is a checking account that

contains a zero cash balance at all times, but which pulls funds from another account, such as the investment account, when checks clear. The only disadvantage to this approach is that the bank reconciliation is made more difficult, because the reconciliation of all checks now flows through a single account, which results in a large amount of check volume to sort through.

- *Controlled disbursements.* It is also possible to retain cash through the accounts payable function without suppliers realizing that cash is being withheld from them for an extra day or two. This approach is called controlled disbursements, and involves the payment of checks from banks so isolated that it takes longer for checks to clear through them. This additional float period is minor but allows a company to retain its cash for slightly longer than normal, so it can keep the funds in short-term investments and earn slightly more interest income than otherwise would be the case. This approach can also be expanded to include the mailing of checks from company locations that are farthest from supplier locations, in order to take advantage of a few days of additional mail float. However, this delaying tactic is more obvious to suppliers and tends to meet with stiff disapproval by them.

An item that was mentioned at the beginning of this section was the sale of fixed assets as a source of cash flows. Selling assets is a task that most companies address only sporadically, resulting in assets' losing value over time while they lie ignored in odd corners of the company. However, if dealt with in a systematic manner, the periodic review of fixed assets will result in the prompt identification of unused assets and continuing attention to their disposal, which results in the highest possible sale prices for the assets, thereby contributing to cash flows. The basic process is to schedule a periodic asset review, certainly no less than annually, in which the management team reviews the list of fixed assets to determine which items can be sold off at once. One person should be in charge of this process, so the system will not be dropped for lack of attention. Also, this person should be required to report to the management team regularly regarding the progress of asset sales. This simple system will ensure that a company realizes the greatest possible cash flow from the sale of its unused assets.

Outflows

The largest volume of cash outflows generally is referred to on the income statement as expenses, although some "accrued" expenses may not yet have been paid in cash. Other non–cash flow expenses shown on income statements are such things as depreciation. Another item to be added to "other expenses" is the principal portion of loan payments, which, although not an expense item, is still a use of cash.

The business must be concerned with the timing and nature of the demands made on its cash. The timing of cash inflows and the importance of shortening the "float" were discussed earlier. For cash outflows, the corollary is that you want to ride the float or use the delay in cash transfers to your advantage. Some businesses capitalize on the float by writing checks on accounts without sufficient funds available to cover those checks. They may in fact have adequate reserves of cash maintained in high-yield accounts until needed to meet a draw. In this way, the business is maximizing its return by using float to its advantage. Extreme care must be exercised to avoid "kiting," (illegally benefiting from the deliberate creation of a float between accounts at two banks) an illegal act.

How do you plan for the use of float? A reasonable float pattern to study is that of paychecks. Some employees have automatic deposits to credit unions; others deposit their checks immediately, some even in the employer's bank; some employees will hold their checks for several days; and a few hardy souls may hold their checks for a week or more. To determine the necessary balances, you should gather some data:

• Collect the number of checks and the amount presented for payment on each day after the payday.
• Calculate the amount presented by day.
• Repeat the process for successive pay periods.
• Construct a frequency distribution of funds demanded by day.

From this frequency distribution, you can plan for having the appropriate amount of cash in your account at the right time. In order to ensure that you are not embarrassed by insufficient funds, maintain a safety margin in the account. (Even this safety margin can be determined statistically if there is sufficient data to determine variations in returned checks.) If the payroll is significant, holding portions of that payroll even for a day or two in a high-yield account amounts to significant returns. In the case of automatic deposits, you can determine with certainty the delay in funds transfer and can earn extra interest on this systematic float. You probably should have an agreement with your bank either to notify you if your account is underfunded, to make automatic transfers from another account, or to "cover" you with a line of credit.

Introduction to Cash Flow Budgets

Before you attempt a cash flow budget for the business, it is useful to do a cash flow analysis. Preparing a cash flow analysis often gives managers a much better understanding of the operation of their business. It is particularly important for some small businesses to get an understanding of cash flows because they are especially vulnerable to problems dealing with cash. Smaller businesses tend to operate with inadequate cash reserves or none at all.

Perhaps the most critical element to be considered is the timing of cash flows. If all of the cash outflows occur in the first six months and most of the cash inflows occur during the second six-month period, the business may fail before it has an opportunity to receive sufficient cash inflows to sustain itself. Timing of flows is critical.

Indications of Cash Flow Problems

Many businesses never achieve cash flow control. These businesses are always in trouble, chronically overdrawn and slow in paying bills. Many eventually fail. Some could survive if managers would take the necessary planning steps to create a cash flow budget and manage their cash flows as they manage other portions of the business with the following steps:

- *Decreased liquidity.* Running out of working capital. Some symptoms include too little inventory to meet demand and stretching payables.
- *Excessive turning.* Turning inventories over more than other businesses of comparable size in the industry. This can be an indication of good management, but in extreme cases it may be caused by too little working capital to support adequate inventories.
- *Excess reliance on short-term debt.* Here you may be rolling over short-term debt to raise needed working capital. Contrary to popular belief, not all working capital is short term. In most businesses, a level of working capital is required for the reasonable operation and growth of the business. We call this *fixed working capital.*
- *Dropped discounts.* Past-term payments and failure to take advantage of timely payment discounts could indicate poor management of payables or the lack of cash necessary to pay in a timely way.
- *Slow collections.* A high percentage of old receivables probably indicates poor management of receivables. It certainly indicates a potential cash problem.

These problems may be caused by insufficient cash, or the insufficient cash may be the result of poor management. In some cases, low cash balances might even indicate a planned result. For example, rapid inventory turns may be advantageous. In the grocery business, with a low margin per sale, the more frequently sales are made and inventory is turned over, the more profit is earned. Thus indicators of cash flow problems may signal nothing more than that further investigation is warranted.

Managing Cash

The control of cash is not mysterious, nor is the process itself complex. What is required is a systematic and organized approach. A few simple guidelines, set out in the next eight steps, help organize the process.

1. Identify all your sources of cash inflows: operations, debt, sale of assets, and investment.
2. List the uses to which you put the cash.
3. Identify the timing of cash flows, both in and out.
4. Calculate the difference between cash inflows and cash outflows. It is important to identify time delays in receiving cash.
5. Identify any bottlenecks to getting cash in quickly and determine how to open up the inflow.
6. Enumerate any constraints on the use of cash, such as bank loan covenants.
7. Identify those cash inflows and outflows that can be rescheduled or whose timings may be changed.
8. Most important, establish a plan for positive cash flows. This step cannot be accomplished until the other seven steps have been completed and analyzed. Each of these steps will require time and effort to complete. However, like most planning, the rewards in the long run significantly outweigh the costs to gather and analyze the information. It may save your business.

In order to effectively carry out the design and implementation of a cash flow analysis, a flowchart of how cash flows through the business is helpful. The flowchart shown in Figure 4.1 serves as an aid in the development of a cash flow budget. An analysis of each step contained in the flowchart follows.

Step 1. Identify all sources of cash inflow.
- New investments and debt are sources of cash. However, they are infrequent and cannot be relied on as continuing sources of cash.
- The sales of fixed assets are like new investments. The sale of fixed assets is not a source of recurring cash. You can sell the asset only once. While these sources cannot be ignored, they are secondary to operating profits. Consequently, it is important to focus on operating profits as your main source of cash. It

FIGURE 4.1

Cash Budgeting Flowchart

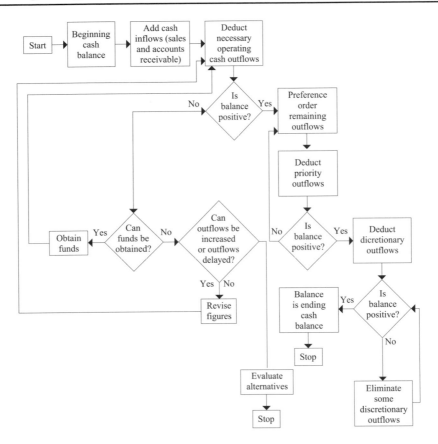

should be noted, however, that operating profits probably will not be the source of capital for major plant expansions.

- Operating profits, unlike new investments or debt, are ongoing and also harder to track. They must be monitored and controlled constantly. Even growing businesses, with increasingly larger amounts of cash inflows, must review the budget and related variances periodically and maintain control, or they may suffer from shortages of cash. As your business grows, you will often suffer from liquidity problems. Such problems may cause your business to fail to meet its short-term obligations even when it is quite viable and profitable.

As you advance through the business or product life cycle, cash demands will vary with the stages of the cycle. Typically, a company's life cycle graph will look like that in Figure 4.2.

For example, in periods of fast growth, the business probably will need growing inventories, receivables, and transactions cash. These inventory growth periods demand the commitment of large amounts of working capital, much as would be the case for adding to a building. This fixed working capital problem is illustrated in Figure 4.3.

Notice that inventory turns improve as more sales produce faster turns. Also notice that receivables turns degenerate as sales are made to marginal customers and staff is not available to perform proper credit checks and follow-up. Unfortunately, these are typical scenarios. Assume that these numbers are indicative of trends in many businesses and could apply to you.

On sales of $1 million with profits at, say, 15 percent of sales, you generate $150,000 to contribute to your working capital needs. On sales of $2 million (assuming you have to "deal" to get the

FIGURE 4.2

Life Cycle Graph

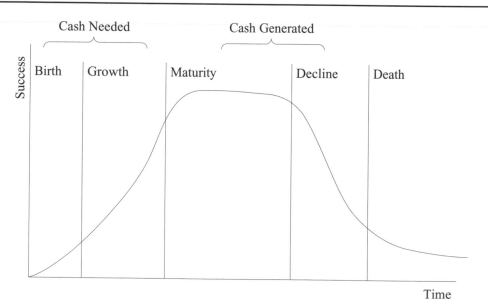

FIGURE **4.3**

Typical Growth Company

Sales Level	Inventory Turn	Inventory Amount	Receivables Turn	Receivables Amount	Transactions Cash	Working Capital
$1,000,000	6.0	$100,000	10	$100,000	$10,000	$210,000
1,250,000	6.2	121,000	9	139,000	12,500	272,500
1,500,000	6.5	138,500	8	187,500	15,000	341,000
1,750,000	7.0	161,500	7	250,000	17,500	429,000
2,000,000	7.0	185,000	7	285,000	20,000	490,000

other sales), your average profit percentage drops to 13 percent, so you generate $260,000. Your working capital needs increased by $280,000 ($490,000 − $210,000) while your profit contribution increased by only $110,000. How do you finance this growth?

The "fixed" working capital issue is that there is some minimum amount of investment in working capital that is required and should be financed as a long-term asset, not on a short-term basis. In our illustration, if base sales stay around $1.5 million with peaks and valleys, then the "fixed" component of working capital is about $340,000.

Rather than being a source of net cash inflow, the period of rapid growth may be a problem period. In periods of fast growth, inventory, receivables, and so on might not only consume all of your profits but might also require debt financing.

Part of the problem might result from offering extended payment terms to customers while at the same time being required to pay material suppliers on short terms. This difference between the time when you must pay suppliers and when you receive payment from your purchasers could mean the difference between continuing to operate and having the business fail.

The problems just outlined in regard to the increase in working capital that are associated with rapid growth may also arise in a company that is not growing at all, but for different reasons. For example, a company's investment in inventory will increase if the purchasing staff is buying parts in excessively large quantities, if finished goods are not being sold, or if the engineering staff has made a number of parts obsolete by switching to new parts on existing products. Similarly, a more liberal customer credit granting policy or a weakened collections effort will increase the investment in accounts receivable, whereas taking early payment discounts will reduce the amount of accounts payable outstanding. Since any of these issues can arise at any time, no matter what the growth stage of a company, it is best to monitor changes in the balances of all working capital items on a weekly basis and immediately investigate the reasons for sudden jumps in the investment in this category. Otherwise, a company may find itself in need of far more cash than its cash flow forecast would lead it to expect.

Step 2.   List cash outflows or uses.

A good place to start considering cash outflows is the cash journal or, if you don't have one, the checkbook. The important activity for this step in the process is to determine where the cash is going.

Many businesses experience lengthy delays between the time they pay for goods for resale and when they actually receive cash from the sale. To some extent, the delay is unavoidable. By analyzing the delay, however, you can plan for the amount of cash necessary

FIGURE 4.4

Analysis of Delay

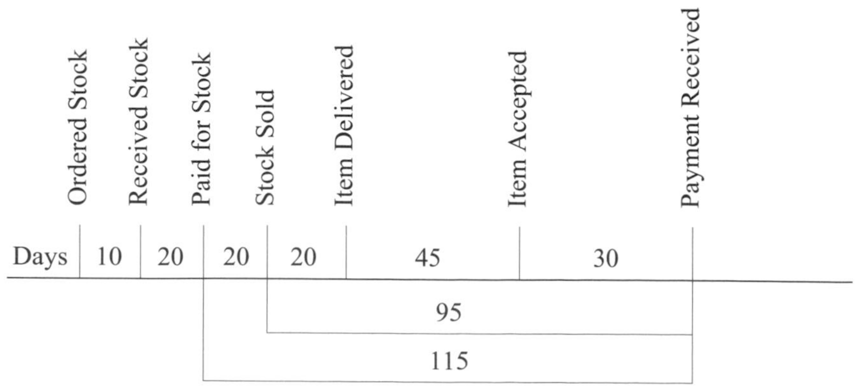

	Ordered Stock	Received Stock	Paid for Stock	Stock Sold	Item Delivered	Item Accepted	Payment Received
Days	10	20	20	20	45	30	
					95		
			115				

to sustain this short-term investment in inventory and receivables. An example of the analysis of delay is shown in Figure 4.4.

In the figure, you paid for the item of inventory but do not receive payment from the customer until 95 days later. Built into the system is some unavoidable delay. But the problem can become worse, since the item may sit on the shelf for multiple months before being purchased.

All expenditures of cash should be listed and carefully considered. Then the effort must be made to determine whether all of those cash expenditures are necessary. Pertinent questions are:

- Can we get along without it?
- Can we postpone this expenditure?
- Is the timing proper?
- Would it make more sense to pay for it earlier or later?
- Can it be done less expensively?

We often get into the rut of believing there are only two ways of doing something: our way and the wrong way. People typically act according to habit simply because doing so takes less mental effort than to think out every action in the day. The way to be innovative is to ask *why*.

When addressed to business activities, probing questions might uncover areas in which significant savings can be realized. For the computer system dealer in Figure 4.4, several questions can be asked:

- Why do we have a 45-day acceptance period?
- Why do we have a 30-day credit period after acceptance?
- Why does it take so long to deliver the product?
- Why do we carry this item in inventory?

The answers to these questions may save both expense and cash immediately. If you cannot determine where the cash is going, it may be necessary to consult your accountant and get help establishing controls. However, for many small businesses, a checkbook can provide adequate daily records of cash disbursements.

Step 3.   Identify when cash is received and expended.

The most useful tool in identifying cash inflows and outflows is a calendar. Because most businesses deal in a cyclical variation, a year is generally a useful period for which to examine expenditures and receipts of cash. To begin with, a list should be made of those outflows that have fixed dates:

- Paydays
- Tax deposits
- Bank debt repayments
- Insurance payments
- Other periodic obligations

Continue to list those items for which cash is expended until you are sure that you have accounted for all of the periodic expenditures that occur annually.

Once the cash outflows are listed, you may begin listing inflows. In doing so, you must consider the delays in receiving accounts receivable payments and your seasonal and periodic sales fluctuations. It may be necessary to consider mean or average receipt times for some of these items.

Step 4.   Examine the timing of cash inflows minus cash outflows.

A positive cash flow period is one in which the inflows of cash exceed the outflows of cash. This may not happen in all circumstances. However, it should average out over the year. For any operating period in which the business experiences a negative cash flow period, funds must be obtained from some other source.

Negative cash flow periods will occur occasionally—for example, during growth spurts. Many businesses experience sales rhythms. If you are experiencing such a rhythm, look to see if it is typical for the industry. In such cases, you must understand the rhythm and time-discretionary cash inflows in order to properly plan for those periods in which you may experience a negative cash flow period. Understanding the phenomenon of delayed cash inflow as a result of growth will help to determine how fast the business can afford to grow. It may be better to sustain a slower growth rate in order to avoid significant negative cash flow problems.

By looking at the timing of cash inflows and cash outflows, you may find ways to improve profitability by both cutting costs and increasing your opportunities.

Step 5. What effect does the current cash flow have on the business?

Plan payments to maximize the utilization of cash. That is, consider extending payments for as long as practical without incurring adverse consequences from the creditors.

Everyone in business knows that the way to improve cash flow is to slow down the outflow of cash while speeding up the inflow. This is particularly true in a tightening economy. However, before blindly following this path, consider the consequences of slowing down payment to vendors. In business, terms for payment are still commonplace. In fact, 2/10, N/30 is a commonly offered discount. In order to monitor discounts taken and discounts missed, you should establish a regular reporting mechanism to control this process.

The chart in Figure 4.5 can be expanded or redesigned to meet the specific discounts available and the payment schedules you use. In this way, you can effectively monitor performance.

The intent of discounts is to encourage early payment. But what are the consequences of not taking the discount? Let's assume a 2/10, N/30 discount. For one thing, if you wait the full 30 days to pay, you are still incurring, in essence, a 36.9 percent annualized interest rate on that money. Even if the payment period is extended for a full 50 days without adverse consequences from the vendor, you have merely cut the interest rate to 18 percent. This figure is

FIGURE 4.5

Annualized Interest Equivalent Cost of Not Taking a Cash Discount

If Paid In:	1/10, N/30	2/10, N/30
Day 10	0%	0%
Day 20	36.9%	73.8%
Day 30	18.5%	36.9%
Day 40	12.3%	24.6%

derived from the following relationship: Under the 2/10, N/30, you receive a 2 percent discount on the money due if you pay within the first 10 days. However, in the event you wait the full 30 days to pay the bill, you incur interest of 2 percent of the amount due for holding the money for an additional 20 days. Because there are approximately 18 such 20-day periods per year, the annualized interest rate of 2 percent per 20 days amounts to an annual interest rate of 36 percent. This is hardly an equitable interest rate to incur for borrowing money for such a short period. Even if you extend the period for a full 50 days, you are, in a sense, borrowing at 2 percent for 40 days. Since there are approximately 9 such 40-day periods per year, the 2 percent for each of these periods amounts to 18 percent per annum. Most businesses can afford to borrow from a bank at less than 18 percent interest.

Other consequences may result from delaying payment for up to 50 days. The creditor may institute proceedings for collection. But even if it doesn't, you will not become a favored customer by holding the vendor's money for a 50-day period. In times of tightening economies or shortage of the materials provided by this vendor, the slow-paying customer will not sit high on the list of most favored customers. You may find shortages of necessary materials or none at all coming from that vendor if you are more costly to do business with than other customers.

In managing accounts payable, there are four rules to be considered.

1. Do not buy necessary material too early; buy no unnecessary materials at all.
2. Plan your buying to balance needs with some measure of safety stock.
3. Pay so that unnecessary costs are not incurred. In doing so, consider vendor relationships and the interest rates associated with early payment discounts.
4. Set up an accounting system to monitor discounts lost or not taken. Most accounting systems list discounts taken. While this has some benefits, you will fail to take advantage of the opportunity costs. These lost opportunities may, in the long run, be

more important than discounts taken. Since it should be policy to take discounts, exception reporting would dictate capturing discounts lost.

Step 6. Identify which cash inflows or outflows cannot be changed.

Many payments made periodically by the business may not be rescheduled. In addition, collection policies might fail to achieve their objectives. Identify the extent to which payments and receipts are inflexible. Consider methods intended to speed up cash inflows. It is possible to identify particular clients who are for the most part reliable in payment and others who are dilatory. It may be more profitable to discontinue sales to purchasers with late payment records than to continue to provide them with goods. Remember, in shipping goods to a purchaser, you are in effect loaning that purchaser money. Those goods represent a cash investment by you and can be considered a loan to that purchaser.

An important consideration here is to establish a credit policy. Having a credit policy and exercising that policy consistently is a major point of control. Before extending credit, you have the maximum leverage on a particular purchaser. Once credit has been extended, much of that leverage is lost. Although there is legal recourse against the purchaser, that will not improve the cash flow in the short run.

Four rules for credit extensions follow.

1. Have a written credit policy.
2. Have a business collection policy that everyone understands.
3. Know your legal rights when it comes to collections.
4. Know the legal restraints and conditions when offering credit.

It is important to maintain an aged accounts receivable file. Knowing which accounts to either collect or receive payment from and in what period of time is very important for estimating cash inflows. Remember these points about aged accounts receivable:

- The older the account gets without payment or collection, the less likely you are to receive payment or make collection. The age of the account has a direct effect on the efforts that must be made in collecting.

- You may want to establish rules for termination of further shipments based on the age of receivables.

When establishing a collection policy, consider these points.

- Categorize the steps you wish to take in making a collection. This may include "first letters," first phone calls, referral of the collection to the legal department, and so on.
- Do not establish fixed time frames for advancing from step to step. If the time frames are known, many customers will wait to pay until the last possible moment before you move on to the next collection step.
- Do not be predictable in collection efforts. Once your collection efforts become normalized, debtors will behave accordingly.

Step 7. Identify those cash inflows and cash outflows that can be rescheduled.

By identifying those cash inflows and outflows that can be rescheduled, you may be able to balance payments and receipts to avoid unnecessary negative cash flow situations. Sometimes talking with your creditors and working out payment schedules that meet your needs and theirs can be an effective compromise. A surprising number of banks and large companies are willing to work out such payment schedules, because a smaller payment that can be expected with some degree of certainty is preferable to uncertainty or no payment at all. Also, if creditors know that there may be a nonpayment period, they are able to work out their own cash flow requirements to not be adversely affected.

Very often, businesses get into trouble with their accounts payable. You may end up spending more time talking with the people to whom you owe money than you spend in producing the money to pay your bills. This can become a cycle that gets you deeper into trouble. The solution may be to sort through all the creditors and identify all the small bills under some particular cutoff. Creditors of less than the cutoff can prompt as many phone calls as the large creditors. Often it is less expensive to borrow an amount of money and pay off all of the small creditors than to try to pay off each one separately. In this way, time becomes available to get back to the business of earning money. The bank may be able to help you out of short-term financial problems. Often grouping together many small bills into one large bill with a fixed payment period may resolve some of the intermediate cash flow problems. Be careful about lumping nonrevolving payments (due on billing) into revolving or longer-term, periodic payments in order to avoid:

- Building in an interest payment (perhaps lower than the penalty or interest due on all the small bills).
- Paying off many nonrevolving accounts. This may encourage the incurring of further liabilities on these accounts. In doing so, you simply restart the cycle.

Trade associations may be good sources of information on how to improve the business's cash outflow and inflow picture. Other businesses in the same industry may have had similar experience with collections and have ready advice on how to improve collections.

Step 8. Plan for positive cash flow.

A major tool available for planning cash flow is a cash budget. Cash budgets involve projections of future cash needs as well as cash receipts. This budget reveals the timing and amount of expected cash inflows and outflows over a particular period. For example, most businesses use a one-year business cycle. You may want to consider a two-year cash budget with modifications to the second year's budget after significant experience in the first year. The cash flow budget should take into account seasonal variations in sales and cash outflows. If cash flows are extremely volatile, short time period increments should be used in the budgeting process. If the budgeting shows a more stable period, the time periods may be longer, depending on the stability of the data. Remember that the farther into the future you try to predict cash flows, the more uncertain the forecast is. The cash budget is only as useful as the accuracy of the forecast that is used to make the predictions. If your cash flows are subject to high levels of uncertainty, you should provide for either a cash cushion, ready borrowing, or both.

Preparation of the Cash Budget

A key to the accuracy of most cash budgeting is a forecast of sales. When using an internal approach for the generation of a sales forecast, the salespeople must be asked to project sales for the forthcoming periods. The product sales manager or other appropriate person gathers these estimates and consolidates them into a sales estimate for a particular product line, thereby building up data into useful information. Often, however, internally generated sales forecasts may be too narrow in scope and overly optimistic. They may miss important trends in the economy and the industry generally. For these reasons, many companies use externally generated sales forecasts. Advisory or consulting businesses are available that use econometric modeling techniques to approximate future industry and economy conditions. These businesses may be helpful only to larger, multioperational, multiproduct, multisectional companies.

Given the basic predictions of business conditions and industrial sales, the next step is to estimate market share by individual product, price, and the expected customer reception of the new products. These estimates should be made in conjunction with the business's marketing managers. By using a consolidated approach with the sales forecast generated in conjunction with internal and external marketing personnel, a more accurate projection may be realized. The importance of the accuracy of sales forecasts cannot be overstated, as most of the other budgets, projections, and forecasts are based on expected sales.

The next step in generating a cash budget is to determine the cash receipts from the expected sales. Consider your past history of cash and credit sales to determine offsetting factors and time delays associated with each. Some probabilities may be applied to projected sales in order to generate expected receipts. In this way, you are considering the credit terms used and offsetting the timing of receipt of those sales dollars.

Disbursements

Given a sales forecast, another important body of information to be generated is a production schedule. Decisions must be made whether to gear production closely to sales or to produce at a relatively constant rate over time, ignoring the periodic fluctuations in demand. Remember that with a level production schedule, inventory carrying costs are generally higher than when the business tends to match production to sales. However, level production generally is more efficient than fluctuating production. Therefore, it is important to consider the trade-off in inventory carrying costs versus the efficiencies that can be realized in various production schedules.

Another important consideration is whether you intend to produce just enough to meet demand or to commit the resources to build inventory levels. The sales forecast is a valuable tool in determining expected future production needs. You should consider the generation of a production forecast based on some strategy for meeting this expected need. Almost all strategies will require a commitment of resources. Even production tailored to meet demand exactly requires a commitment of cash and other resources before you expect to receive cash inflows. If you plan to build a buffer inventory, you must expect an even greater delay in receipt of compensating cash inflows.

Once a production schedule has been established, estimates can be made concerning the necessary materials to be purchased, the labor required for that production, and any additional fixed assets you may need to meet the demand. From the production schedule you can evaluate the expected cash outflows and even the timing of those outflows. There is a lag between the time a sale is made and the time of actual cash payment.

Wages are assumed to increase with the amount of production. Another factor of wages is the trade-off of overtime versus increased production staff. Very often, production peaks can be taken care of more cost effectively by using overtime rather than incurring the cost of hiring new employees. Establish a policy concerning the amount of overtime you will tolerate before hiring additional employees. This can be calculated on a cost basis. For example, if the cost to the business for overtime is 2.5 times the cost of regular time (adding in overtime benefits, wages, premiums, etc.), how many hours of additional labor justify the addition of another employee?

$$\text{Breakeven for new employee} = \frac{40 \text{ hrs/wk}}{2.5} = 16 \text{ hours of overtime}$$

If your business sustains more than 16 hours of overtime for a particular function, it may be cheaper to hire another employee.

In calculating the trade-off between overtime hours and the decision to hire additional labor, we have simplified the problem for example purposes only. The problem actually is more complex. In the example, we have considered only the variable cost component of adding an additional employee. There are still fixed and semi-variable components. When you decide to add a new employee, you will incur additional costs associated with recruitment, training, insurance, administrative processing, health examinations, and other factors. In making the overtime versus hire decision, consider the costs of additional overtime hours against these fixed and semi-variable cost components as well. Obviously, this is only a first approximation. You must also consider the duration of the need and the learning time for new employees to become productive.

In addition, you will have other demands on cash. Included in other expenses are general administrative and selling expenses; property taxes; interest expenses; utilities; and maintenance expenses. These expenses tend to be reasonably predictable over the short run.

You must also take into account capital expenditures, dividends, federal taxes, and other cash outflows. As shown in Chapter 2, a business should plan as far in advance as possible for its capital expenditures. These forecasted expenditures should be predictable for the short-term cash budget. Dividend payments, if appropriate, for most companies are discretionary and are paid on specific dates. Estimation of federal income taxes can be based on projected profits, which a bookkeeper can readily generate. These cash outlays must be combined with the total cash expenditures in order to obtain a schedule of total cash disbursements. The four most critical categories to be included in the schedule of cash disbursements are:

1. Total cash expenses
2. Capital expenditures
3. Dividend payments
4. Income taxes
   These should be listed on a month-by-month basis for the fiscal year.

Many accounting software packages include a report that itemizes short-term future cash flows based on the billing and payment information already entered into the system. These systems review the open accounts receivable and determine the most likely cash receipt dates from customers, based on the dates when these invoices are due for payment. The systems also analyze open accounts payable in a similar manner, to determine the dates when supplier invoices must be paid. The information usually is presented in weekly time buckets for as far into the future as there is available information in the system to add to the forecast. Although this information is based on detailed underlying information and should be quite accurate, there are several reasons why it must be heavily supplemented by manual adjustments.

- *Missing accounts payable.* Many companies do not enter their accounts payable into the computer system until shortly before they are due for payment, because the accounting staff prefers to match supplier invoices to supporting purchasing and receiving documentation prior to making any computer entries. Because this information is not included in the computer, there will be an insufficient amount of accounts payable forecasted for payment by the computer.
- *Missing capital expenditure payments.* The accounts payable system may not include payments for capital expenditures, since many of these purchases require either cash in advance or cash on delivery, or several periodic payments; in all these cases, the

payments may not be entered into the system until the day they are due for payment, which does not allow the system to include them in forecasted cash flows.

- *Accounts receivable timing.* The actual dates on which payments arrive from customers will vary significantly from the scheduled dates itemized by the computer because there is always a mix of late payments caused by a variety of factors that delays cash receipts. Also, there are always delayed cash receipts coming in from earlier billings, the receipt of which the computer had already predicted in some earlier period, which will impact the forecasted cash flow in a positive manner.
- *Does not include payroll.* Many companies use outside payroll services or payroll software that is not integrated into the remainder of their accounting systems. For these reasons, the accounting software cannot access any information about cash outflows to pay for employee salaries and wages.

For these reasons, it is best to use the computer-generated cash forecast as a tool in constructing a more accurate manual forecast. If a detailed version of the report itemizes the specific timing of individual accounts payable and receivable, it may be of use in verifying the cash forecast that is being derived manually.

Net Cash Flow and Cash Balances

An enterprise must review its schedules carefully in order to ensure that it has taken into account all foreseeable cash inflows and outflows. By combining the cash receipts and the cash disbursements schedules, you can obtain the net cash inflow or outflow for each period. Once you have identified the months in which you will have difficulty in meeting your cash needs, you must find the means to address the cash deficiencies and to plan for them. This is further discussed in Chapter 5. Before seeking additional cash to meet these demands, you may be able to delay your capital expenditures or your payments for purchases in order to prevent the negative cash flow months from occurring.

Knowing what the cash position will be in each month allows you to consider such options as when to make capital investments, investments of excess funds in marketable securities, and other forms of cash planning.

Exceptions to Expected Cash Flows

A cash budget merely represents an estimate of future cash flows. Depending on the care devoted to preparing the budget, the volatility of the market, and the accuracy of the data used, there may be considerable deviation between the actual cash flows and the expected cash flows. When considering such uncertainty, it is necessary to provide information about the range of possible outcomes. Considering cash flows using only one set of assumptions may result in a faulty perspective of the future and misinformation for planning purposes.

In order to consider deviations from expected cash flows, it may be important to work out additional cash budgets using different forecasted sales levels. Such cash budget scenarios help you plan for contingencies. In addition, you may want to generate budgets for best-case, most likely, and worst-case scenarios.

One of the benefits of discussing the cash budget within the business is that management is better able to plan contingencies for possible consequences and probable events. These discussions tend to sharpen the perspective of management on the future. Finally, management will be encouraged to realize the magnitude and impact of various occurrences on the profitability of the business.

Computers can be used to evaluate different scenarios. An example of such a computer-generated budget is included in the appendix to this chapter. The cash budget can be designed for easy substitution of different probabilities for outcomes, thus generating a probable cash budget more rapidly and with more flexibility than by trying to adjust by hand for all the alternatives. In this manner, cases may be rerun on a computer, allowing extensive analysis of minimum cash balances, the maturity structure of needed debt, the borrowing power of the business, and the ability of the business to adjust to deviations in expected outcome. For example, these and other questions may be asked:

- How flexible are expenses?
- What can be cut or eliminated?
- How quickly can we respond?
- How much effort should be devoted to the collection of receivables?
- What additional purchases will be required for unexpected increases in business?
- Can labor be expanded and at what cost?
- Can the current plant handle the additional demand?
- How much money will be needed to finance buildup?

The answers to these and other questions will show the efficiency and flexibility of the business under varying conditions. By relying on numerous budgets with different ranges of possible outcomes, you have the option to consider and be prepared for many more contingencies.

Summary

Your working capital is principally composed of cash, accounts receivable inventory, accounts payable, and other short-term payables.

Cash serves many functions within the business and actually is the medium of exchange for all transactions. The investment of excess or temporarily idle cash should be made with a consideration for the expected yield, the associated risk, the liquidity of the investment, and the transactional costs associated with the exchange of investment with cash. There are many ways to invest excess cash, each of which has a risk-and-return relationship and other conditions and constraints. Many of the constraints deal with liquidity and transactional cost considerations.

A business selling its product in a large geographic area has to be concerned with the time delays associated with the physical transfers of payment (cash). This delay, or float, costs the business money. Many methods have been developed to minimize the delay and to speed up the receipt of cash: concentration banking, lockboxes, and others. In addition, you can delay cash outflows in order to earn additional interest.

You should have a cash flow budget. Determining how cash flows within the business may best be envisioned as an actual flow of dollars for each transaction. Cash management should consider how things are being done and question all cash expenditures: Can we get along without it? Can we postpone it? Can it be done more cheaply?

As with cash, you can profit from managing your accounts receivable. One of the easiest methods of gaining an understanding of how well collections are being made is to establish a frequency distribution of the age of the receivables. It may be more profitable to discontinue sales to delinquent customers than to continue to advance credit, tying up valuable assets. An unpaid account receivable is an outstanding loan.

The other side is your policy about paying your bills. Another simple tool is a chart showing discounts taken and, more important, discounts not taken. A common discount, 2/10, N/30, means that it costs you 2 percent of the invoice amount to extend payment for 20 days. This can be equated to a 37 percent per annum interest rate. Discounts lost can have serious cost implications.

Timing is all-important in transactions. Many businesses experience cycles that affect their cash status. Planning for these timing variations may allow you to earn more interest during periods of excess cash while having enough cash available in times of poor cash flow to avoid cash borrowing.

Appendix: Cash Flow Example

In this appendix, we review a typical cash forecasting model that uses a series of assumptions to arrive at a monthly prediction of cash inflow and outflow. The model begins with assumptions regarding sales levels, collection periods, and debt interest rates in the sections entitled "Sheet 1.1" and "Sheet 1.2." These assumptions are then used to arrive at predicted cash receipts and cash disbursements by month, as noted in the sections entitled "Sheet 2.1" and "Sheet 3.1." We bring this information together in "Sheet 4.1" to arrive at a net cash change per month. The final section, "Sheet 5.1," notes the amount of cash the company expects to invest in its working capital and other key accounts over the course of the year. This format is short and easily readable, so managers can quickly grasp the reasons for changes in cash flows.

We will note the reasons for using each line item in the cash forecast, as well as how the information is derived. This line-by-line explanation gives you a thorough understanding of the model, allowing you to duplicate it easily. The line item descriptions follow.

Sheet 1.1: Revenue

- *Total dollar sales.* This information comes from the sales department's forecast and is extremely important; the sales figures are used later in the cash forecast to determine the timing of cash receipts and the amount of likely cash expenditures. Because it affects so much of the cash forecast, a company must be sure to enter the most accurate information possible into this line.
- *Collections, cash sales.* This is a percentage and is multiplied by the total dollar sales figure in the preceding line to derive the "cash sales" figure that is listed under the *Cash Receipts Detail* section. This figure represents the cash inflow that has no timing delay, since customers pay at the time of product receipt.
- *Collections, collect in 30 days.* This is a percentage and is multiplied by the total dollar sales figure in the first line of this section to derive a portion of the "Collections of Receivables" figure that is listed under the *Cash Receipts Detail* section. This figure represents the proportion of cash inflow that has a delay of approximately 30 days in arriving and represents that portion of accounts receivable that arrives on time. Those businesses using different payment terms on their billings should use their stated number of payment days instead of the 30 days used in this example.
- *Collections, collect in 60 days.* This is a percentage and is identical to the preceding one in its usage, except that it represents the proportion of accounts receivable that are collected later than normal. This figure tends to fluctuate with the looseness of a

company's credit granting policy and in inverse proportion to the aggressiveness of its overdue accounts receivable collection efforts.

- *Collections on November sales.* The sample cash forecast we are reviewing begins with December, so any late cash receipts from preceding months must be entered in this line. Based on the dollar quantities entered in the example, we can estimate that the sales in November were $100,000, since the standard proportion collected in 30 days is 40 percent, and $40,000 is entered as having been received in December.
- *Average gross margin percentage.* This is a percentage and represents the average cost of sales in each month. In this model, it is used to derive the Total Purchases on Credit, which is the first line in the *Assumptions* section. For example, by multiplying the February sales figure of $140,000 by 70 percent, we arrive at total purchases for the month of $98,000, to which we add an inventory buildup for the month of $94,000 (as noted in the Inventory line in the *Balances in Key Accounts* section). When added together, this equals total purchases of $192,000, which is the number listed under February in the Total Purchases on Credit line in the *Assumptions* section.

Sheet 1.2: Assumptions

- *Total purchases on credit.* The derivation of the amounts in this line were described for the Average Gross Margin Percentage in the *Sheet 1.1* section. The total purchases number is later used in the Payment for Purchases on Credit line in the *Cash Disbursements Detail* section, with a delay of one month (since we assume supplier payment terms of 30 days). This is the chief component of the cash disbursements total.
- *Line-of-credit interest rate.* This is a percentage, and is used later in the *Cash Disbursements Detail* section to determine the interest payment on the line of credit, which is a cash disbursement.
- *Line-of-credit balance in December.* The last line of the cash forecast includes a calculation of the balance in the line of credit; however, this figure will be incorrect unless the model already contains the balance from the previous year. Therefore, we include this preliminary debt figure.

- *Long-term debt interest rate.* This is a percentage and is used later in the *Cash Disbursements Detail* section to determine the interest payment on the long-term debt, which is a cash disbursement. Unlike the interest rate for the line of credit, there is only a single entry for this amount, rather than an entry in every month of the year; the reason for the difference is that most long-term debt is fixed at the beginning of the debt agreement, so there is no need to adjust the rate over the course of the year.
- *Long-term debt balance in December.* The *Cash Disbursements Detail* section includes line items for the interest and principal payments on long-term debt. Those payments are derived from the December debt balance, since it reveals the total amount that the company still has left to pay on its debt.
- *Long-term debt payment schedule.* This line item lists the grand total payment to lenders each month that is required to fulfill debt payment obligations on the long-term debt total that was listed in the last line item. If there are debt balloon payments, they should be entered in the correct month in this line.
- *Minimum acceptable cash balance.* This figure is the minimum amount of cash that the management team has decided must be kept on hand at all times, perhaps to meet short-term cash needs. This figure is needed to calculate the Cash Needs Comparison line in the *Analysis of Cash Requirements* section.

  The figure also appears in the Ending Cash Balance line of the same section, where we have borrowed enough funds through the line of credit to ensure that the cash balance never drops below the minimum acceptable cash balance.

Sheet 2.1: Cash Receipts Detail

- *Cash sales.* The numbers in this line denote the total amount of cash received from cash payments for sales. These cash receipts have no timing delay, since they come from customers as immediate payment for sales to them. The numbers are derived by multiplying the sales figure in the Total Dollar Sales line in *Sheet 1.1* times the cash sales percentage in the same section, and for the same month.
- *Collections of receivables.* This line is a calculation that summarizes the delayed cash receipts from sales in the past two months.

Specifically in this model, it is 50 percent of the sales from two months ago, plus 40 percent of the sales from the preceding month. (These collection percentages were listed in the *Sheet 1.1* section.)

- *Other.* There are always miscellaneous cash receipts that can come in from a variety of sources, such as tax rebates or proceeds from asset sales. These figures are entered manually in this line.

- *Total cash receipts.* This line summarizes all the cash receipts previously noted in this section.

Sheet 3.1: Cash Disbursements Detail

- *Payment for purchases on credit.* The numbers in this line are drawn directly from the Total Purchases on Credit line in the *Assumptions* section. However, their timing is moved forward one month, since we are assuming that purchases made in the preceding month have payment terms of 30 days and so must be paid in the following month. For example, purchases made in July of $90,000 do not appear in the cash forecast as payments until August.

- *Operating expenses.* The numbers in this line are entered from the annual budget, and contain the salaries, facility expenses, and other miscellaneous administrative costs associated with running the business.

- *Long-term debt interest.* This line item and the next one, Principal, are based on an electronic spreadsheet command. The command is derived from the debt payment amount listed in the Long-Term Debt Payment Schedule line and the Long-Term Debt Interest Rate line, both located in the *Assumptions* section. You can use the IPMT command in Microsoft Excel to determine the proportion of the monthly debt payment that is ascribed to interest expense, while you can subtract the interest expense from the total debt payment to derive the principal payment that is listed in the next line. These two lines can be merged if management is not interested in the interest and principal components that comprise a debt payment.

- *Principal.* See the preceding line item.

- *Interest payment on line of credit.* This line item is based on the month-end line-of-credit balance from the preceding month, multiplied by the interest rate for the month, which results in the interest payment due to the lender during the current month. For example, the February interest payment is derived by multiplying the January debt total of $58,250 by the interest rate of 15% (reduced to one-twelfth, since this is a single-month payment), which results in an interest expense of $728.

- *Income taxes.* This line contains the estimated income tax payments for each quarter of the year, and is usually inputted directly from the annual budget.
- *Other.* There are always additional cash payments that do not fall into the standard categories previously noted in this section. This line item is used for manual entries of these extra cash outflows.
- *Total cash disbursements.* This line summarizes all of the cash disbursements previously noted in this section.

Sheet 4.1: Analysis of Cash Requirements

- *Net cash generated this period.* The numbers in this line are calculated by subtracting the amounts in the Total Cash Disbursements line in the preceding section from the amounts in the Total Cash Receipts line in the *Cash Receipts Detail* section.
- *Beginning cash balance.* This figure comes from the Ending Cash Balance line at the end of this section, but for the preceding month. It is netted against the Net Cash Generated This Period line to arrive at the Cash Balance Before Borrowings line, which follows.
- *Cash balance before borrowings.* As just noted, this line is derived by netting the Net Cash Generated This Period line against the Cash Balance Before Borrowings line. The resulting numbers show the cash inflow or outflow resulting from operations.
- *Cash needs comparison.* This line compares the Cash Balance before Borrowings line to the Minimum Acceptable Cash Balance in the *Assumptions* section to arrive at a total amount of borrowings needed or cash available for an additional debt payment. For example, in the month of April, we have a preliminary cash need of $32,450, but then increase it by $20,000, since we

require an internal cash balance of $20,000, resulting in a total cash need of $52,450.

- *Current period short-term borrowings.* This line is a calculation that is essentially the inverse of the preceding line. It itemizes a borrowing requirement that exactly matches the cash need we have just calculated in the Cash Needs Comparison line. However, note that the amount of debt paid down in August is lower than the amount of cash spun off by operations, because we are paying off the line of credit in August and have surplus cash left over.

- *Total short-term borrowings.* The numbers in this line are cumulative from month to month. For example, the total short-term borrowings at the end of January are $58,250 but are increased by $47,478 in February (see the Current Period Short-Term Borrowings line), resulting in a total borrowings figure of $105,728.

- *Ending cash balance.* The numbers in this line are based on a minimum cash balance of $20,000 (as noted earlier in the Minimum Acceptable Cash Balance line in the *Assumptions* section), or a higher cash balance, if the line of credit has been paid off. For example, the ending cash balance in July is $20,000, but this increases to $67,404 in August, because the line of credit has been paid off, leaving an extra $47,404 to add to the beginning cash balance for the next month.

Sheet 5.1: Balances in Key Accounts

- *Cash.* The numbers in this line are drawn directly from the Ending Cash Balance line in the preceding section. Its purpose in this section is to be part of the summary of key accounts that most affect monthly cash flows.

- *Accounts receivable.* The numbers in this line are derived from the sales and collection figures at the top of the *Sheet 1.1* section. For example, the December accounts receivable figure is composed of two calculations. The first is 90 percent of the current month's sales, which is derived by assuming that only 10 percent of sales are paid for in cash (as noted in the Cash Sales line in the *Sheet 1.1* section). The remaining amount comes from previous month sales, which in this example are 40 percent of the November sales. After adding the two calculations together, we arrive at an estimated accounts receivable balance of $152,900.

- *Inventory.* The numbers in this line are derived manually and are normally input from the production or inventory budget page in the annual budget. Many manufacturing companies will build inventory levels prior to the commencement of their main selling seasons, and so the inventory level will not necessarily bear a direct relationship to sales levels each month. This line item is part of the calculation for the Payment for Purchases on Credit line in the *Cash Disbursements Detail* section, as explained earlier in the bullet for that line.
- *Accounts payable.* The numbers in this line are drawn directly from the Total Purchases on Credit line in the *Assumptions* section and represent the total source of funds from suppliers that will offset cash used by the other line items in this section (e.g., accounts receivable and inventory).
- *Line of credit.* The numbers in this line are drawn directly from the Total Short-Term Borrowings line in the preceding section. Its purpose in this section is to be part of the summary of key accounts that most affect monthly cash flows.

Review the following cash flow example in detail, consulting the explanations section to clarify any points of uncertainty, for as long as it takes to obtain a thorough understanding of how a cash flow forecast works. We highly recommend that every company create a cash flow forecast and update and consult it regularly, because cash flow is the lifeblood of a business and can rapidly lead to a cash flow coronary that results in a business heart attack.

Revenue Sheet 1.1

	Dec	Jan	Feb	Mar	Apr	May	Jun	Jul	Aug	Sep	Oct	Nov	Dec
Total Dollar Sales	110,000	120,000	140,000	180,000	240,000	242,000	187,000	154,000	121,000	110,000	110,000	110,000	21,000
Collections: Cash Sales as Percent	10	10	10	10	10	10	10	10	10	10	10	10	10
of Sales Collect in 30 Days	40	40	40	40	40	40	40	40	40	40	40	40	40
Collect in 60 Days	50	50	50	50	50	50	50	50	50	50	50	50	50
Collections on November Sales	40,000	50,000											
Average Gross Margin Percentage	70	70	70	70	70	70	70	70	70	70	70	70	70

Assumptions Sheet 1.2

	Dec	Jan	Feb	Mar	Apr	May	Jun	July	Aug	Sep	Oct	Nov	Dec
Total Purchases on Credit	112,000	144,000	192,000	198,000	153,000	126,000	99,000	90,000	81,000	90,000	90,000	90,000	17,000
Line-of-Credit Interest Rate:	14	14	15	17	18	16	16	16	16	16	15	14	12
Line-of-Credit Balance in December:	0												
Long-Term Debt Interest Rate:	14												
Long-Term Debt Balance in December:	100,000												
Long-Term Debt Payment Schedule:	2,500	2,500	2,500	2,500	2,500	2,500	2,500	2,500	2,500	2,500	2,500	2,500	2,500
Minimum Acceptable Cash Balance:	20,000	20,000	20,000	20,000	20,000	20,000	20,000	20,000	20,000	20,000	20,000	20,000	20,000

Cash Receipts Detail Sheet 2.1

	Jan	Feb	Mar	Apr	May	Jun	Jul	Aug	Sep	Oct	Nov	Dec
Cash Sales	12,000	14,000	18,000	24,000	24,200	18,700	15,400	12,100	11,000	11,000	11,000	12,100
Collections of Receivables	44,500	103,000	116,000	142,000	186,000	216,800	195,800	155,100	125,400	104,500	99,000	99,000
Other												
Total Cash Receipts	56,500	117,000	134,000	166,000	210,200	235,500	211,200	167,200	136,400	115,500	110,000	11,100

Cash Disbursements
Detail   Sheet 3.1

	Jan	Feb	Mar	Apr	May	Jun	Jul	Aug	Sep	Oct	Nov	Dec
Payment for Purchases on Credit	112,000	144,000	192,000	198,000	153,000	126,000	99,000	90,000	81,000	90,000	90,000	90,000
Operating Expenses	12,250	12,250	12,250	12,250	12,250	12,250	12,250	12,250	12,250	12,250	12,250	12,250
Long-Term Debt Interest	1,167	1,151	1,135	1,119	1,103	1,087	1,071	1,054	1,037	1,020	1,003	985
Principal	1,333	1,349	1,365	1,381	1,397	1,413	1,429	1,446	1,463	1,480	1,497	1,515
Interest Payment on Line of Credit	0	728	1,498	2,700	3,099	2,601	1,372	198	0	0	0	0
Income Taxes	3,000	0	0	0	0	0	2,000	0	0	3,000	0	0
Other	0	5,000	0	2,000	3,000	0	5,000	0	2,000	0	25,000	0
Total Cash Disbursements	129,750	164,478	208,248	218,450	172,849	143,351	123,122	104,948	97,750	107,750	129,750	104,750

Analysis of Cash
Requirements   Sheet 4.1

	Dec	Jan	Feb	Mar	Apr	May	Jun	Jul	Aug	Sep	Oct	Nov	Dec
Net Cash Generated This Period		-73,250	-47,478	-74,248	-52,450	37,351	92,149	88,078	62,252	38,650	7,750	-19,750	6,350
Beginning Cash Balance		35,000	20,000	20,000	20,000	20,000	20,000	20,000	20,000	67,404	106,054	113,804	94,054
Cash Balance Before Borrowings		-38,250	-27,478	-54,248	-32,450	57,351	112,149	108,078	82,252	106,054	113,804	113,804	100,404
Cash Needs Comparison		-58,250	-47,478	-74,248	-52,450	37,351	92,149	88,078	62,252	86,054	93,804	74,054	80,404
Current Period Short-Term Borrowings	0	58,250	47,478	74,248	52,450	-37,351	-92,149	-88,078	-14,848	0	0	0	0
Total Short-Term Borrowings	0	58,250	105,728	179,976	232,426	195,075	102,926	14,848	0	0	0	0	0
Ending Cash Balance	35,000	20,000	20,000	20,000	20,000	20,000	20,000	20,000	67,404	106,054	113,804	94,054	100,404

Balances in Key
Accounts   Sheet 5.1

	Dec	Jan	Feb	Mar	Apr	May	Jun	Jul	Aug	Sep	Oct	Nov	Dec
Cash	35,000	20,000	20,000	20,000	20,000	20,000	20,000	20,000	67,404	106,054	113,804	94,054	100,404
Accounts Receivable	99,500	152,000	174,000	218,000	288,000	313,800	265,100	213,400	170,500	147,400	143,000	143,000	152,900
Inventory	35,000	95,000	189,000	261,000	246,000	202,600	170,700	152,900	149,200	162,200	175,200	188,200	220,500
Accounts Payable		144,000	192,000	198,000	153,000	126,000	99,000	90,000	81,000	90,000	90,000	90,000	117,000
Line of Credit	0	58,250	105,728	179,976	232,426	195,075	102,926	14,848	0	0	0	0	0
		64,750	85,272	121,024	168,574	215,325	253,874	281,452	306,104	325,654	342,004	335,254	356,804

Financing

When considering business financing, it is important to distinguish between businesses just beginning their life cycle and those that have an established business record on which to build.

New Businesses

Many new businesses begin operations using "stolen funds," which means funds diverted from other normal financial activities unrelated to the project. With the inception of a new business, the capital for start-up often comes from personal resources. Even in larger businesses, start-up funds may come from stolen funds. As such, they may appear in another budget, not directly earmarked for the project to which they are applied.

Another source of stolen funds may be personal loans advanced by individuals using homes and items of personal property as collateral. Finally, an ultimate source of venture capital for a small business may be funds invested by, or loaned from, friends or family.

In all events, these funds represent a source not to be counted on for long-term or continued financing. As businesses start to grow, additional funds from these sources probably will not be available for continuing operations and growth. Additional resources and capital will be needed for inventory, equipment, operations, and to support accounts receivable. Many people with new businesses are surprised to learn how much money is needed to support accounts receivable. As the business grows, accounts receivable may seem to eat money.

Later in the chapter, we discuss sources of equity capital. At this point, however, it is important to mention that, in many circumstances, it is better to borrow money than to seek money from outside equity sources. Equity sources often dilute entrepreneurial control—a significant potential problem for smaller businesses.

Debt may be the best form of financing for at least two reasons:

1. *It is sometimes cheap.* Interest payments on debt are made in before-tax dollars. Dividends paid on equity are in after-tax dollars. However, interest payments are mandatory, and dividends can be discretionary.
2. *Debt has an amplifying effect on earnings.* Provided the business is profitable "after debt service," as the percentage of debt to equity increases, the earnings available to stockholders increase for a given amount of earnings. That is, once debt is serviced, the additional earnings on that capital go to the stockholders, not the creditors.

Zero Working Capital and Zero Fixed Assets

Before we delve into the various forms of financing, it is worthwhile to note several approaches for avoiding the need for financing. One of the best is the concept of zero working capital, which is a state in which the sum of a company's investments in accounts receivable, inventory, and accounts payable nets out to zero. This is made possible by using different management techniques for each of these elements of working capital:

- *Accounts receivable.* The goal in managing accounts receivable is to shorten the time needed for customers to pay the company. This can be done through several approaches. One is to use a very aggressive collections team to contact customers about overdue payments and ensure that payments are made on time. Another approach is to tighten the credit granting process, so that potential customers with even slightly shaky credit histories are kept on a very short credit leash or granted no credit at all. A final approach is to drastically shorten the standard customer payment terms, which can even go so far as requiring cash payments in advance.

- *Inventory.* The goal in managing inventory is to reduce it to the bare minimum, which can be achieved in two ways. One is to outsource the entire production operation and have the production supplier drop ship deliveries directly to the company's customers, so that the company never has to fund any inventory—the company never purchases raw materials or work-in-process. Instead, it pays the supplier when finished goods are delivered to its customers. A different approach is to use a manufacturing planning system, such as just-in-time (JIT). Under this concept, the inventory levels needed to maintain a proper flow of inventory are reduced to the bare minimum through a number of techniques, such as many small supplier deliveries straight to the production line, kanban cards to control the flow of parts, and building to specific customer orders.

- *Accounts payable.* The goal in managing accounts payable is to not pay suppliers for as long as possible. One way to do this is to stretch out payments, irrespective of whatever the supplier payment terms may be. However, this will rapidly irritate suppliers, who may cut off the credit of any company that consistently abuses its designated payment terms. A better approach is to formally negotiate longer payment terms with them, perhaps in exchange for slightly higher prices. For example, terms of 30 days at a price point of $1.00 per unit may be altered to terms of 60 days and a new price of $1.02 per unit, which covers the supplier's cost of the money that has essentially been lent to the company. Although there is a cost associated with lengthening supplier terms, this may be a good deal for a company that has few other sources of funds.

Forcing longer payment terms on suppliers is much easier if a company knows that it comprises a large part of its suppliers' sales, which gives it considerable negotiating power over them. The same situation exists with a company's customers if it has a unique product or service that they cannot readily find elsewhere, so they must agree to abide by the short payment terms. If a company does not have these advantages, or if competitive pressures do not allow it to make use of them, the best option left is the reduction of inventory, since this is an internal issue that is not dependent on the vagaries of suppliers and customers.

Dell Computer Company has achieved a *negative* working capital position, which means it makes money from its working capital. It does this by keeping only a day or two of inventory on hand and by ordering more from suppliers only when it has specific orders in hand from customers. In addition, Dell pays its suppliers on longer terms than the terms it allows its customers, many of whom pay by credit card. The result is an enviable situation in which this rapidly growing company can not only ignore the cash demands that normally go along with growth, but actually take in cash from it.

Working capital is not the only drain on cash that a company will experience. It must also invest in fixed assets, such as office equipment for its staff, production machinery for the manufacturing operation, and warehouses and trucks for the logistics department. Although these may seem like unavoidable requirements that are an inherent part of doing business, there are a few ways to mitigate or even completely avoid these investments.

- *Centralize operations.* If a company adds branch offices or extra distribution warehouses, it must invest in fixed assets for each one. This is a particular concern when extra distribution warehouses are added, since a company must absorb not only the cost of the building but also the cost of the inventory inside it. A better approach for a cash-strapped company is to centralize virtually all operations, even if there is a cost associated with *not* decentralizing. For example, shifting to a central warehouse will eliminate the cost of a subsidiary warehouse, but will increase the cost of deliveries from the central warehouse, assuming that shipments must now travel a farther distance.
- *Rent or lease facilities and equipment.* With so many leasing companies in the market today, as well as manufacturers financing

the lease of their own equipment, a company has a wealth of financing choices that allow it to avoid the purchase of its facilities and equipment. These arrangements can be a straight rental, wherein the company has no ownership interest in the assets it uses (also very similar to an operating lease), or a capital lease, in which the terms of the lease agreement assume that the company will take possession of the asset being leased at the end of the payment term. In either of these cases, the total of the rental or lease payments will exceed the cost of the asset if a company chose to purchase the asset; this is due to the maintenance and interest costs of the lease supplier, as well as its profit. The main advantage is that there is no large lump-sum payment required at the time of asset acquisition.

- *Outsource operations.* Some portion of every department can be outsourced to a supplier. Although the main reasons for doing so are related more to strategic and operational issues, you can also make a strong case for outsourcing because it reduces the need for fixed assets. By using outsourcing to avoid the hiring of clerical staff, a company no longer has to invest in the office space, furniture, or computer systems that they would otherwise require. Also, shifting the distribution function to a supplier can completely eliminate a company's investment in trucking and warehouse equipment, whereas outsourcing production will eliminate the massive fixed asset investment that is common for most manufacturing facilities. Similarly, shifting a company's computer operations to the data processing center of a supplier will eliminate its investment in its own data processing center, which may be considerable. By using outsourcing, a company avoids not only an initial investment in fixed assets but also the update and replacement of those same items.

- *Use partnerships.* If a company can enter into a partnership with another company, it may be possible to use the other company's assets to transact business. For example, if a drug research company has a new drug to market, it should enter into a partnership with an established drug manufacturing firm, so that the research firm does not have to invest in its own production plant. This arrangement works well for both parties: The research company can avoid additional cash investments in fixed assets, while the other company can more fully utilize its existing assets. If a company brings a particularly valuable patent or process to a partnership, it can use this to extract a large share of the forthcoming partnership profits, too.

This list includes many cases in which fixed assets could be eliminated, but at the cost of increased variable costs. Examples of this were heightened distribution costs in exchange for eliminating an outlying distribution warehouse, renting equipment rather than buying it, and outsourcing services rather than attempting to operate them in-house. These are acceptable approaches for many companies, and for several reasons. One is that avoiding the fixed costs associated with a fixed-asset purchase will keep a company's total fixed costs lower than would otherwise be the case, which allows it to have a lower break-even point, so that it can still turn a profit if sales take a turn for the worse. Also, if there are few and meager funding sources, the added variable costs will not seem like much of a problem when weighed against the amount of cash that a company has just avoided investing in fixed assets. Finally, the centralization of operations and use of outsourcing will reduce the amount of management attention that would otherwise be wasted on the outlying locations that are now no longer there or the departments that have been shifted to a supplier. In smaller companies with a dearth of managers, this is a major advantage. Consequently, the increased variable cost of some of the fixed-asset reduction options presented here should not be considered a significant reason for not implementing them.

Types of Financing

Typically, businesses are financed using either or both of two forms of capital investment: debt and equity. Within these two general classifications, there is an array of alternatives as diverse and creative as human imagination. The first and most common form of financing is debt.

Debt

Debt—borrowing—can be structured with repayment in the short, intermediate, or long term. It can be unsecured or (as is more commonly the case) secured by the assets of the business and/or owners. It typically has conditions or covenants that define the terms of the commitment and repayment of the loan.

Short-term debt generally is intended to be self-liquidating in that the asset purchased with that loan will generate sufficient cash flows to pay off that loan within one year. It is often used to finance inventory buildups and seasonal increases in accounts receivable. Trade credit, lines of credit, and commercial paper (for the large firm) are sources of short-term, unsecured financing. With some forms of short-term, unsecured financing, some extra compensation is required. For example, for a line of credit, a bank may require a compensating balance to be deposited. If you wish to establish a line of credit for $200,000, many banks require you to maintain a balance of, say, 15 percent, or $30,000, in a demand-deposit account during the year. If the compensating balance is above the amount you ordinarily would have on deposit, the cost of the incremental amount represents an additional cost of borrowing. In the above example, if you wish to borrow $200,000 and the bank rate is 12 percent, with the compensating balance of $30,000 *more* than you ordinarily have on deposit, you would net only $170,000 to use. The nominal annual dollar cost is 12 percent of $200,000, or $24,000. The actual cost of the loan as a percentage is:

$$\frac{\$24,000}{\$170,000} = 14.11\%$$

The use of compensating balances is falling with the advent of variable interest rates. Some banks are charging higher interest rates more in line with their incremental cost of money and deemphasizing compensating balances.

Another method used by banks to improve their return is discounting. For example, under a "regular" loan, a bank lends $20,000 for one year at 14 percent simple interest. At the end of the year, the borrower repays the $20,000 plus $2,800 in interest. If the loan is discounted, the bank collects its interest at the time of lending. The borrower receives a net loan of $17,200. At the end of the year, when the borrower repays the loan of $20,000, the actual effective interest rate is higher. It computes to:

$$\frac{\$2,800}{\$17,200} = 16.28\%$$

Secured Loans and Intermediate Financing. Many new firms cannot obtain credit on an unsecured agreement because they have no proven track record. First, banks look to your cash flow ability. Failing that, the security of the collateral pledged to insure payment must be considered. The lender will seek collateral in excess of the loan value to guarantee a margin of safety. The greater the margin of safety, the more liquid the collateral, because the asset can be discounted further (and still realize full repayment) and sold more quickly to meet the call on the debt.

One method that may be employed to secure the debt is borrowing against accounts receivable. The collateral to the lender is the debt owed the borrower on goods or services provided to customers. From the lender's standpoint, there is a cost to process the collateral and there is a risk of fraud and default. Therefore, this may be an expensive method of borrowing.

A loan against accounts receivable generally is made through a commercial bank because the interest rate is lower than that offered by finance companies. The lender discounts the face value of the receivables and may even reject from consideration some that have low credit ratings, are unrated, or are slow to pay.

Another factor of concern to the lender is the size or amount of each receivable. There is a trade-off: the larger the amount of the receivable, the larger the amount of potential default. But with fewer accounts to keep track of, the cost of administration is less. A large number of small accounts have higher administrative costs, but any single default has less overall impact.

Accounts receivable financing is a continuous financing arrangement because as new accounts are added and assigned, additional security is added to the base. New receivables replace old, and the amount of the loan may fluctuate with each change in the base. This form of financing is advantageous to growing companies that have growing receivables.

Selling or factoring receivables is another form of financing. When receivables are sold (with notification), the purchaser steps into the place of the seller and the customers pay the purchaser of the receivables. The sale of receivables may be with or without recourse against the seller. When the sale of receivables is without recourse, the discounting will be much higher than when the buyer of the receivable still may see recovery from the seller. Sometimes receivables are sold "without notification." In this case, customers continue to pay the goods or service provider who acts as agent for the purchaser.

The problem with selling accounts receivable is that companies that are in financial trouble often do it. If you are not in financial trouble and you attempt to sell accounts receivable, you may send a signal that will be incorrectly interpreted by both the customers and your lending institutions. This may have a detrimental effect despite the offsetting benefits received from the sale. You may lose customers as a result of selling their accounts. Sometimes firms that purchase accounts receivable do not have the same equitable treatment of customers in mind when they undertake collection policies. Their rigidity in collection is based on one and only one premise: collecting their money. Your interest in collecting from your customer includes maintaining ongoing business with the customers for a long time. The goals of the collection department of the receivables purchasers are not congruent with your goals.

As was stated earlier, accounts receivable financing is expensive. And selling or factoring receivables is quite expensive for several reasons:

- The firm purchasing receivables incurs substantial costs in collecting.
- It also incurs front-end costs in analyzing the worth of the receivables. This analysis cost has to be recovered somewhere, and that somewhere is in the discount rate for the receivables.

- The collection firm stands the risk of noncollections. Because there is a risk associated with noncollections, the purchasing firm will discount the receivables additionally to compensate for the percentage of potential bad debt.
- The purchasing firm might not purchase high-risk-of-default accounts, leaving the selling firm with the "worst" receivables still on its books.

Inventory Loans. Inventories represent a significant investment. The lender making a loan secured by inventory generally discounts the market value of the inventory based on a perception of the ease of liquidation. The advance on an inventory secured loan may be as high as 90 percent. However, lenders do not want to be in the sales business and prefer to have the loan repaid rather than have to seek foreclosure on the inventory. These loans can be ongoing and variable in amount depending on the size of the inventory.

Long-Term Financing. Long-term financing generally is considered an equity-based investment. Acquiring such investment often requires the services of investment bankers who act as middlemen between a firm issuing securities and sources of funds wishing to make an investment. Investment bankers take some of the risks associated with the selling of a company's offering. Investment banking firms are used because of their expertise.

Investment banks use two methods of obtaining offerings: bidding and negotiation. In either case, the investment banker makes a margin in the issue between the selling price and the price at which the banker purchases the offering. This margin may be small—often less than 1 percent of the offering price. This function is called underwriting and relieves the offering company of the risk of selling the issue.

Convertible Debt. The firm may issue bonds that are convertible to common stock at a given ratio. One of the arguments against convertible debt is that it may lead to further stock dilution. Other conversion options are available to corporations besides conversion of long-term debt to common stock. For example, short-term debt may be converted to long-term debt or vice versa. This latter conversion can have dangerous consequences but is really no different from a creditor's accelerating payments as a result of failure to meet a loan covenant.

Common Stock

Common stock represents an ownership right in the firm issued to investors in return for the input of capital. Common stock has two statements of value: that which the stock certificate says and that which the market says. The stock certificate may indicate a par value, a stated value, or that the stock is issued without par or stated value. These values have legal ramifications as to the required legal capital in the company. Because various state laws govern in these cases, a competent corporate attorney should be consulted concerning state requirements.

The truly important value is the market value, which is what someone will pay to acquire a share of the stock. This is the perception of worth that governs how much ownership percentage you must surrender to acquire sufficient funds.

The advantage of common stock is that there is no obligation for the corporation to pay dividends in any given year. Dividends are declared at the discretion of the board of directors, assuming the company is profitable and there are sufficient additional dollars to pay the dividend.

Unlike debt, there is no maturity date on a stock. Therefore, common stock is a financial cushion for the firm. The common stockholders are the ones who absorb the bad times and enjoy the profit in the good times. Common stock ownership is considered residual ownership and should be thought of as a risky investment.

Companies can have approximately the same yields but different dividends and growth rates. A formula for yield or cost of stock equity (depending on whether you are a buyer or seller) is:

$$\text{Yield, or cost of stock equity} = \frac{\text{Annual dividend}}{\text{Stock price}} + \text{Growth}$$

Thus, the real cost of common stock cannot be measured by the dividend alone; consideration should be given to the growth rate in the stock's value as well.

When a company issues more stock, it is in effect selling ownership interests in the business. The problem with the sale of new stock is that it dilutes the percentage ownership of existing stockholders. For example, take a company that has three stockholders who own these respective interests:

Shareholder	Percentage	Dollars	Shares (@ $100/share)
A	23%	$23,000	230
B	41%	41,000	410
C	36%	36,000	360
Total	100%	$100,000	1,000

If 300 additional shares are sold at $100 per share to D, the resulting ownership looks like:

Shareholder	Percentage	Shares
A	17.7%	230
B	31.5%	410
C	27.7%	360
D	23.1%	300
	100%	1,300

By selling 300 new shares of common stock to D, the percentages of ownership for A, B, and C have been reduced. Sometimes the price of the stock will also drop to reflect the additional stock selling on the market. This reaction is caused by the perception (or misperception) that the total value of the business has not changed but is just being spread over more shares. This dilution in value may give existing stockholders certain legal rights. In the preceding example, if the market believes the business is worth $100,000, by selling 300 additional shares the price might drop from $100 per share to, say, $77. This happens because the business is perceived to be worth $100,000/1,300 shares. The value of each shareholder's interest would then be:

Shareholder	Shares	Value	Change in Value
A	230	$17,692	(5,308)
B	410	31,537	(9,463)
C	360	27,692	(8,309)

The initial stockholders may file a lawsuit against the company for these losses through a proceeding called a *derivative suit.* They can claim a real loss in value as a result of a sale of additional stock by the company. For example, stockholder A claims a loss of $5,308 because the firm sold 300 shares of new issue. To protect against such a suit, the company could offer the option to purchase a pro rata share (usually this preemptive right is granted to shareholders by covenant) of the new issue to existing stockholders. In this example, these options would be offered:

A: 23% of 300 shares, or 69 shares
B: 41% of 300 shares, or 123 shares
C: 36% of 300 shares, or 108 shares

In this way, their ownership percentages could be maintained, but the value per share still may decline. One of the governing criteria of the market price (or price per share) will be the use to which the additional funds are put and whether the value of the business appears to increase in the eyes of the market. It comes down to what the potential buyers *believe* the value of the business is. The decision to sell additional stock should be considered carefully and planned for in advance of issue. You should consider an information release indicating what plans the company has for the funds. The intent is to let the market know that the value will increase with the new issue.

There are other problems with issuing stock. First, common stockholders are the last to receive a return if the company liquidates. Second, because there is no legal obligation to pay dividends, the business may choose not to pay them to shareholders. Finally, when the business is forced to liquidate assets to capital contributors, common stock owners are the last in line to share in the asset distribution.

The question, then, might be: Why not always use debt financing? These points show the dangers of debt financing.

- The stockholder may lose the expectation of future returns if new debt capitalization is added. Additional debt increases the debt service against gross profits and decreases earnings, which translates directly into a risk of reduced dividends.
- There may be a decrease in the amount of managerial freedom. Debt reduces the amount of unaccounted-for profits by increasing debt service and the fixed obligations of interest payments. This may also reduce management's operating latitude because of the covenants to which management agrees when accepting the debt.
- As a company issues more debt, it approaches its debt capacity. As it nears this limit, it reduces the margin of safety available to issue more debt if it needs additional capital, particularly if it needs capital quickly. Thus, the company has reduced its financial flexibility.

Preferred Stock

Often called a compromise investment, preferred stock has some of the attributes of common stock and some of the features of debt. Usually a company's interest in selling preferred stock increases under these conditions:

- The company cannot issue further debt but wants to use further leverage.
- The company does not want to dilute the interests of current common stockholders but wants more stock equity.

In either case, the company may wish to sell preferred stock. Some of the distinguishing characteristics of preferred stock follow.

- Although it may have a fixed rate of return (like debt), the dividend is optional and paid only when declared by the directors (but the dividend may be "cumulative" and therefore payable before any common stock dividends are paid).

- Preferred stock may have sinking fund provisions for the repurchase of the stock.
- Debt holders have a superior claim to assets in case of liquidation and have first claim to earnings. However, preferred stockholders' claims are superior to common stockholders'.

Taxes affect the amount of earnings needed to meet debt service and preferred stock dividends. However, because they receive different tax treatment, they affect earnings differently.

Suppose that both debt and preferred stock command a return of 12 percent and the applicable corporate tax rate is 46 percent. To pay the 12 percent interest rate on debt, the firm has to earn 12 percent before taxes. Interest on debt is paid in before-tax dollars. To pay the 12 percent dividend for preferred stock, the firm has to earn 12 percent in after-tax dollars.

For a 12 percent earnings after taxes, 22.2 percent—12 percent/ (1 − .46)—is required in before-tax dollars. Because dividends are paid in after-tax dollars, the firm has to earn more to pay a dividend of comparable worth to an investor than it has to earn for interest.

The tax rate the company pays will have a great deal to do with the amount of dividend paid for two reasons:

1. The lower the company's real tax rate, the more disposable cash it will have to reinvest and pay dividends.
2. The lower the company's tax rate, the more flexibility it can have in designing dividend policies to be attractive to investors and enhance the goodwill and value of the firm.

Private Placement of Stock

A company may find itself with an excessive proportion of debt in relation to its equity, or there is no way to obtain additional debt, forcing the owner to go in search of equity. A private company accomplishes this through a private stock placement, where shares are sold to a limited number of individuals or business entities. It may be possible for company management to sell shares on an informal basis to friends and family, but this is at best a limited source of equity. When more equity is needed, you must search outside your circle of acquaintances.

A formal private placement of stock may require the services of an investment banker with far-reaching connections. A reputable investment banker will require an in-depth review of the company to ensure that it is an acceptable investment vehicle for potential investors. Next the banker will construct an offering memorandum, which describes the type and terms of stock to be offered, its price, the company, and how the company plans to use the funds. The offering memorandum will then be sent to a group of prospective investors, followed by investment meetings where the management team makes presentations to investors. If all goes well, the investment banker then coordinates a closing where the investors pay the company for the proffered stock.

Sounds easy? It is not. Finding the right investment banker who works well with the company is difficult, as is the writing of an offering memorandum, and presentations require long preparation and role-playing. And do not forget the investment banker's fee. This can vary substantially, but expect some variation on the Lehman Formula, which is 5 percent of the first $1 million raised, 4 percent of the second $1 million, 3 percent of the third $1 million, 2 percent of the fourth $1 million, and 1 percent of all funds raised above that amount. For example, the fee for an investment banker who raises $5 million on behalf of the company will be $150,000. In addition, a banker may request a large number of warrants on the purchase of company stock in order to take advantage of any potential increase in the company's value at a later date.

Swapping Stock for Expenses

Often equity is obtained to pay off short-term expenses. This is a two-step process of obtaining the equity from one party and using the resulting cash to pay off suppliers. You sometimes can short-cut this process by issuing stock directly to suppliers in exchange for their services. Although this can be an effective way to eliminate debts, it also sends a clear message to suppliers that the company is short on cash. Thus, this approach usually only works once: when suppliers have already sent their bills to the company, and it responds by negotiating a stock payment in lieu of cash. If a company tries to convince suppliers in advance to take stock as payment, it is unlikely to have many takers.

Stock Warrants

A stock warrant is a legal document that gives the holder the right to buy a specific amount of a company's shares at a specific price, and usually for a limited time period, after which it becomes invalid. The stock purchase price listed on the warrant is usually higher than the current market price at the time of issuance.

A stock warrant can be used as a form of compensation instead of cash for services performed by other entities to the company, and it may be attached to debt instruments in order to make them appear to be more attractive investments to buyers. For example, say you are interested in obtaining debt at an especially low interest rate and attach stock warrants to a new bond offering in order to do so. Investors attach some value to the warrants, which drives them to purchase the bonds at a lower effective interest rate than would have been the case without the presence of the attached warrants.

A company rarely sells stock warrants on their own in the expectation of receiving a significant amount of cash in exchange. Consequently, this is not a good way to directly obtain equity funding; rather it is used to reduce the cost of other types of funding or to reduce or eliminate selected supplier expenses.

Stock Subscriptions

Stock subscriptions allow investors or employees to pay a company a consistent amount over time and receive shares of stock in exchange. When such an arrangement occurs, a receivable is set up for the full amount expected, with an offset to a common stock subscription account. When the cash is collected and the stock is issued, the funds are deducted from these accounts and shifted to the standard common stock accounts.

Stock subscriptions can be arranged for employees, in which case the amount invested tends not to be large, and is not a significant source of new equity financing. When it is used with investors, it typically involves their up-front commitment to make payments to the company as part of a new share offering and so tends to occur over a short time period, rather than involving small incremental payments over a long time frame.

How to Obtain a Bank Loan

A businessperson making a first-time loan application has greater reporting responsibilities and requirements than does a borrower who has been dealing on a continuing basis with a bank for short-term financing. Once a bank has had good experience with a borrower, a loan request is much simpler. Usually the borrower need only provide updated information for an application that is on file.

Bankers are also interested in information that is not always reflected in the financial statements. For example, they like to be informed about the borrower's management capability, organizational strength, experience, and reputation. However, in addition to this reputation information, the bank generally will require completion of certain standardized reporting forms in order to evaluate the creditworthiness of the borrower. Some of these filing requirements will be discussed next.

Projected Cash Flow Statements

One of the most effective tools to determine the amount of the loan needed and its repayment date is the projected cash flow statement. The projections should disclose the significant assumptions used by management in preparing the cash forecast. Generally, past performance will serve as the basis for preparation, but it should be adjusted to reflect current trends. Two ways of making these adjustments are (1) pro forma and (2) an attrition allowance. Pro forma adjustments reflect changes in a company's projected cash flow that are nonrecurring; an attrition adjustment can be used to reflect recurring changes and expenses. For example, if the company has an agreement with labor for an annual increase of 7 percent, this would be treated as an additional allowance and grouped together with other recurring costs as an overall percentage adjustment to expenses. Nonrecurring expenses can be treated as one-item adjustments to individual expenses. An example of a typical nonrecurring item may be the payment of damages due to a loss in a personal injury lawsuit. It is not anticipated that in any succeeding period the company will lose a similar lawsuit. If it does, it should be treated as an attrition allowance.

The cash flow statement should show a monthly estimate of receipts from all sources, such as cash sales, accounts receivable, miscellaneous income, and loans. The estimated expenditures should include capital improvement, accounts payable, taxes, payroll, other operating expenses, and repayment of loans.

Financial Trends

When bankers look at a company's financial results, they are concerned not only with cash flow but also with other financial trends. The question may not be what the ratios are for the year, but rather how they compare with those of the previous years. The question that will be asked is: How does your financial picture (past, present, and projected) relate to the general economy and to the borrower's industry? Banks generally keep a record of clients' financial trends by periodically transcribing all of the vital balance sheet and operating statistics to a worksheet.

Banks may calculate some of these key financial factors:

- Profitability
- Net working capital
- Working capital or current ratio
- Net quick ratio
- Ratio of debt to net worth
- Number of days of sales in accounts receivable
- Number of days of purchases in accounts payable
- Number of days of supply of inventory (related to cost of sales)

These are discussed in Chapter 6, but the relevant ones are defined and briefly discussed here.

Profitability. Profitability is a measure of how well the business has been doing. At least three ratios generate meaningful potential measures of a firm's profitability:

1. Net profit to net sales
2. Gross profit to sales
3. Net profit to net worth

It is important that a company be able to earn profits in a manner consistent with the capital invested and the expected growth. When the company shows that it has a high net profit, not only does it have debt-paying dollars, but it also has fresh capital to reinvest and support its own growth. These are indications of good management. A bank will be interested in looking at year-to-year profitability and noting any trends in ratios.

Bankers will also want to see if the company's flow of net profits into its working capital is growing. They will be interested in whether profits must be reinvested constantly in fixed assets. Also, a company that pays out all of its profits in dividends and salaries will be unable to show growth in net worth from this source.

Bankers usually will add back noncash items, such as depreciation, to the net profit of the company to arrive at the cash flow or debt-servicing dollars available from profit. Caution must be emphasized here, for what the bank might be doing is looking to funds that are earmarked as a "reserve" for equipment replacement. Although the bank may be interested in the potential use of those funds for debt servicing in the worst case, enlightened bankers will also care about replacement of worn-out assets. The best bankers are concerned with the long-term needs of the business as well as protecting their own interests.

Net Working Capital. The net working capital of the company is defined as the excess of the current assets over the current liabilities and is a significant factor to be considered for credit purposes. A bank expects a company to provide enough of its own normal working capital to carry its inventory, accounts receivable, and other current assets at prudent levels. The company should be able to meet these obligations during nonpeak sales periods of the year. Thus, even during slow times, the bank expects the company to cover its current liabilities within the customary terms of trade.

Working Capital or Current Ratio. This is the ratio of current assets to current liabilities. It is even more significant in the bank's appraisal than in the working capital budget. For example, company A has current assets of $200,000, current liabilities of $100,000, and net working capital of $100,000. The working capital ratio is $200,000 to $100,000, or 2 to 1. Company B has current assets of $500,000, current liabilities of $400,000, and net working capital of $100,000. The working capital ratio is $500,000 to $400,000, or 1.25 to 1.

Both firms show the same net working capital of $100,000, yet the first company is in a more favorable position because it has $2.00 in current assets from which to pay for each $1.00 in current liabilities in the event that it must liquidate assets. The second company has only a $1.25 to meet its current liabilities of $1.00. Therefore, based on this ratio, company A would be considered to be in a much stronger financial position.

Net Quick Ratio. Another indicator bankers use to determine the ability of a company to pay its bills is the net quick ratio. This ratio is determined by taking the total of cash, short-term marketable securities, and net receivables, and dividing it by the total of current liabilities. This is a simple measure of the firm's liquidity or the company's ability to pay its debts. Again, a bank will be more concerned with the trend established by several years of net quick ratios. This will show the bank whether the company is increasing or decreasing its liquidity and hence its ability to meet its debt. Since cash and accounts receivables are far more current than inventory, this ratio is a good indicator of the relative short-term liquidity risk of the company.

Ratio of Debt to Net Worth. Another test of the adequacy of the company's net worth is the ratio of total debt, including current liabilities, to net worth. Banks, again, generally will rely on the trend in the ratio as well as the specific number itself.

Other debt ratios are discussed in Chapter 6.

Number of Days of Sales in Accounts Receivable. In calculating this number, these assumptions are made:

- An even flow of sales
- A uniformity in collecting accounts receivable

The question here is the average number of days it takes the company to collect its accounts as compared with other firms within the same industry. The banks will factor in the number of days normal for the terms of the sale and those of the industry. For example: Assume a firm has average daily credit sales of $20,000 and accounts receivable are $1.8 million. The terms of the sale are 30 days. The first step is to divide the accounts receivable of $1.8 million by $20,000, the average daily credit sales. This indicates that 90 days of sales are still in accounts receivable and that the accounts receivable are taking longer to collect than the normal 30-day terms. In fact, on average, this company is collecting its accounts receivables 60 days after the expiration of the due date. This is 60 days more than the pricing policy allows; it is probably having considerable financial effects on cash flow.

This also indicates that management may not be doing a good job of managing its accounts receivable. However, this may also be typical for the industry. If this is your situation, you should take some steps to try to improve your accounts receivable collection policy. You are loaning money to your customers for *an average* of 60 days *more* than you intended when you set your terms of sale.

Number of Days of Purchases in Accounts Payable. This figure is computed by dividing the average daily purchases into the accounts payable. If, for example, the average daily purchases are $5,000 and the accounts payable are $150,000, the number of days purchases in accounts payable is 30 days. This number tells a banker quickly if the company is paying its bills promptly. Significant variations from normal trade terms must be explained. If the company is on a net 30-day cycle, then it is meeting its obligations and perhaps obtaining all of the discounts it is entitled to under the terms of its purchase agreements. That question requires further examination. The ratio is helpful, but you should also be concerned with those accounts payable for which discounts were lost and not only the average payments.

The company should be examining its aging of payables and monitoring discounts lost.

Number of Days of Supply of Inventory.   This number is computed by dividing the *cost* of the inventory by the average daily cost of sales, assuming an even flow of sales. The answer gives the banker the average number of days it takes the company to turn over inventory. The abuse that the bank is looking for here is excess inventory. This ratio will vary substantially from business to business. Supermarkets generally have very short inventory cycles, whereas automobile dealers have longer cycles.

Other Supplemental Data.   Other information that should be considered for submission in the loan request presentation includes:

- A summary of insurance coverage.
- An analysis of profitability by product line, if available and applicable.
- Unusual events, historical or prospective, affecting the company.
- Concentration, if any, of sales within a small number of customers. This shows the bank the reliance on a few select customers. If sales are concentrated in very few buyers, as in the aerospace industry, the risk associated with that industry may be considered to be somewhat higher.
- Analysis of the effect of special situations on the company, such as a last-in, first-out (LIFO) method of inventory evaluation.

Letters of Credit

A company may not want to borrow any money from a bank; however, a prospective subcontractor or provider of raw materials may be unsure as to the company's creditworthiness. A method for improving assumed creditworthiness that may be available at low cost is to purchase a letter of credit.

If the company is new or is experimenting with a new product or product line, some vendors will refuse to sell it materials on a trade accounts payable basis. They would instead prefer to have the company establish creditworthiness by showing good payment records. A possible way around this problem is to obtain a letter of credit and, in effect, to use the good credit standing of a bank. By obtaining a letter of credit, the company is saying: "If we fail to pay you, the bank will pay you." The bank then has recourse to the company for its money.

In this way, the company is advancing the bank's creditworthiness. Typically, letters of credit cost 1 percent of the amount the company wishes to advance, and a letter of credit normally is good for one year. The real cost of a letter of credit depends on how frequently the company wishes to purchase while using the letter of credit as a guarantee of payment.

For example, suppose a supplier of raw materials wants money net 30 days but is willing to extend credit for 90 days if the company provides a letter of credit. Also, suppose that the letter of credit costs 1 percent. Because the company is having money advanced for two additional months for the cost of 1 percent, this is the same as borrowing money at 6 percent per annum, assuming the letter of credit and the materials purchased are the same amount. However, each time the company uses the guarantee of the letter of credit during the year, it is still taking advantage of that one-time payment of 1 percent. The more the firm uses the letter of credit, the cheaper (on a cost-per-transaction basis) the cost of the guarantee.

The company may consider joint ventures. Joint ventures are, essentially, a technique whereby a company changes its organizational structure. However, this is still a form of financing whereby the financial creditworthiness of a collective entity is used to improve the market appearance to lenders and investors. The financial strength of two or more entities is put behind the joint venture entity.

Sources of Debt Financing

A business may consider a number of financial institutions as possible lenders. The large and popular ones include:

- *Banks.* Both commercial banks and savings and loan associations grant a significant portion of all the available credit they have on hand to businesses.
- *Commercial finance companies.* Most commercial finance companies have a specialty, such as discounting accounts receivable. Interest rates are generally higher with finance companies because as a financing source they seem to be institutions of last resort. Companies that are unable to find other means of financing may resort to commercial finance companies.
- *Insurance companies.* Many large insurance companies participate in investment banking both directly and indirectly. Typically, insurance companies loan substantial blocks of money. Because of this, the typical insurance company borrower is a large company. They do not as often or as readily extend credit to smaller companies. Insurance companies prefer transactions of $1 million or more. Some insurance companies are interested only in transactions greater than $5 million.
- *Brokerage houses.* Many stock brokerage houses offer or arrange financing that ranges from bonds and commercial paper to private loans from individual investors. Brokerage houses do just as their name suggests: They broker money from sources to ultimate users.
- *Investment bankers.* Investment banking may be a function of any of the previously named lenders. They generally facilitate the sale of security issues, through either a bidding process or a contractual arrangement. For a fee, they use their expertise and market contacts to sell securities.

  In some financing agreements, the lender takes an equity position in connection with a loan or takes an option or warrant to buy stock in the event that the company grows. This is known as a kicker or sweetener and generally is viewed by borrowers as giving up some possible future control over the business in exchange for controlling current costs. Many investors wish to have some financial or managerial say over the direction and nature of the business. Typically, when substantial funds are loaned to a business, it has to give up some measure of control.

- *Venture capitalists.* Venture capitalists may be investment bankers when they invest capital, make loans, and give management advice intended to assist the company to achieve significant growth. Many companies financed by venture capitalists convert from closely held corporations to public corporations during the course of their growth.

- *Government loans and grants.* The federal government offers a wide variety of loan programs. Some are direct loans, others are government-sponsored or guaranteed loans channeled through banks. Small Business Administration loans are available to smaller businesses. Additionally, the federal government has a program for small business innovation research grants. These grants are intended to assist small businesses in obtaining financing for the development of specific ideas.

Types of Loan Arrangements

Several types of loans are possible. Some of these are:

- *Commercial loans.* The terms of a commercial loan are designed to repay the loan on the basis of specific assets or business-cycle activities. These loans may take the form of either short-term or long-term commitments.

- *Leases.* Many lending institutions offer a choice between debt and a lease. Leases are obligations for the specific assets, and are generally fixed as to rate and payment. In addition, most offer a purchase option. Some caution must be exercised in selecting between leasing and outright purchase with a mortgage. Very often, under the terms of the lease, significantly higher costs are incurred over the costs of the outright purchase of the item.

- *Mortgages.* A mortgage secures a loan by pledging an asset as collateral, with an associated repayment schedule. Amortization schedules of repayment show the principal and interest payments over the life of the mortgage.

- *Balloon loans.* Balloon loans are very similar to mortgages except that an unpaid balance or balloon payment is due and payable after a specified time. A typical example of a balloon payment is a 20-year mortgage with a requirement that after 5 years of payment on the mortgage, the unpaid balance of the principal is due. The advantage to a lender of a balloon mortgage is that it obtains significant interest payments during the early years of the mortgage. It is during this period that the interest constitutes the bulk of the payment. The benefit to borrowers is that they expect to pay off the principal without incurring further interest liabilities after a few years of operation. In addition, these interest payments represent significant deductions for tax purposes. Remember that if the firm is paying taxes at the rate of 46 percent on profits, the federal government is returning $.46 on *each* dollar of interest paid. Very often, these loans provide for refinancing in the event that the balloon payment cannot be met.

- *Leverage-financed loans.* These loans are used to acquire businesses. The largest percentage of funds used to acquire a business is supplied by a lender, who secures all assets. These loans ostensibly are attractive to borrowers because if a firm is heavily leveraged, a smaller increment of profit yields a much higher percentage return on equity. For example, compare: Firm A makes $100,000 profit (after taxes) and is capitalized for $1 million. It has 50 percent debt and 50 percent equity. The firm realizes a return on equity of:

$$\frac{\$100,000}{50\% \times \$1,000,000} \text{ or } \frac{\$100,000}{\$500,000} \text{ or } 20\%$$

- Firm B makes $100,000 profits (after taxes) and is capitalized for $1 million. It has 80 percent debt and 20 percent equity. The firm realizes a return on equity of:

$$\frac{\$100,000}{20\% \times \$1,000,000} \text{ or } \frac{\$100,000}{\$200,000} \text{ or } 50\%$$

- For the same level of after-tax profits, for the same size firms, the higher the leverage, the greater the percentage return on equity. The fallacy in the cited example is that Firm B would have to pay interest on the additional $300,000 of debt.

- The greater the debt to equity ratio the greater the risk, because the fixed obligation to pay debt service increases. However, this relationship to risk may be incorrect if you can show substantial cash flow ability to service the debt. Therefore, the debt to equity ratio can be misleading without additional information.

- *Bonds.* Bonds represent debt sold to lenders either privately or through public underwriting. Usually a business needs to be fairly substantial in size to float a bond issue. Bonds typically are not available to small businesses except in some special cases, where they are backed by local governmental units.

- *Commercial paper.* Commercial paper is offered by large, stable companies intent on raising working capital for short periods of time. Commercial paper generally is sold in a public market and is in the form of short-term, unsecured promissory notes. The usual denominations are $25,000 and over.

- *Small Business Administration (SBA) loans.* The SBA generally guarantees a bank loan, thereby lowering the risk and interest cost for the borrower. These loans are intended for businesspeople who can qualify based on certain profiles. These loans may be based on needs such as a business in a hardship area or areas where unemployment is high. Occasionally these loans are extended for areas in which a natural disaster has occurred.

- *Economic Development Authority (EDA) loans.* EDA loans generally relate to social goals promoted by the authority, such as increasing minority employment or employment in depressed areas. These loans are made and administered through state agencies. The nature of these loans is to obtain working capital allowances and not generally to purchase specific assets.

- *Industrial revenue bonds (IRBs).* IRBs are issued through governmental agencies and are intended for use in the acquisition of real estate and equipment. The governmental agency issues the bonds, which are then purchased by investors, often banks. Because they are governmental bonds, they are tax exempt. As such, the prevailing interest rate on IRBs is lower than the prevailing market rate. A great deal of criticism has been leveled against IRBs because some businesses, which compete with others that get IRBs, complain they are unable to acquire similar low-interest money and thus are less able to compete.

- *Research and development (R&D) financing arrangements.* Often companies and private investors have entered into creative financing arrangements in order to raise necessary funds to pay for research and development. In recent years these have taken the shape of limited partnerships. Typically, the sponsoring company contributes the right to a product in a limited partnership, in exchange for an interest in the partnership, often as the general partner. Capital contributions by limited partners usually provide funds for R&D that may be subcontracted to the sponsoring company or even to other entities. The limited partners expect to receive income in the form of royalties from the sale and development of the product. They may also receive income tax breaks in the form of capital gains rates. The major advantage to the sponsor is that if the project fails, no repayment of the loan is required and there is no liability for interest cost.

Restrictions on Loans

When an institution is considering making substantial loans to a company, it often requires, as part of the loan, agreements to control the business activities and obtain reports about the current status of the firm. Typically these arrangements include:

- *Limitations on the purchase of new assets.* Some lenders have a policy to keep additional expenditures low after a loan has been made. This has the effect of slowing or stopping growth. Negotiate with the lender to ensure that this is not an absolute limitation on acquisition of new assets. Be sure that additional new assets can be purchased on a regular basis if there is provable growth associated with the need for those purchases. Show the lender that through planned growth, the risk of default is lessened. Planned growth can be accomplished only by the acquisition of additional assets based on a good business plan.
- *Limitations on additional debt.* Once again, a lender may try to restrict the incurring of additional debt. This too has the detrimental

effect of limiting growth. When negotiating with the lender, make it clear that additional debt may have to be incurred in order to sustain regular growth. An adequate business plan will certainly help as bargaining leverage for the execution of the appropriate terms in the lending agreement. The selling point to the lender is that additional debt supports additional income through growth. As the company grows, so does the lender's security of repayment.

- *Salary restrictions.* Because salaries of chief executives and other executives are a direct expense, lenders typically will want some restriction on these salaries so they do not skyrocket. Large increases in these salaries will dig into the profits of the firm, sometimes radically increasing expenses. Counter with a reasonable alternative, which may include tying the increases to the profitability of the firm. This also has the beneficial effect of motivating management.

- *Dividend restrictions.* If the company pays dividends, you should attempt to negotiate a reasonable formula for payment. The company is confronted with the competing interests of debt holders and holders of equity. The lender may prohibit the payment of any dividends. This allows for the additional retained earnings to be used for debt servicing. But it may have a chilling effect on the raising of additional equity capital. A company's attraction as an equity investment opportunity is based on two factors: its absolute growth in net worth and the income stream of dividends. A no-dividends policy reduces the attractiveness of an equity investment possibility.

Typically firms will be required to provide lenders with regular financial reports. Lenders generally will require financial statements accompanied by a certified public accountant's (CPA's) report. Audited reports certified by CPAs are costly and time-consuming documents to prepare. Look to reduce the requirement to a cheaper alternative such as a review or a compilation.

Some people think that when they incorporate, they absolve themselves of any personal liability for the debt incurred by the business in its operation. Legally, that might be true. However,

lenders too have learned that people try to limit their personal liability by incorporating and often require certain personal guarantees by the business owner. Some banks may want you to sign a
general guarantee of the business loan as a sign of "good faith" or
as a "personal commitment" to the business. Here are some points
to consider regarding collateral and loan guarantees.

- *Specific personal assets.* It is not wise to risk everything you own.
  If a pledge of "good faith" is required by the lender, pick one
  particular asset to risk. Do not risk more than you are willing to
  lose in any situation.
- *The value of business collateral already offered.* Typically lenders will
  require as much collateral as they can reasonably get. They may
  even seek collateral that is unreasonable. In such cases, it may
  be beneficial to prepare reports showing the extent and valuation of those assets pledged to secure the loan. Often appraisals
  by independent groups as to the value of real estate and other
  assets tend to dissuade the bank from seeking further collateral.
- *Stock in the business as collateral.* If the business has some attractiveness and a reasonably high probability of success, the lender
  may take back some stock as collateral. Be wary that you are not
  giving up so much stock that you lose control of your business.

Conditions That a Borrower Should Seek

The success of the business depends on you. Too much reliance on
the lending institution to help run the business may prove disas-
trous. There should, therefore, be flexibility in the agreement to let
the business grow and be successful. Advice and help from the
lender should not be overlooked. Lenders may have had experience with other similar businesses, and you can profit from that
experience. As a borrower, you should request these considerations
in the lending agreement:

- *There should be an option available to you to refinance at any time.*
  Often the lender will qualify this provision to permit refinancing

only after a certain period of time or with a prepayment penalty. You may need this provision in order to take advantage of lower prevailing interest rates should they occur.

- *A conversion agreement should allow for more favorable loan conditions once certain "growth forecasts" have been met.* This provision takes into consideration the fact that as your business grows, its risks may decrease. Because interest rates should be tied to perceived risk, as you prove your viability and success, you are entitled to pay less of an interest premium; arguably, your riskiness has been reduced.

- *Agree on no prepayment penalty.* Changing financial conditions may provide you with sufficient cash to prepay the loan. This may be done to realize significant tax benefits, as a requirement for the obtaining of additional financing, or to put you in a better business posture. Prepayment generally will work no hardship on the lender other than to take away the guarantee of expected future earnings. There would be nothing to stop the lender from reloaning this money to other individuals and thus recovering the future earnings from someone else. The lender's risk is that the money cannot be reloaned at equal or better rates.

- *Request limitation on interest rates.* Banks prefer to charge a variable interest rate. You should negotiate limitations or caps on rates and make this a major consideration in determining whether to enter into the financing agreement.

- *Agree on the possibility of an increased loan based on meeting certain tests.* Often, if you are successful and the business is growing within certain predictable ranges, additional debt financing may be necessary to continue the growth pattern. As such, you may want the loan agreement to provide for additional advances of debt to aid in sustaining that growth. A lender should consider itself an ongoing business partner in these agreements. As you grow, so does the income of the lender. Some loans have an absolute upper credit limit, and you may borrow up to that limit without further formal application.

- *The agreement should specify identifiable assets that are pledged as collateral.*

- *Seek a loan "grace" period of 30 to 60 days for noncompliance with debt arrangements.* Very often this provision requires you to notify the lender in advance that you will use the provision. There probably will be a limit on how frequently this can be done. Lenders may be more willing to permit minimum defaults when you submit a plan showing how you will make it up after appropriate notice to the lender. The worst thing you can do is surprise your lender. In most cases, a lender would rather work out a mutually agreeable accommodation than seek legal redress.

Summary

Financing is in some respects similar to the operational side of the business. They each have associated risks and returns. Each has strategic consequences for a firm.

There are two fundamental sources of financing: debt and equity. Each has certain consequences. Debt, either secured by property or unsecured, is the most common form of financing. It has fixed repayment requirements for both principal and interest. Failure to make interest payments, unless otherwise provided for, generally results in default. Additionally, interest payments are made with before-tax dollars. As such, depending on the tax rate, interest payments are in effect discounted by a company's federal tax liability. The relative amount of debt financing has a multiplying effect on earnings. The greater the percentage of debt to equity for a fixed amount of profits, the greater the percentage return on equity.

A company may seek to raise capital through the sale of ownership. This is done through the issuance and sale of stock. Businesses generally sell two forms of certificates: common and preferred stock. Common stock carries with it no obligation to pay a dividend. Preferred stock, however, may have a fixed rate, as does debt, but payment is optional if no dividends are declared. Dividends on preferred stock (sometimes cumulative over a period of years) have to be met *before* payment can be made to common stockholders.

Obtaining financing is a matter of convincing conservative lenders or investors to part with their money. As in all selling, it is a process of convincing these people that risks are low and that reasonable returns will compensate them for taking the risk. The best method of selling is through the use of a good business plan showing good ratios and a sound financial picture. One of the chief objectives should be to build a lasting, sound financial relationship with these sources.

Remember that many of the terms of a financial agreement are negotiable. Therefore, when approaching any such situation, try to be prepared to negotiate from strength. The more preliminary work that you do in getting ready to deal with lenders and investors, the greater the likelihood of a favorable financial agreement.

Section III

Evaluating the Operations of the Business

The first two sections addressed the tasks to be accomplished before the business, or operating period, begins and those that are ongoing during the operating period. Naturally, there is a close connection between what you determine to do—your plan—and what you actually do.

In this section, we discuss what happens when the operating period is completed. This may be an intermediate time—not necessarily the end of a complete fiscal year. For example, some of what is discussed in these final chapters is equally appropriate to monthly or quarterly considerations.

As Sections I and II were closely related, so Section III is closely linked to both of them. The topics to be covered here include:

- Performance measurement systems
- Financial analysis
- Taxes and risk management

These flow directly out of your intended accomplishments as well as actual ones during the fiscal period.

Chapter 6

Performance Measurement Systems

Performance measurements, like many of the tools discussed earlier, can be used to make rational decisions in keeping with a company's objectives. Measurements are analytical tools used by outside suppliers of capital, creditors and investors, and by the company itself to evaluate how well it is doing. Measurements may also be used to evaluate how the business appears to the investor. The type of analysis undertaken varies according to the specific interest that the party seeks to satisfy.

- A trade creditor who has supplied goods, services, or raw materials generally would be interested in liquidity—the company's ability to pay bills.
- A bondholder is more interested in long-term financial stability. As such, he or she would be interested in cash flow and the company's ability to service its debt.
- The present and expected future earnings and the stability of these earnings may be primary concerns to an investor in common stock.

Depending on the planning horizon of each person interested in the performance measurements, the value of trend analysis may be greater than any point-in-time measurements. How well the company has done over time and is expected to do in the future are pieces of information necessary to make reasoned decisions.

Finally, the company too should be concerned with the trend depicted through performance measurements. In order to bargain more effectively for outside funds, you should be aware of all of the aspects of financial analysis that outsiders use in evaluating the business. Financial and operating ratios can also be effective tools for managing and controlling the business.

Two broad categories of measurements will be of concern in this chapter. The first set is financial ratios. Financial ratios were discussed briefly in Chapter 5. Therefore, we will not endeavor to repeat that material, but rather only supplement it here. The second set of measurements are operating ratios, which can be designed to meet the specific needs of the user. These ratios are intended as a tool for analysis and control of business operations.

Financial Ratios

Some unit of measure is necessary to evaluate the financial condition or the performance of the business. A system frequently used is a ratio, or index, which connects two pieces of financial or operational information. Interpreting a ratio correctly gives the analyst an understanding of the financial condition and performance of the firm, which may not be readily apparent from the traditional forms of reporting. It is important to remember that a single ratio in itself may not be a particularly meaningful piece of information. Often a trend showing past historical ratios will indicate more than will the current individual ratio alone. When financial ratios are listed on a spreadsheet for a period of years, a study of the composite change will quickly indicate whether there has been an improvement or deterioration in the financial condition over time. In addition, the productivity, profitability, or performance of the firm relative to past performances is demonstrated easily. For example, by arraying the last five years of current ratios—that is, the ratio of current assets to current liabilities—you can compare the ability of the business to pay its bills and determine if that is improving or deteriorating.

The second comparison method involves evaluating the ratio

of one company against others similarly situated for the same period. Such a comparison, if properly done, will give some insight into the relative financial condition of the company. If improperly done, the information derived from this study may be worse than meaningless—it may be harmful. The primary problem is comparability.

Avoid using "rules of thumb" indiscriminately. The comparison of your financial ratios with the ratios published by major sources may be inaccurate. For example, you may have multiple product lines and may not have the same product mix as other companies in the industry. You may be differently diversified, crossing industry boundaries. It is preferable to build comparable numbers over time for your own business rather than seek comparisons with others. However, sometimes outside comparisons, properly used, can be helpful. A rule of thumb, if it is to be used, should be from your industry. Trade associations can be a source of good financial ratio information.

For example, the standard rule of thumb for the current ratio—that is, the ratio of current assets to current liabilities—is 2:1. It is considered advisable for a small business to maintain a current ratio of at least 2:1 for the sake of sound cash flow and healthy financial condition. Remember, however, that rules of thumb are averages. As such, there may be as many companies above the average as below it. To show how this rule of thumb may be misapplied, take the example of a fast food outlet. It may have a current ratio of 1:2 or even 1:3. Comparing this current ratio with the rule of thumb, you quickly conclude that the business has a liquidity problem and may not have sufficient liquid assets available to meet all of the debts falling due. However, this is probably not the case. A typical fast food outlet has:

- *Receivables.* There are generally no credit sales and no delayed payments at a fast food store.
- *Inventory levels.* Fast food stores generally carry very small inventories and deliveries are small, frequent, and fresh.
- *Normal or extended trade payables.* Some profitable franchises can delay payments to local suppliers for longer than is normal because of their volume of business.

Fast food outlets, therefore, turn over inventory at a tremendous rate and generate continuous streams of cash. At any one point, the company may not have large amounts of cash on hand if it is using cash to retire longer-term debt or to acquire additional fixed assets. By comparing the company's own historic trend in the current ratio, and examining those ratios with other fast food outlets, you can perhaps see that a 1:4 ratio may be even better than a 1:2 ratio. The traditional rule of thumb may not be applicable or representative of the fast food industry. The point of this example is that you should consider those ratios that make sense for the business, give usable management information, and can be obtained on a timely basis.

Figure 6.1 shows a balance sheet and statement of earnings that will be used to demonstrate the financial ratios.

Types of Financial Ratios

Liquidity Ratios

Liquidity ratios give an indication of a company's ability to meet short-term obligations. These ratios give some insight into the present cash solvency and are a measure of the company's ability to meet adversity. Generally, liquidity ratios look at the short-term assets or resources and the short-term debts and obligations.

Current Ratio. As discussed in Chapter 5, the current ratio is the ratio of:

$$\frac{\text{Current assets}}{\text{Current liabilities}}$$

For Fruit Crate Manufacturing Co., Inc., the current ratio for 2006 is:

$$\frac{\$276,055}{\$98,294} = 2.81:1$$

Supposedly, the higher the ratio, the better the company's ability to pay bills. However, the ratio does not take into account how

FIGURE **6.1**

Sample Balance Sheet and Statement of Earnings

Fruit Crate Mfg. Co., Inc.

Assets

	2006	2005
Current Assets		
Cash and marketable securities	$21,285	$20,860
Accounts receivables	83,473	91,155
Inventories	164,482	157,698
Prepaid expenses	2,554	2,049
Accumulated prepaid tax	4,261	3,475
Current assets	$276,055	$275,237
Fixed Assets		
Fixed assets	$198,760	$192,666
Less: Accumulated depreciation	107,330	99,030
Net fixed assets	$91,430	$93,636
Long-term investment	$8,229	$-0-
Other Assets		
Goodwill	$23,839	$23,839
Debenture discount	751	833
Other assets	$24,590	$24,672
Total Assets	$400,304	$393,545

Liabilities and Net Worth

	2006	2005
Current Liabilities		
Bank loans and notes payables	$53,638	$42,544
Accounts payable	17,560	16,271
Accrued taxes	4,321	15,186
Other accrued liabilities	22,775	19,608
Current liabilities	$98,294	$93,609
Long-term debt	$75,562	$74,262
Stockholders' equity		
Common stock @ $1 par value	$50,420	$50,420
Capital surplus	43,179	43,016
Retained earnings	132,849	132,238
Total stockholders' equity	$226,448	$225,674
Total Liabilities and Net Worth	$400,304	$393,545

(continued)

FIGURE 6.1 *(continued)*

Fruit Crate Mfg. Co., Inc.

Statement of Earnings

	2006	2005
Net sales	$492,374	$464,383
Cost of goods sold	$330,383	$311,601
Selling, general and administration expense	98,475	90,555
Depreciation	13,786	14,396
Interest expense	10,340	8,823
Expenses	$452,984	$425,375
Earnings before taxes	$39,390	$39,008
Less: Income taxes	18,907	19,114
Earnings after taxes	$20,483	$19,894
Less: Cash dividend	12,495	12,732
Retained earnings	$7,988	$7,162

liquid the "current" assets really are. For example, if the current assets are mostly cash and current receivables, these are more liquid than if most of the current assets are in inventories. To refine the ratio as a measure, we eliminate the effect of inventories, prepaid expenses, and prepaid tax, which gives us this acid test ratio:

Acid Test Ratio

$$\frac{\text{Current assets} - (\text{Inventories} + \text{Prepaids})}{\text{Current liabilities}}$$

For Fruit Crate Manufacturing Co., Inc.:

$$\frac{\$276,055 - 171,297}{\$98,294} = 1.066{:}1$$

The acid test ratio eliminates the least liquid components of the current assets and therefore focuses on the assets most easily converted to debt payment.

Liquidity of Receivables.   Analyzing the current assets by components enables the company to detect problems in its liquidity. One thing that can be examined is how current the receivables are.

Receivables are a liquid asset only if they can be collected in a reasonable time. The first of two ratios that examine receivables is *average collection period ratio*:

$$\frac{\text{Receivables} \times \text{Days in year}}{\text{Annual credit sales}}$$

For Fruit Crate Manufacturing Co., Inc., the average collection period rate for 2006 is (assuming all sales are credit sales):

$$\frac{83{,}473 \times 365}{492{,}374} = 62 \text{ days}$$

This tells that the average collection period receivables are outstanding, in other words, how long, on average, the company waits to convert receivables to cash.

The second basic receivable ratio is the *receivable turnover ratio*:

$$\frac{\text{Annual credit sales}}{\text{Average receivables}}$$

For Fruit Crate Manufacturing Co., Inc., the receivables turnover ratio is:

$$\frac{\$492{,}374}{\$83{,}473} = 5.90 \text{ times}$$

If there is no figure for the amount of credit sales, you must resort to the total sales figure. Care should be taken to analyze all ratios, especially receivables ratios. Often the numbers available are year-end numbers, which may not recognize seasonal fluctuations or significant, steady growth. If there are significant seasonal sales, the average of the monthly closing balances may be a more appropriate figure to use. If the company is experiencing a steady growth in sales, the year-end receivables will not match accurately with the annual sales figure. If this is the case, the number may be calculated based on the annualized sales from the last six months and the end-of-year level of receivables.

Some questions to ask when analyzing these ratios are:

• How does the average collection period compare with the sales terms? For Fruit Crate Manufacturing Co., Inc., the credit terms are 2/10, n/60. The bulk of the collections are made around the due date.

- How does the collection period compare with others in the industry? This can give some insight into the investment in receivables.
- Is the average collection period so low that it may be inhibiting sales? The firm may have an excessively restrictive credit policy.
- How old are the receivables? Here you must ask "What does the average tell us?" Fruit Crate Manufacturing Co., Inc., had 433 accounts and found the average collection period ratio was 62 days. But when it grouped the accounts by age it discovered these statistics:

Number of Accounts	Paid in How Many Days?
110 (25%)	10
80 (18%)	30
170 (39%)	60
73 (18%)	180 days

Eighty-two percent of the receivables are collected before or by the due date, and only 18 percent extend beyond the due date. But the late receivables are *really* late: averaging six months after shipment of goods and four months after payment was due.

Adding an aging of receivables provides more usable information than the average collection period ratio alone. This tells:

- Where collection efforts need to be concentrated
- How much investment the company has in receivables
- Accounts that may require discontinuation of service
- Whether the terms are speeding up the recovery of receivables

Another question the aging would raise is: "Are the good accounts paying in the 10–30 period taking the cash discounts even though they have no right to it?" If the answer is yes, the cash discount terms are really 2/30, n/60.

Debt Ratios

Up to now, we have been concerned with short-term liquidity measures. Depending on the use, certain long-term solvency ratios may be of interest to a company and its investors. These ratios give an indication of the company's ability to meet long-term obligations.

Debt to Net Worth.   This ratio is computed by dividing the total debt, including current liabilities, by the net worth (total stockholders' equity). For Fruit Crate Manufacturing Co., Inc.:

$$\frac{\text{Total debt}}{\text{Net worth}} = \frac{\$98{,}294 + 75{,}562}{\$226{,}448} = \frac{\$173{,}856}{\$226{,}448} = .77{:}1$$

Frequently, intangible assets, if relatively large, are deducted from net worth to obtain the tangible net worth. Note that for the liquidity ratios discussed earlier, we used assets divided by liabilities. Here we are creating debt ratios—putting liabilities over other measures. For liquidity, the higher the number, the "better" the ratio. For debt ratios, the reverse is true: The lower the number, the "better" the ratio. Sometimes in computing this ratio, preferred stock is included with debt instead of net worth. This acknowledges that preferred stock represents a claim superior to the claim of common stockholders. It also points out that when using "comparable ratios," you must be certain that the calculations are truly comparable; that is, you must compare the definitions of the ratios.

The debt to net worth ratio varies from industry to industry. One factor often contributing to this variation is the volatility of cash flows. The more stable and predictable the cash flow, the greater the debt you may be able to service consistently. Because this ratio is a good measure of ability to pay debts over time, it sometimes is used as a measure for approximating financial risk.

Debt to Total Capital.   Another useful debt ratio is the ratio of total debt to total capital. In this ratio, only the long-term capitalization of the firm is considered.

$$\frac{\text{Long-term debt}}{\text{Total capitalization}}$$

The total capitalization is composed of long-term debt and net worth.

For Fruit Crate Manufacturing Co., Inc.:

$$\frac{\$75,562}{\$75,562 + 226,448} = \frac{\$75,562}{\$302,010} = .25:1$$

This ratio shows the importance of long-term debt financing relative to other financing in the capital structure. When computing this ratio, it may be more informative to use market values instead of book values for the stock components. (Book values were used in the preceding calculation.) If market values of stock are available, this computation may indicate a very different leverage factor.

Coverage Ratios

Coverage ratios are used to examine the relationship between finance charges and a company's ability to service them. One of the traditional coverage ratios is the interest coverage ratio. To compute this ratio for a given period, divide the annual earnings before interest and taxes by the interest charges for the period.

Different coverage ratios use different interest charges in the denominator. For example: The overall coverage method considers all fixed interest regardless of the seniority of the claim. By ignoring the seniority of some debt, the implication is that senior debt obligations are only as secure as the ability to meet all debt servicing. A method that gives some consideration to the seniority of debt is the cumulative deduction method.

For cumulative deduction methods, assume these hypothetical data: Fruit Crate Manufacturing Co., Inc., has:

$49,730 = earnings before interest and taxes ($39,390 + 10,340)
$4,210 = interest on 7% senior notes.
$6,130 = interest on 9% junior notes.

The coverage on the senior notes would be:

$$\frac{\$49,730}{\$4,210} = 11.81 \text{ times}$$

The coverage on the junior notes, after the senior debt has been covered, is:

$$\frac{\$49,730 - 4,210}{\$10,340} = 4.40 \text{ times}$$

Using this method, the coverage ratio on the junior notes takes into consideration the fact that there are outstanding senior obligations.

Both of these methods ignore the fact that the payment of interest is only part of the obligation covered by debt service. Debt service includes payment of both interest and principal. And because these payments are made from cash, a more appropriate ratio may be the cash flow coverage ratio. One adjustment should be made in computing this ratio. Interest payments are accounted for before taxes, whereas principal payments are treated as after-tax dollars. To adjust for the tax effect, you must adjust the principal by the factor $[1/(1 - t)]$, where t is the effective tax rate. So:

$$\text{Cash flow coverage ratio} = \frac{\text{Annual cash flow before interest and taxes}}{\text{Interest and principal } [1/(1 - t)]}$$

If you had a $10,000/year principal payment and a 46 percent tax rate, it would require:

$10,000 \times [1/(1 - .46)]$ or
$10,000 \times (1.85)$, or $18,500 in before-tax dollars
to meet that principal obligation

This type of analysis can, in some cases, be expanded to consider other fixed obligations, such as dividends on preferred stock, lease payments, and long-term essential capital expenditures.

Debt ratios or coverage ratios may not give an accurate picture of the company's ability to meet obligations. Because of the timing of the payment of debt obligations, the average interest rates, and other factors, you may wish to calculate other ratios showing the relationship of profitability to sales or to investment.

Profitability Ratios

When the profitability on sales ratio and the profitability on investment ratios are considered, they can give an indication of your efficiency of operation. The first such ratio is the *gross profit margin.*

For Fruit Crate Manufacturing Co., Inc., the gross profit margin is:

$$\frac{\$492,374 - 330,383}{\$492,374} = \frac{\$161,991}{\$492,374} = 33\%$$

This ratio gives the percentage of profit relative to the sales after deducting the cost of goods sold. A more reflective ratio of profitability is the *net profit margin*:

$$\frac{\text{Net profit (after taxes)}}{\text{Sales}}$$

For Fruit Crate Manufacturing Co., Inc., the net profit margin is:

$$\frac{\$20,483}{\$492,374} = 4.2\%$$

This ratio gives a measure of overall efficiency after taking into consideration expenses and taxes but not extraordinary charges. With these two ratios you can, over time, evaluate operational changes. For example, if the gross profit margin remained relatively constant over time, but the net profit margin declined, it shows that either the tax rate has changed or selling and administrative expenses have increased. The relative change between these ratios can identify areas where management attention may be necessary.

As another example, if the gross profit margin declines, the cost of goods sold has increased. This could signal several things:

- The firm may have had to lower its product prices to be competitive.
- The cost of labor, materials, or purchased components may have increased.
- Overall efficiency may have declined.

Another group of profitability ratios relate profits to investment. For example, the formula for the *rate of return on common stock equity* is:

$$\frac{\text{Net profit after taxes} - \text{Preferred stock dividend}}{\text{Net worth} - \text{Par value of preferred stock}}$$

For Fruit Crate Manufacturing Co., Inc. (no preferred stock involved):

$$\frac{\$20,483}{\$226,448} = 0.90 \text{ or } 9\%$$

This ratio gives an indication of the earning power on the book investment of the shareholders' interest. A more general ratio used to analyze profitability is the *return on assets ratio.* Use this formula to calculate this ratio:

$$\frac{\text{Net profits (after taxes)}}{\text{Total assets (tangible)}}$$

For Fruit Crate Manufacturing Co., Inc.:

$$\frac{\$20,483}{\$375,714} = 5.5\%$$

Profits are considered after interest is paid to creditors; to some extent this ratio may be inappropriate because some of these same creditors provide the means by which part of the assets are supported. When the finance charges are large, it may be better for comparative purposes to calculate a different ratio. An arguably more appropriate ratio may be the *net operating profit rate of return.* It is calculated as follows:

$$\frac{\text{Earnings before interest and taxes}}{\text{Total assets (tangible)}}$$

For Fruit Crate Manufacturing Co., Inc.:

$$\frac{\$49,730}{\$375,714} = 13.24\%$$

Turnover and Earning Power Ratios

The asset turnover ratio relates total sales to total tangible assets. Like many of the ratios discussed before, the meaningfulness of this ratio lies in the trend the company establishes and how it compares with similarly situated, comparable businesses in the same industry. The ratio is used as a measure or indicator of how well the company uses its resources to generate output.

The *asset turnover ratio* is calculated as:

$$\frac{\text{Sales}}{\text{Total tangible assets}}$$

For Fruit Crate Manufacturing Co., Inc., the asset turnover ratio is:

$$\frac{\$492,374}{\$375,714} = 1.31$$

A shortcoming of this ratio is that it puts a premium on businesses that have more fully depreciated equipment than on more new investment, which may distort efficiency. New equipment should be producing goods at lower per-unit costs than older, out-of-date equipment. As a consequence, this ratio should be used in conjunction with other ratios.

The earning power ratio on total assets is obtained when the asset turnover is multiplied by the net profit margin, generating the *earning power percentage*:

$$\text{Earning power} = \frac{\text{Sales}}{\text{Total assets (tangible)}} \times \frac{\text{Net profit (after taxes)}}{\text{Sales}}$$

$$= \frac{\text{Net profits (after taxes)}}{\text{Total assets (tangible)}}$$

Because the net profit margin ignores the asset utilization and the turnover ratio does not consider profitability, each by itself is an inadequate measure of operating efficiency. The earning power ratio resolves these shortcomings. From this ratio, it is clear that earning power will increase if there is an increase in turnover, net profit margin, or both.

Using Performance Measurements for Predictions

Any ratio calculation is based on historical information, which may have no bearing whatsoever on future results. For example, the profitability ratio for a Christmas ornaments company may look awful for the first two-thirds of a year, leading you to assume a continuing pattern of losses, only to see a late-season surge in sales volume that completely overturns all assumptions based on previously calculated ratios. Because of their historical foundation, does this mean that ratios are useless for predicting the future? Not at all. However, the results they show must be tempered by your knowledge of the business, as well as a comparison to a variety of other performance measures. For example, if the current ratio suddenly drops from 2:1 to 1:1, this may signify that a company is rapidly using up its available resources to pay its liabilities, which is a clear preliminary signal of bankruptcy. However, the ratio can also be completely misleading, because a company simply may have chosen to use much of its current assets to pay off a long-term debt in advance of its scheduled payment date. The correct interpretation would have required either a complete knowledge of the subject company's financial transactions (which is not always easy to come by) or a more comprehensive view of other ratios. For example,if the current ratio had been supplemented by the debt to equity ratio, then it would have been an easy matter to see the drop in the current ratio being offset by the improvement in the debt to equity ratio. Thus, ratio analysis must be supplemented by other information before it can be used as a predictive tool.

For prediction purposes, the ratio format shown in Figure 6.2 can be of considerable use. Having just noted that a number of measures, combined together, are superior to a single ratio for predictive purposes, we have created a mix of ratios that tell a more comprehensive story of a company's financial condition. The measures are described in month-to-month format, so that the observer can see a clear trend line of financial performance. Figure 6.2 uses a mix of ratios and percentages, as well as the monthly sales figure, to determine what is happening to Company XYZ.

In Figure 6.2, the trend line of sales has gone up substantially, as Company XYZ has clearly obtained much new business, beginning in the month of May. However, this sales increase is coincident with a marked drop in profitability, probably because the company has increased its incremental sales by selling at too low a margin, thereby converting itself from a low-volume, high-margin company into the reverse: a high-volume, low-margin company. Further, to meet the demands of the company's sales growth, note that the return on assets has dropped markedly, probably due to the purchase of new fixed assets that are needed to produce the added volume. The turnover ratios for both accounts receivable and inventory have also dropped, implying that the company's working capital investment has increased, probably due in part to worsening credit problems with its new customers. The increase in assets and working capital have contributed to a shortage of cash, as evidenced by the worsening current ratio, not to mention the increase in debt, as revealed by the debt to equity ratio. To make matters worse, the added expenses and reduced margins associated with these extra sales have resulted in a much higher break-even point, so that the company must maintain a very high sales level in order to cover its costs. This type of more comprehensive analysis, when set up in a multiperiod format, is much more revealing for prediction purposes than a single-ratio examined for a single period. From this wider range of information, we can easily determine the course of a company's future finances, as well as possible reasons for the current situation, and suggestions for further improvements. To use the example in Figure 6.2, we can predict a speedy demise for this company, because its cash requirements for working capital and fixed assets vastly exceed the ability of operations to spin off substantial cash. Our recommendation, based on the analysis, would be to eliminate the new customers and return to the smaller sales levels that also resulted in higher margins.

Only by creating a complete picture of a company's financial condition, which requires a mix of ratios, percentages, and other calculations, can you have a firm basis on which to predict future financial performance.

FIGURE 6.2

Predictive Ratio and Margin Analysis

					Low-Margin Sales Added Here →							
Measurement	Jan	Feb	Mar	Apr	May	Jun	Jul	Aug	Sep	Oct	Nov	Dec
Sales (000s)	$550	$560	$565	$570	$800	$950	$1,150	$1,300	$1,500	$1,780	$2,000	$2,125
Breakeven (000s)	$450	$450	$450	$450	$600	$850	$950	1,150	$1,350	$1,550	$1,800	$1,950
Current Ratio	2.5:1	2.5:1	2.5:1	2.5:1	2.0:1	1.7:1	1.5:1	1.2:1	1.0:1	.8:1	.7:1	.6:1
Receivable Turnover	8	8	8	8	8	6	6	6	5	5	5	5
Inventory Turnover	7	7	7	7	7	6	6	6	6	6	5	5
Debt/Equity	.2:1	.2:1	.2:1	.2:1	.2:1	.4:1	.6:1	.8:1	1:1	1.3:1	1.5:1	1.7:1
Gross Margin	25%	26%	26%	26%	27%	24%	23%	22%	21%	21%	21%	21%
Net Margin	6%	7%	7%	7%	8%	5%	4%	3%	2%	2%	2%	2%
Times Interest Earned	3.0×	3.0×	3.0×	3.0×	2.7×	2.5×	2.4×	2.1×	1.9×	1.7×	1.3×	1.0×
Return on Assets	18%	20%	20%	20%	22%	16%	14%	12%	10%	8%	6%	4%

Operating Ratios

Operating ratios may be even more useful than financial ratios because of the timely nature of their calculation and the decision-specific nature of their use. While these ratios are in keeping with the thinking of most engineers and managers of sales, service *and* manufacturing can also use the principles of operating ratios effectively.

Comparison of Financial and Operating Ratios

Similarities

- Both financial and operating ratios are most useful when the information generated by the ratio is timely. Ratios are like other tools; they are beneficial only if you have them when you need them.
- As with financial ratios, operating ratios can be generated for any two numbers, for example, the number of salespeople and the dollars of sales per month. These two numbers will generate an average sales per salesperson, against which there may be a relative performance index. Also like financial ratios, unless there is a relationship, the resulting ratio is meaningless.
- Like financial ratios, operating ratios should not be accepted at face value. For the sales per person ratio, assume we find the average to be 17 sales per salesperson per day in an automobile dealership. Two of the salespeople make 43 and 53 sales per day, respectively, and the remaining five salespeople make 3 sales, 6 sales, 5 sales, 5 sales, and 4 sales, respectively. It would appear that you could replace the five salespersons with one aggressive person and be better off. However, additional information may reveal that the low-volume employees are automobile showroom salespeople and the other two are in the parts department. The parts room accounts for only 17 percent of the revenues but has 28.6 percent of the sales force. Several more ratios can be generated that would help in determining whether the sales force is well managed, efficient, and economical. Standing alone, no one ratio is as useful as a series of related ratios.

- Ratios for operations, like financial ratios, can be more effective if they are "trended." Taking the salesroom salespeople's past 12 months average ratio of sales per day, we observe these data:

Jan.	3.6	July	4.9
Feb.	4.2	Aug.	2.1
Mar.	5.4	Sept.	4.7
Apr.	6.1	Oct.	7.0
May	7.7	Nov.	6.3
June	6.3	Dec.	4.1

  From this we see a two-peak cycle of automobile sales. The dealership can plan when it should order more cars to increase the inventory in anticipation of seasonal sales. It also may help plan for sales incentives, promotional advertising, vacation schedules, and other operational elements.

- The cost of generating the data necessary for any ratio should not exceed the benefit derived from the information produced from the data. As with any tool, a ratio should itself have a favorable cost-benefit relationship. In other words, the benefits should outweigh the costs.

- Ratios are useless if they do not meet a need. Looking back, the ratio of average sales per salesperson per period was designed to measure the relative performance of sales personnel. It did not do that adequately. It failed to inform management what the meaningful performance was for automobiles versus parts sales personnel.

- Properly structured, an operating ratio or series of ratios can be used for planning and control. As an example, some of the financial ratios mentioned can be used to evaluate credit policy. The same is true for operating ratios. If we monitor how well auto sales personnel are doing individually, compared to the monthly historical figures, we have a quantitative measure of individual performance. If we look at the aggregate sales figures of average sales per person per day against the historical average, we have a measure of how well the business is doing compared with past performance.

Dissimilarities

- Financial ratios relate to numbers from the balance sheet and income statement, whereas operational ratios are oriented more toward production, service, and sales—figures that may not be accumulated in the accounting system. Because of this, standard financial ratios are more likely to be routinely prepared, whereas operating ratios are more often tailored to meet particular needs. There is a greater tendency to compare financial ratios among businesses almost indiscriminately—resulting in bad comparisons among dissimilar businesses. Because operating ratios may be tailored, there is less of a tendency for misapplication and greater reliance on historical trends.
- Operating ratios often can be calculated very quickly from obvious data. For the example of average sales per salesperson, management can have an accurate number for the previous day's sales for each member of the sales force at the start of each workday. It is often more difficult to compile and verify the financial data.

Use of Operating Ratios

Operating ratios can be used to evaluate any function. There may be a very large number of data-gathering efforts necessary to compile the needed input for ratio generation. Data gathering is costly and time consuming. It represents an investment that should have an expectation of a return to justify the expenditure. Therefore, you should first implement the use of ratios that have the greatest return or control. The ability to improve control through ratio generation and evaluation should be directed at critical steps in the process.

Breakdowns at critical steps may halt all production. For example, in a law firm specializing in appeals, time constraints are externally generated by rules of court with limited opportunities for extensions of time or deviations. Operationally, research is accomplished using sophisticated terminals connected to national data banks. Writing and editing is done on word processing software. All work flows through personnel highly skilled in the use of word processors. A breakdown in the word processing function could be very serious for the meeting of critical deadlines. Often the speed of input into the word processor is slower than dictation. Therefore, the ratio of skilled typists to writers may be critical. Ratio analysis can play a key role in determining a proper relationship.

There is a general five-step process for designing and implementing a control system based on ratio analysis. The number of steps may vary based on system complexity.

The five steps are:

1. Analyze the process or system: Write a step-by-step description of the process.
2. Look for and identify critical steps: Is there any one step through which most or all work flows?
3. Analyze the critical step: Is it a potential bottleneck or constriction? Why is it a bottleneck?
4. Set a target performance ratio: Determine from past historical data how well you have done and ask, "How much better can we do?"
5. Evaluate performance and feedback: How well are you now doing? How do you improve the system? What is the justification?

Applications

Operating ratios can be applied to any business. The next case study applies a ratio analysis to a service company (a law firm). Other suggestions will be given for a retail store and a manufacturing firm.

The firm of Simmer, Braize, and Broyle, P.A., is a Midwest law firm composed of 6 partners and 11 associate attorneys. They represent three large automobile insurance companies in defense litigation. The firm's business is basically steady, with two small seasonal variations. The firm has a sophisticated word processing system with satellite terminals; one draft, high-speed printer; one letter-quality printer; and a laser printer. The firm has two senior secretaries, two junior secretaries, and one clerk-typist/receptionist. As the caseload has grown, one senior secretary spends almost all her time setting up new case files.

The firm noticed that the secretaries were putting in more

overtime, and the senior partner was concerned that things were getting done only just in time. Ratio analysis was undertaken by an associate who had an undergraduate degree in business.

- She analyzed the flow of paper from the receipt of a complaint through the final order of the trial court. She prepared a flow-chart of what work was done, when, and by whom.
- She discovered two critical steps:
  1. All work product passed through the two junior secretaries and one senior secretary as they input, edited, and printed out lawyers' work products.
  2. The reproduction and mailing of letters, pleadings, and briefs.
- The technical word processing function was on the verge of becoming a bottleneck. The work just seemed to take too long to process.
- The reproduction facility was a disaster. The equipment was always breaking down; when it worked, people were constantly walking back to work without copies because "the line was too long" or "a long critical job was on the machine."
- After studying the number of words processed by each of the three secretaries, she found an average of 52 words per minute. Not to be fooled by averages, she looked at the distribution. The two junior secretaries typed at 38 and 42 words per minute each and the senior secretary typed at 75. The other senior secretary, who only set up files, could type at 81 words per minute. The associate, told that this secretary had been hired because of her typing speed, calculated that if the senior secretary switched roles with the junior secretary, the firm could target word input at 67 words per minute, average, without changing personnel (a 29 percent increase). The junior secretary and the receptionist would be able to prepare all the files as they came in. The associate found that the senior secretary had started or updated 61 files per day. She set a target of 45 files for the junior secretary and 20 for the receptionist (because of her other duties).
- She ran a study of the copier by asking each user to log in the number of copies made of each original and the number of originals. From this, she learned several things. There were only

two basic types of copying requirements: (1) long runs (many copies of large jobs with many originals) and (2) short runs (few originals, few copies). The long runs, on average, consumed 6 hours a day total time and the short runs 1.5 hours. The average short run took less than 30 seconds, but the average long run took 17 minutes. Twenty-one long runs and about 200 short runs were run each day. With the machine breakdowns considered, the copier (owned by the firm) worked properly on average 8.2 hours each 9-hour day. Often copies were run through lunch hour on a staggered secretarial shift.

- From these ratios, the associate made these recommendations: Buy a highly reliable small copier and dedicate it to short runs. Hire a clerk to do the copying. As justification, she made these findings based on ratio analysis:

  • On average, each secretary saved up five small runs or one long run before going to the machine.

  • On average, the machine was tied up doing long runs or broken down 6.8 hours out of every 9 hours, roughly 75 percent of the time. On three out of every four trips to the machine, a secretary found it occupied by a long run. Because the secretaries made 40 successful trips to the copier per day (200 short runs/5 runs per trip), they were making approximately 120 unsuccessful trips to the machine. If they waited for a long run to finish rather than returning to their desk, they waited 8½ minutes (17/2).

  • By assigning a clerk to copying, all unsuccessful trips were eliminated. Even though an unsuccessful trip to the copier took only 45 seconds, 1.5 hours of secretarial time was saved (120 trips × 45 seconds).

  • By reducing the demand on the copier, the breakdown rate was expected to improve.

  • The biggest bonus to the firm was the actual freeing up of 7.5 hours of secretarial time. Simply to do the copying, a secretary stood at the machine for 6 hours a day for long runs and 1.5 hours per day for short runs. This, coupled with the 1.5 hours of time saved on unsuccessful trips, amounted to enough savings in dollars of overtime to pay for the small-run copier in nine months and still pay the salary and benefits of the clerk.

Ratio analysis improved the operation of the firm, gave it quantifiable measures of performance, and got some control over the operation.

Other Ratios

A list of other operating ratios a firm might generate follows; it is not meant to be complete.

For the law firm, other ratios were considered:
- Total hours worked to hours spent on task for which hired
- Clerical hours to professional hours
- Billable hours to hours worked
- Billable hours brought to firm (new clients, new or repeat work) to hours billed

For a retail store:
- Number of customers making purchases to the number of customers coming through door
- Number of sales to number of customers waited on (by each salesperson)
- Number of sales per hour of the day
- Dollars of sales per dollars of inventory (by product or product type)
- Number of sales to number of salespersons

For a manufacturing firm:

Lower Management
- Hours of setup time to hours of run time
- Hours of downtime to available hours
- Hours of downtime to run time
- Hours of sick time to hours worked
- Labor hours per product produced
- Hours of rework to hours of production
- Number of quality control steps or inspections to hours to produce or steps to produce
- Work area per employee

Middle Management

- Number of supervisors to direct laborers
- Number of indirect laborers to direct laborers
- Scrapped product to good finished goods
- Number of returns to goods sold

Upper Management

- Dollars of profit to cost to produce
- Number of products back-ordered to number delivered
- Dollars of sales to number of employees
- Lost time accidents to hours worked
- Number of service employees to manufacturing employees
- Number of units shipped per day

For the accounting department:
- Purchase discounts taken to total discounts
- Transactions processed per person
- Transaction error rate
- Average time to issue invoices
- Time to produce financial statements
- Percentage of tax filing dates missed
- Bad debt percentage
- Percent of cash applied on day of receipt

For the engineering department:
- Bill of material accuracy
- Labor routing accuracy
- Percentage of existing parts used in new products
- Average number of distinct products per design platform
- Ratio of actual cost to target cost
- Warranty claims percentage
- Time from design inception to production

For the logistics department:
- Production schedule accuracy
- Days of inventory on hand
- Obsolete inventory percentage
- Inventory accuracy
- Percentage of certified suppliers

- On-time parts delivery percentage
- Purchased component defect rate
- Picking accuracy for assembled products
- On-time delivery percentage

For the production department:
- Utilization percentage for bottleneck operation
- Break-even plant capacity
- Unit output per direct labor hour
- Average equipment setup time
- Unscheduled downtime percentage
- Scrap percentage
- Maintenance expense to fixed assets ratio

For the sales and marketing department:
- Market share
- Customer turnover
- Browse to buy conversion ratio
- Direct mail effectiveness ratio
- Quote to close ratio
- Sales per salesperson
- Days of backlog

Each manager or supervisor concerned with the operations of the firm or store should monitor at least two or three critical ratios on a continuous basis. This information may be plotted on a daily basis to accumulate historical information that could be used for planning, control, and budgeting. Often this information will point up areas of critical concern before it has a fatal effect. Therefore, ratios, if properly structured and monitored, can be powerful management tools.

The Balanced Scorecard

Too often, a company focuses exclusively on its financial results. By doing so, it may be forcing attention away from other key measures that ultimately have a strong impact on financial performance and enhance that performance in the long run. To counteract this problem, Robert Kaplan and David Norton published *The Balanced*

Scorecard (Harvard Business School Press, 1996). In this book, the authors make a strong case in favor of splitting up a company's key performance measurements into four areas—the financial, customer, internal business processes, and learning and growth areas. These areas are designed to build on each other, so that a proper level of attention to the three nonfinancial measurement areas will result in an improved set of financial measurements as well. An example of this measurement system is shown in Figure 6.3. In it, we see that the learning and growth measurements, shown in the lower left-hand corner, are designed to improve the performance of employees through training as well as reduced turnover (on the grounds that fewer employee departures results in fewer new employees, hence a more experienced staff). Measurements for the last month are compared to those from previous periods, so that employees can see trends in the measurements. Success in the learning and growth area should result in an improvement in the company's internal business processes, which are itemized in the lower right corner of the figure. In this area, increased employee training has led to improved processing time for customer orders as well as the near completion of a just-in-time manufacturing system. These process changes should result in improved customer-related measurements, which are noted in the upper right corner. With improved product quality, on-time shipments, and customer satisfaction, we assume that financial performance will improve, which will be reflected in the final box in the upper left corner. In this area, the financial measures are closely tied to the corporate goal, which is listed at the top of the page: to spin off enough cash from operations to fund new facilities and acquire competitors. Thus, the balanced scorecard reporting system results in a coherent set of interlocking measurements that are directly tied to a company's goals.

The balanced scorecard must be individualized for each company that uses it, since each one operates within a unique set of constraints. The measurements used in the example are designed for a manufacturing facility, and so would be inappropriate for use by a service company. To obtain the correct set of measurements for a balanced scorecard, a company's senior management group should compile a short list of the most appropriate measures, possibly with the assistance of a trained facilitator who can keep the discussion

FIGURE 6.3

The Balanced Scorecard

XYZ Company
Balanced Scorecard

Goal: To spin off enough cash flow to build new facilities and acquire competitors.

Financial:

	Actual	Goal
Net profits		**6%**
This Month	4.5%	
This Quarter	3.4%	
Last Year	2.6%	
Inventory Turns		**20%**
This Month	16.0%	
This Quarter	12.5%	
Last Year	12.0%	
Receivable Turns		**9.0%**
This Month	8.2%	
This Quarter	7.6%	
Last Year	8.1%	

Customer:

	Actual	Goal
Customer Satisfaction		**95%**
This Month	59.5%	
This Quarter	54.0%	
Last Year	50.0%	
On-Time Shipments		**98%**
This Month	71.0%	
This Quarter	68.0%	
Last Year	42.0%	
Quality Percentage		**99.5%**
This Month	94.5%	
This Quarter	91.3%	
Last Year	89.2%	

Learning & Growth:

	Actual	Goal
Employee Turnover		**10%**
This Month	19.0%	
This Quarter	21.0%	
Last Year	38.0%	
Training Hours per Employee Annualized		**40**
This Month	29	
This Quarter	25	
Last Year	21	

Internal Business Processes:

	Actual	Goal
Just-in-Time System Percentage Complete		**100%**
This Month	65%	
This Quarter	45%	
Last Year	20%	
Average Time to Process Orders		**2 Days**
This Month	2.9 Days	
This Quarter	3.2 Days	
Last Year	3.5 Days	

on track. Once everyone has agreed on the most appropriate measures, there must be further agreement on how each one should be calculated, as well as when the measures will be sent back to the management team for periodic review. These up-front decisions ensure that the correct measures will be calculated and that they will be used by managers to improve the business.

The balanced scorecard should not supplant all previous measurement systems that a company uses to track its performance. Dozens or even hundreds of measures may be in place already that are extremely useful for the conduct of daily operations and that should be continued. The balanced scorecard is more for the management group, who can use it to see how well they are directing the company's performance in reaching its major goals. To this end, it should be treated as a high-level set of measurements, under which lie a great many other measures that still must be used to transact daily company business.

Summary

Ratios are an analytical tool used for reporting and control. They have external and internal applications. Externally, trade creditors, bondholders, and banks are interested in the ratios and the trends depicted by a historical progression of those ratios. Internally, financial and operating ratios depict how well the firm is doing and serve as an instrument of feedback for control.

In trying to determine what a ratio means, analysts sometimes resort to rules of thumb, which are nothing more than averages. As such, they may be inapplicable, thus generating faulty comparisons and conclusions. Financial ratios generated internally over time may be the most useful for the firm's purposes. Next, you might compare other similar firms' ratios generated by trade associations.

For financial ratios, you might generate liquidity ratios, debt ratios, long-term liquidity measures, coverage ratios, and profitability ratios.

After financial concerns, operating ratios may be generated as a measure of how well the firm is doing, where bottlenecks occur, and where objective measures of performance can be established.

Creating operating ratios is an individual endeavor for each business. Although some of the ratios established—for example, acceptable parts to parts produced—may be common, what is acceptable will vary from business to business. Also, where you want to emphasize control will vary according to individual costs.

A five-step analysis of a process or system helps point out areas where a company may have critical steps or potential bottlenecks. These may be areas where you should expend some effort in generating ratios for control and reporting.

The generation of *useful* ratios is the guiding star for this analysis. If you undertake to generate the information necessary for implementation of a ratio control or feedback system, the ratio should be meaningful and the information useful.

Ratios are guides, and that implies movement over time. Taking a snapshot look at ratios may tell management something, but that something may be misleading. Trends in ratios indicate what is going on with the business, and they may even indicate what might go on in the future.

Properly applied, analyzed, and interpreted, ratios are a powerful tool for internal and external reporting, control, and evaluations.

7

Financial Analysis[1]

The business owner should be aware of several financial analysis topics. The first is risk analysis, which addresses the variability of data made to make decisions. Another is capacity utilization, which is of great importance when determining the ability of an organization to change the amount of revenue it produces, as well as to monitor its bottleneck operations. The final analysis tool is the break-even chart, which is addressed in increasing levels of complexity in order to show how it can be modified to incorporate a variety of variables. These tools are all useful for managing a business.

Risk Analysis

It is customary to make decisions based on *projected* information. This happens whenever a business forecast or sales projection is issued. In particular, it is a primary element of any cash flow projection for a capital expenditure. If there is even a small difference between actual and projected cash flows from a project, it may result in a negative net present value, which means that an implemented project should not have been approved initially. To avoid this problem, you must have a good knowledge of the risk of any

---

[1] Adapted with permission from Chapters 8, 13, and 17 of Steven M. Bragg, *Financial Analysis* (Hoboken, NJ: John Wiley & Sons, 2000).

projection, which is essentially the chance that the actual value will vary significantly from the expected one.

There are several rough measures of data dispersion. They tell how spread out the projected outcomes are from a central average point. By reviewing the several measurements, you can obtain a good feel for the extent to which projections cluster together. If they are tightly clustered, then the risk of not meeting the estimated outcome is low; a large degree of dispersion reflects considerable dissension over the projected outcome, and a greater degree of risk is associated with this situation.

The first task when determining data dispersion is to determine the center, or midpoint, of the data, to see how far the group of estimates vary from this point. There are several ways to arrive at this point.

- *Arithmetic mean.* This is the summary of all projections, divided by the total number of projections. It rarely results in a specific point that matches any of the underlying projections, because it is not based on any single projection—just the average of all points. It simply balances out the largest and smallest projections. It tends to be inaccurate if the underlying data include one or two projections that are significantly different from the other projections, resulting in an average that is skewed in the direction of the significantly different projections.
- *Median.* This is the point at which half of the projections are below and half are above. On the assumption that there are an even number of projections being used, the median is the average of the two middle values. By using this method, you can avoid the effect of any outlying projections that are radically different from the main group.
- *Mode.* This is the most commonly observed value in a set of underlying projections. As such, it is not impacted by any extreme projections. In a sense, it represents the most popular projection.

When selecting which to use for the midpoint of the data, you must remember why you are using the midpoint. Because the determination of the level of risk is the goal, you want to determine how far apart the projections are from a midpoint. As you will be including the extreme values in the next set of measurements, you do not have to include them in the determination of the center of the projections. Accordingly, you will use the median, which ignores the size of outlying values, as the measurement of choice for determination of the middle of the set of projected outcomes.

The next step is to determine how far apart the projections are from the median. Given the small number of projections, this is easy enough. Just pick the highest and lowest values from the list of outcomes, then determine the percentage by which the highest and lowest values vary from the median. To do so, you divide the difference between the lowest and median values by the median, and calculate the same variance between the median and the highest value. This is a good way to determine the range of possible outcomes. For example, these cash flow projections were collected as part of risk analysis determination:

- The set of projections for estimated cash flow is:
  $250, $400, $675, $725, $850, and $875
- The median is the average of the third and fourth values, which is:
  $700
- The percentage difference between the median and highest projection is:
  ($875 − $700)/$700 = 25%
- The percentage difference between the median and lowest projection is:
  ($700 − $250)/$700 = 64%

If the difference between the median and the highest possible estimate is only 25 percent, but the difference between the median and the lowest possible estimate is 64 percent, then there is a modest chance that the actual result will be higher than the estimate but there is a significant risk that it may turn out to be lower than expected.

Another way to determine dispersion is to calculate the *standard deviation* of the data. This method measures the average scatter of data about the mean. In other words, it arrives at a number that is the amount by which the average data point varies from the midpoint, either above or below it. You can divide it by the mean of the data to arrive at a percentage that is called the *coefficient of variation*. This is an excellent way to convert the standard deviation, which is expressed in units, into a percentage. It is a much better way of expressing the range of deviation within a group of projections, since you cannot always tell if a standard deviation of $23 is good or bad; when converted into a percentage of deviation of 3 percent, you can see that the same number indicates a very tight clustering of data about the center point of all data. Figure 7.1 uses the data just noted to determine the standard deviation, the mean, and the coefficient of variation.

The calculations in Figure 7.1 reveal that the set of projections used as underlying data vary significantly from the midpoint of the group, especially in a downward direction, indicating that there is a high degree of risk that the expected outcome will not be achieved.

Sometimes the management team to whom risk information is reported will not be awed by a reported coefficient of variation of a whopping 80 percent or by a standard deviation of 800 units. They do not know what these measures mean, and they do not have time to find out. For them, a graphical representation of data dispersion

FIGURE **7.1**

Calculating the Standard Deviation
and Coefficient of Variation

1. The standard deviation formula in Excel, using data set, is:
   = STDEV(250, 400, 675, 725, 850, 875)
   = 252

2. The calculation of the mean of all data is:
   = (sum of all data items)/(number of data items)
   = (250 + 400 + 675 + 725 + 850 + 875)/6
   = 629

3. The calculation of the coefficient of variation is:
   = (standard deviation)/(mean)
   = 252/629
   = 40%

may be a better approach. They can see the spread of estimates on a graph and then decide for themselves if there appears to be a problem with risk.

When constructing a graph that shows the dispersion of data, you can lay out the data set in terms of the percentage difference between each item and the midpoint. Figure 7.2 takes the projection information used in Figure 7.1 and converts it into percentages from the median.

When translated into a graph, Figure 7.2 gives a wide percentage distribution of data on either side of the X axis that gives a good indication of the true distribution of data about the mean. The top graph of Figure 7.3 restates the data in Figure 7.2.

Note that there are two additional graphs in Figure 7.3. The middle graph assumes that there are a number of projections clustered under each of the variance points. The example arbitrarily expands the number of projections to 26, with 8 clustered at the median point, 6 each at the –4% and +4% variance points, and lesser amounts at the outlying variance points. This is close to a classic "bell curve" distribution, where the bulk of estimates are clustered near the middle and a rapidly declining number are located at the periphery. This is an excellent way to present information, but small business owners rarely have a sufficient number of projections to use this type of graph. If there are enough projections, a variation shown in the graph at the bottom of the exhibit may result: Data are skewed toward the right-hand side of the chart.

FIGURE 7.2

Data Dispersion, Measured in Percentages

Projection	Percentage Variance from the Median
$250	–64%
$400	–43%
$675	–4%
$700 (median)	0%
$725	4%
$850	21%
$875	25%

FIGURE 7.3

Graphical Illustration of Data Dispersion

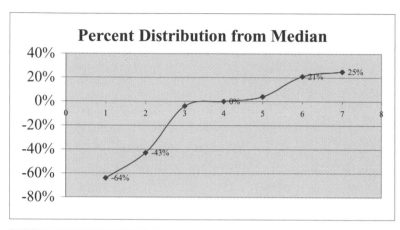

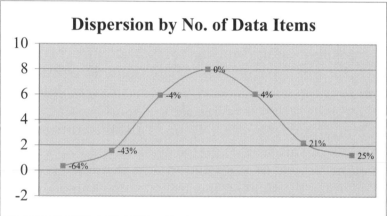

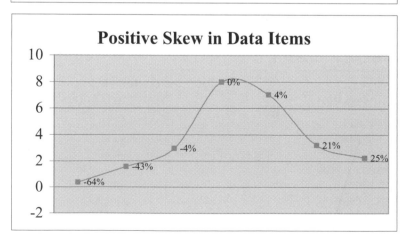

This indicates a preponderance of estimates that lean, or "skew," toward the higher end of the range of estimates. A reverse graph, which had negative skew, would present a decided lean toward the left side.

Of the graphs presented in Figure 7.3, only the first one, the "Percent Distribution from Median," is likely to be used consistently, because in most situations there are so few data points available to work with. Nonetheless, you can use any of these graphs when making presentations to management about the riskiness of projections, because they all are so easy to understand.

Capacity Utilization

The term *capacity* covers both human and machine resources. If those resources are not used to a sufficient degree, there are immediate grounds for eliminating them, either by a layoff (in the case of human capacity) or selling equipment (in the case of machines). A layoff usually has a short-term loss associated with it, which covers severance costs, followed by an upturn in profits, since there is no longer a long-term obligation to pay salaries. The sale of a machine does not have much of an impact on profits, unless there is a gain or loss on sale of the asset, but it will result in an improvement in cash flow as sale proceeds come in; these funds can be used for a variety of purposes to increase corporate value, such as reinvestment in new machines, a loan payoff, a buyback of equity, and so on. Consequently, you should keep a close eye on capacity levels throughout a company. Whoever makes recommendations to keep capacity utilization close to current capacity levels will have a significant impact on both profits and cash flows.

When making such analyses, an issue to be aware of is that a business owner tends to be conservative—he or she wants to maximize the use of current capacity and get rid of everything not being used. This may not be a good thing when activity levels are projected to increase markedly in the near term. If management eliminates excess capacity just prior to a large increase in production volumes, some exceptional scrambling, possibly at high cost, will be required to bring the newly necessary capacity back in house.

Consequently, be sure to work with the sales staff to determine future sales (and therefore production) trends before recommending any cuts in capacity.

Capacity utilization also reveals the specific spots in a production process where work is being held up. These bottleneck operations prevent a production line from attaining its true potential amount of revenue production. You can use this bottleneck information in two ways:

1. To recommend improvements to bottleneck operations in order to increase the potential amount of revenue generation
2. To point out that any capital improvements to other segments of a production operation are essentially a waste of money (from the perspective of increasing the flow of production), since all production still is going to create a log-jam in front of the bottleneck operation

Another use for capacity utilization information is in the determination of pricing levels. For example, if a company has a large amount of surplus excess capacity and does not intend to sell it off in the near term, it makes sense (and cents) to offer pricing deals on incremental sales that result in only small margins. This is because there is no other use for the equipment or production personnel. If low-margin jobs are not produced, the only alternative is no jobs at all, for which there is no margin at all. However, if the business owner knows that a production facility is running at maximum capacity, it is time to be choosy on incremental sales, so that only those sales involving large margins are accepted. It may also be possible to stop taking orders for low-margin products in the future, thereby flushing such products out of the current production mix in favor of newer, higher-margin sales. Although this approach is highly profitable, it can irritate customers who are faced with take-it-or-leave-it answers by a company that refuses new orders unless the customer accepts higher prices. Consequently, incremental pricing for new sales is closely tied not only to how much production capacity a company has left, but also to its long-term strategy for how it wants to treat its customers.

Companies have a variety of activities in which the capacity utilization may be important enough to track. The area most commonly measured is machine utilization, because management teams are always interested in keeping expensive machinery running for as long as possible, so that the invested cost is not wasted. Thus, capacity tracking for *expensive assets* is certainly a common activity. However, another factor that many organizations miss is the capacity utilization measurement for any *bottleneck operation*. This has nothing to do with a costly asset, but rather with determining whether a key operation in a process is interfering with the successful processing of a transaction. For example, if a number of production lines feed their products to a single person who must box and ship them, and this person cannot keep up with the volume of production arriving at her workstation, then she is a bottleneck operation that is interfering with the timely completion of the production schedule. Because she is a bottleneck, her capacity utilization should be tracked most carefully. This worker is not an expensive machine, and may in fact be paid very little, but she is potentially holding up the realization of a great deal of revenue that cannot be shipped to customers. Consequently, using a capacity utilization measure makes a great deal of sense in this situation.

To amplify on the concept of capacity planning for bottleneck operations, it is not sufficient to track the utilization of a single bottleneck operation, because the bottleneck will move to different steps in the production process as improvements are made to the system. For example, the key principle of the just-in-time concept is that management works to identify bottleneck operations and fix them. As a result, each specific bottleneck will be eliminated, but now the second most constrictive operation comes to the fore for review and improvement, which in turn will be followed by a third operation, and so on. Consequently, it is better to identify *every* work center and track the utilization of them all. By using this more comprehensive approach, management can spot upcoming bottleneck problems and address them before they become serious problems.

In the case of machinery, the tracking of utilization for virtually all of them is also useful, not just because they are also potential bottleneck operations, but because of the reverse problem—a machine that is not being used is a waste of invested capital and should be sold off if possible. A detailed capacity utilization report will note those machines that are not being used and tell management what can potentially be eliminated. This information is especially useful when machines are clustered on the report by type, so that a subtotal of capacity utilization is noted for each group of machines. If the machines within each cluster can be used interchangeably to complete similar work, management can determine the total amount of work required of each cluster and add or delete machines to meet that demand, which results in a very efficient use of capital. Such a report is described later in Figure 7.4.

A company frequently thinks of its production capacity only in terms of the current number of shifts being operated, and tracks its capacity utilization accordingly. For example, a production facility that operates for one eight-hour shift and uses all machinery during that time thinks that it is operating at 100 percent capacity utilization. In fact, it is only using one-third of the available hours in a day, which leaves lots of room for additional production. Accordingly, when developing a utilization measurement, always use the maximum amount of theoretical capacity as the baseline, rather than the amount of time during the day that is currently being used. For a single day, this means 24 hours, and for a week, it is 168 hours. On a monthly basis, the total number of hours will vary, since the number of days in a month can vary from 28 to 31. To get around this problem, it is easier to track capacity on a weekly basis and use either four or five full weeks for individual months, depending on where the final month-end dates fall, so that all months of the year (except the last) on the capacity report show full-week results for either four or five weeks.

Once the decision is made to create a capacity utilization analysis, what format should be used to present it? The capacity report in Figure 7.4 lists the utilization hours of 28 plastic injection and blow molding machines. The identification number of each machine is listed down the left column, with the tonnage of each machine noted in the next column. The next cluster of four columns shows the weekly utilization in hours for each machine. The final three columns show the average weekly utilization by machine for the preceding three months. In addition, there are subtotals for all blow molding machines and for five clusters of injection molding machines, grouped by tonnage size.

FIGURE 7.4

Capacity Utilization Report

Machine ID	Machine Description	Run Hrs	Run Hrs	5/9–5/15 Run Hrs	5/2–5/8 Run Hrs	Month of Apr. Run Hrs	Mar. Run Hrs	Feb. Run Hrs
B1100/BM04	Blow Mold	150	142	139	132	112	122	104
B2000/BM03	Blow Mold	149	135	137	152	114	154	119
		89%	82%	82%	85%	67%	82%	66%
01-25	25 Ton	123	125	126	132	138	125	111
02-90/TO11	90 Ton	150	158	152	137	117	132	144
03-90/TO10	90 Ton	129	168	164	129	126	111	120
04-90/TO09	90 Ton	75	50	94	138	142	167	147
16-55/AG01	55 Ton	132	168	163	59	125	109	102
		73%	80%	83%	71%	61%	62%	61%
05-150/TO08	150 Ton	141	150	147	162	133	139	133
06-150/TO07	150 Ton	119	130	137	152	122	124	127
07-198/TO06	198 Ton	147	135	133	77	114	132	54
08-200/TO05	200 Ton	110	120	124	141	117	101	113
17-190/TA05	190 Ton	138	141	127	116	97	106	91
		78%	80%	80%	77%	69%	72%	62%
09-300/TO04	300 Ton	168	168	168	133	148	125	148
10-300/TO03	300 Ton	0	50	79	143	135	142	129
11-330/TO02	330 Ton	148	149	129	136	93	125	100
20-390/TA04	390 Ton	110	127	121	158	128	136	154
21-375/C106	375 Ton	92	100	102	84	78	77	102
26-400/TO01	400 Ton	47	85	124	116	101	78	120
		56%	67%	72%	76%	68%	68%	75%
12-500/CI05	500 Ton	91	168	166	137	113	62	50
14-500/CI04	500 Ton	74	85	100	96	107	142	96
18-450/VN02	450 Ton	168	162	163	164	103	111	119
24-500/VN01	500 Ton	125	0	167	163	161	96	106
25-500/TA03	500 Ton	132	139	145	162	146	128	89
		70%	66%	88%	86%	75%	64%	55%
13-700/CI03	700 Ton	168	151	146	142	106	78	60
15-700/VN03	700 Ton	0	153	107	152	133	118	118
19-720/TA02	720 Ton	102	109	115	161	115	58	113
22-700/CI01	700 Ton	111	59	74	154	74	76	144
23-950/TA01	950 Ton	104	168	126	159	110	91	112
		58%	76%	68%	91%	64%	50%	65%
		66%	74%	78%	80%	71%	66%	66%
		68%	74%	78%	81%	70%	67%	66%

This report format allows management to look across the report from left to right and determine any trends in capacity utilization, while also being able to look down the page and determine usage by clusters of machines. This second factor is of extreme importance in the molding business, because each machine is very expensive and must be eliminated if it is not being used to a sufficient degree. For example, look at the tonnage range of 300–400 tons, located midway through the report. A cluster of six machines is consistently showing between 68% and 76% percent of usage. Is it possible to eliminate one machine, thereby spreading the work over fewer machines and raising the overall usage percentage for all the machines? To determine the answer using data for the highest utilization reporting period, which is for the first week of May, at 76%, add up all the reported hours of usage for that cluster of machines, which is 770, and divide the total number of hours that the machine cluster has available, assuming that one machine has been removed. The total number of hours available for production will be 168 (which is seven days multiplied by 24 hours per day) times five machines, which is 840. The result is a utilization of 92 percent for the maximum amount of work that has appeared in the last quarter of a year. Consequently, the answer is that it is theoretically possible to remove one machine from the 300–400 ton range of machines and still be able to complete all work.

However, when using a capacity report to arrive at such conclusions, there are several additional factors to consider. One is the reliability of the machines. If they have a history of failures, then a standard number of hours per operating period for repair work must be factored into the utilization formula, which will reduce the theoretical capacity of the machine. Another problem is that a machine usually is eliminated in order to realize a cash inflow from sale of the machine; but what if the machines most likely to be sold will fetch only a minor amount in the marketplace? If so, it may make more sense to retain equipment, even if unused, so that it can take on additional work in the event of an increase in sales volume. Yet another issue is that there may be some difficulty in obtaining a sufficient number of staff to maintain or run a machine during all theoretical operating hours. For example, it is common for those organizations with a reduced number of maintenance personnel to cluster those staff on the day shift for maximum efficiency, which means that any machine failures during other hours will result in a shut-down machine until the maintenance staff arrives the next day. Finally, the example shows management taking actual capacity utilization of its machinery to 92 percent. Is this wise, if management has essentially removed all remaining available capacity by selling off the excess machine? What if an existing customer suddenly increases an order and finds that the company cannot accommodate the work, because all machines are booked? Not only lost revenues will result, but perhaps even a lost customer.

One way in which a capacity analysis can be skewed is if there are either a large number of small jobs running through a process, each of which requires a small amount of downtime to switch over to the new job, or a small number of jobs that require a very lengthy changeover process. In either case, the amount of reported capacity will never reach 100 percent, for the required setup time will take up the amount of capacity that is supposedly available. One action that management can take to alleviate this problem is to work on reducing the changeover time needed to switch to a new job. Doing this typically involves videotaping the changeover process and then reviewing the tape with the changeover team to identify and implement process alterations that will result in reduced setup times.

A revenue-related problem that arises when setup times eat up a large portion of total capacity is that the sales department may promise customers that work will begin very soon on their orders, because the capacity utilization report appears to reveal that there is lots of excess capacity. When excessive changeover times do not leave any time for additional customer orders, customers may take their business elsewhere. To counteract this problem, it is necessary to determine the amount of *practical capacity,* which is the total capacity less the average amount of changeover time. If the setup reduction effort noted in the preceding paragraph is implemented, the practical capacity number will increase, because the time available for production will increase as changeover times go down. Consequently, a review of the practical capacity should be made fairly often to ensure that the correct figure is used.

A problem with using practical capacity as the standard measure of how much work still can be loaded into the production system is that it is based on an average of actual capacity information over several weeks or months. However, if there are one or more jobs scheduled for a changeover that require inordinate amounts of time to complete, the reported practical capacity measure will not reflect reality. Similarly, if the actual changeover times are quite small, the true capacity will be higher than the reported practical capacity. Because practical capacity is a historical average, the actual capacity will be somewhat higher or lower than this average nearly all of the time. Although a company with a lot of excess capacity might call this hair-splitting, a company that is running at maximum production levels may find itself blindsided by a lack of available time or some amount of unplanned downtime. In either case, there is a cost to having inaccurate capacity information. Those companies with well-maintained manufacturing resources planning software can avoid this problem by accurately scheduling jobs and changeover times, and updating the data as soon as changes are made.

Breakeven Analysis

A company usually operates within a very narrow band of pricing and costs in order to earn a profit. If it does not charge a minimum price to cover its fixed and variable costs, it will quickly burn through its cash reserves and go out of business. In a competitive environment, prices drop to the point where they only barely cover costs, and profits are thin or nonexistent. At this point, only those companies with a good understanding of their own breakeven points and those of their competitors are likely to make the correct pricing and cost decisions to remain competitive. This section shows how breakeven (also known as the cost-volume-profit relationship) is calculated, as well as a variety of more complex variations on the basic formula.

The breakeven formula is an exceedingly simple one. To determine a breakeven point, add up all the fixed costs for the company or product being analyzed, and divide it by the associated gross margin percentage. This results in the sales level at which a company will neither lose nor make money—its breakeven point. The formula is shown in Figure 7.5.

FIGURE 7.5

The Breakeven Formula

Total Fixed Costs/Gross Margin Percentage = Breakeven Sales Level

For those who prefer a graphical layout to a mathematical formula, a breakeven chart can be quite informative. In the sample chart shown in Figure 7.6, the horizontal line across the chart represents the fixed costs that must be covered by gross margins, irrespective of the sales level. The fixed-cost level will fluctuate over time and in conjunction with extreme changes in sales volume, but we will assume no changes for the purposes of this simplified analysis. Also, an upward-sloping line begins at the left end of the fixed-cost line and extends to the right across the chart. This is the percentage of variable costs, such as direct labor and materials, that are needed to create the product. The last major component of the chart is the sales line, which is based in the lower left corner of the chart and extends to the upper right corner. The amount of the sales volume in dollars is noted on the vertical axis, while the amount of production capacity used to create the sales volume is noted across the horizontal axis. Finally, a line that extends from the marked breakeven point to the right, which is always between the sales line and the variable cost line, represents income tax costs. These are the main components of the breakeven chart.

It is also useful to look between the lines on the graph and understand what the volumes represent. For example, as noted in Figure 7.6, the area beneath the fixed-cost line is the total fixed cost to be covered by product margins. The area between the fixed-cost line and the variable-cost line is the total variable cost at different volume levels. The area beneath the income line and above the variable cost line is the income tax expense at various sales levels. Finally, the area beneath the revenue line and above the income tax line is the amount of net profit to be expected at various sales levels.

Although this breakeven chart appears quite simplistic, additional variables can make a real-world breakeven analysis a much more complex endeavor to understand. One of these variables is fixed cost. A fixed cost is a misnomer, for any cost can vary over

FIGURE 7.6

Simplified Breakeven Chart

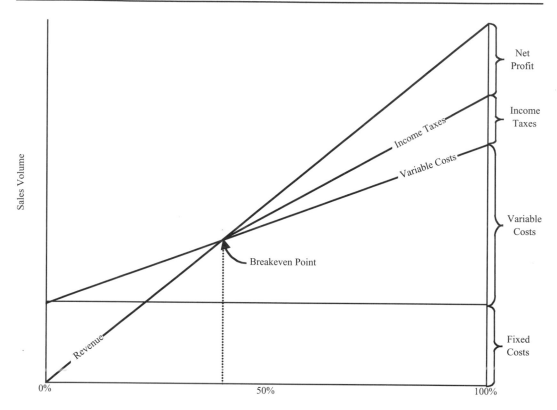

Percentage of Production Utilization

time, or outside of a specified set of operating conditions. For example, the overhead costs associated with a team of engineers may be considered a fixed cost if a product line requires continuing improvements and enhancements over time. However, what if management decides to gradually eliminate a product line and milk it for cash flow, rather than keep the features and styling up-to-date? If so, the engineers are no longer needed, and the associated fixed cost goes down. Any situation where management is essentially abandoning a product line in the long term probably will result in a decline in overhead costs.

A much more common alteration in fixed costs is when additional personnel or equipment are needed in order to support an increased level of sales activity. As noted in the breakeven chart in Figure 7.7, the fixed cost will step up to a higher level (an occurrence known as step costing) when a certain capacity level is reached. An example of this situation is when a company has maximized the use of a single shift and must add supervision and other overhead costs, such as electricity and natural gas expenses, in order to run an additional shift. Another example is when a new facility must be brought on line or an additional machine acquired. Whenever this happens, management must take a close look at the amount of fixed costs that will be incurred, because the net profit level may be less after the fixed costs are added, despite the extra sales volume. In the figure, the maximum amount of profit that a company can attain is at the sales level just *prior to* incurring extra fixed costs, because the increase in fixed costs is so high. Although step costing does not always involve such a large increase in costs as noted in the next exhibit, this is certainly a major point to be aware of when increasing capacity to take on additional sales volume. In short, more sales do not necessarily lead to more profits.

The next variable in the breakeven formula is the variable cost line. Although you would think that the variable cost is a simple percentage that is composed of labor and material costs, and which never varies, this is not the case. This percentage can vary considerably and frequently drops as the sales volume increases. The reason for the change is that the purchasing department can cut better deals with suppliers when it orders in larger volumes. In addition, full truckload or railcar deliveries result in lower freight expenses than would be the case if only small quantities were purchased. The result is shown in Figure 7.8, where the variable cost percentage is at its highest when sales volume is at its lowest and gradually decreases in concert with an increase in volume.

Because material and freight costs tend to drop as volume increases, it is apparent that profits will increase at an increasing rate as sales volume goes up, although there may be step costing problems at higher capacity levels.

Another point is that the percentage of variable costs will not decline at a steady rate. Instead, and as noted in Figure 7.8, there will

FIGURE 7.7

Breakeven Chart Including Impact of Step Costing

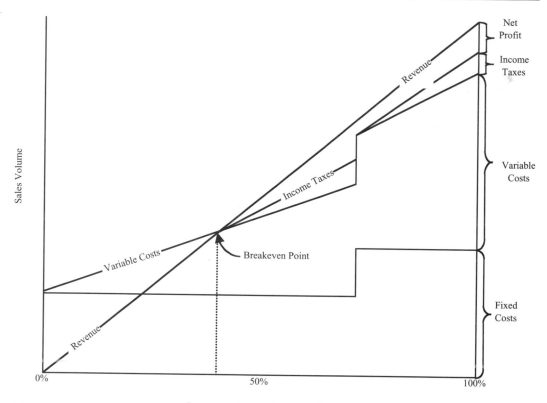

Percentage of Production Utilization

be specific volume levels at which costs will drop. This is because the purchasing staff can negotiate price reductions only at specific volume points. Once such a price reduction has been achieved, there will not be another opportunity to reduce prices further until a separate and distinct volume level is reached once again.

The changes to fixed costs and variable costs in the breakeven analysis are relatively simple and predictable, but now we come to the final variable, sales volume, which can alter for several reasons, making it the most difficult of the three components to predict.

The first reason why the volume line in the breakeven chart can vary is the mix of products sold. A perfectly straight sale volume

FIGURE 7.8

Breakeven Chart Including Impact of Volume Purchases

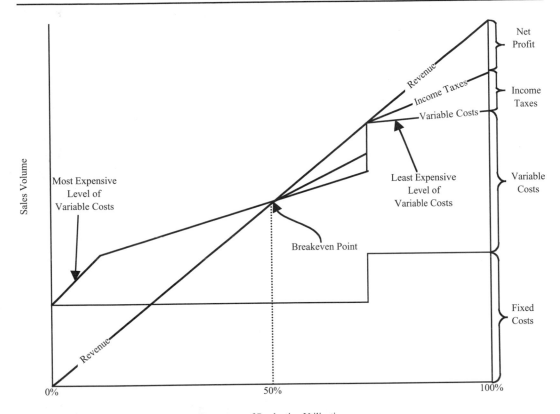

Percentage of Production Utilization

line, progressing from the lower left to the upper right corners of the chart, assumes that the exact same mix of products will be sold at all volume levels. Unfortunately, it is a rare situation indeed where this happens, because one product is bound to become more popular with customers, resulting in greater sales and variation in the overall product mix. If the margins for the different products being sold are different, then any change in the product mix will result in a variation, either up or down, in the sales volume achieved, which can have either a positive or negative impact on the resulting profits. As it is very difficult to predict how the mix of products sold will vary at different volume levels, most company owners do not attempt to alter the mix in their projections, thereby accepting the risk that some variation in mix can occur.

The more common problem that impacts the volume line in the breakeven calculation is that unit prices do not remain the same when volume increases. Instead, a company finds that it can charge a high price early on, when the product is new and competes with few other products in a small niche market. Later, when management decides to go after larger unit volume, unit prices drop in order to secure sales to a larger array of customers or to resellers who have a choice of competing products to resell. For example, the price of a personal computer used to hover around $3,000 and was affordable for less than 10 percent of all households. As of this writing, the price of a personal computer has dropped to as little as $400, resulting in more than 50 percent of all households owning one. Thus, higher volume translates into lower unit prices. The result appears in Figure 7.9, where the revenue per unit gradually declines despite a continuing rise in unit volume, which causes a much slower increase in profits than would be the case if revenues rose in a straight, unaltered line.

The breakeven chart in Figure 7.9 may make management think twice before pursuing a high-volume sales strategy, since profits will not necessarily increase. The only way to be sure of the size of price discounts would be to begin negotiations with resellers or to sell the product in test markets at a range of lower prices to determine changes in volume. Otherwise, management is operating in a vacuum of relevant data. Also, in some cases the only way to survive is to keep cutting prices in pursuit of greater volume, because there are no high-priced market niches in which to sell.

The chart in Figure 7.9 is a good example of what the breakeven analysis really looks like in the marketplace. Fixed costs jump at different capacity levels, variable costs decline at various volume levels, and unit prices drop with increases in volume. Given the fluidity of the model, it is reasonable to revisit it periodically in light of continuing changes in the marketplace in order to update assumptions and make better calculations of breakeven points and projected profit levels.

FIGURE 7.9

Breakeven Chart Including Impact of Variable Pricing Levels

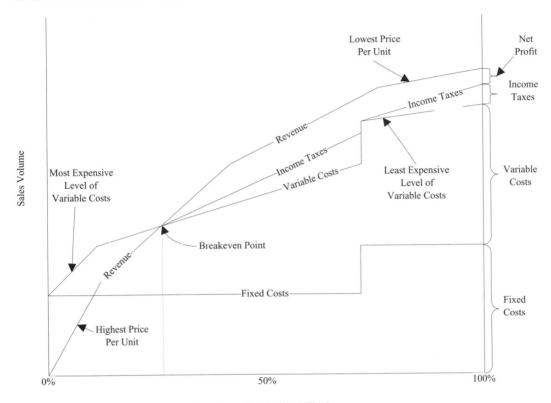

Percentage of Production Utilization

Summary

From a practical perspective, you should use capacity analysis regularly. Doing so can involve the monitoring of: revenue per person, usage levels of various machines, sales per salesperson, or the need for requested capital purchases. All of these issues involve changes in staffing or machinery, which are exceedingly expensive. Accordingly, regularly verify that the organization does not expend too much for excess capacity, instead keeping capacity levels at the highest possible level while ensuring that there is some excess capacity available for short-term growth.

Breakeven analysis should be a required part of any proposal to alter the underlying structure of a business. By reviewing it, you can tell if any alterations, such as to price points, capital expenditures, or the incurrence of new expenses, will have a significant impact on the ability of the organization to exceed its breakeven point on a regular basis.

Chapter 8

Taxes and Risk Management

Many of the tax consequences to a firm are covered in Chapter 9, "Reporting." This chapter points out how to manage taxes on a continuous basis in order to take advantage of the benefits associated with various liability-limiting provisions in the tax code. Without consideration on an ongoing basis, taxes can become a significant drain on the business's cash flow.

If you consider that under the federal corporate tax rates, one of the largest percentage deductions from a company's profits may come as payment of taxes on an annual basis, you quickly realize that significant gains can be made if taxes can be deferred or, better still, eliminated. There are many tax choices available to businesspeople that may eliminate or defer payment of income taxes. Although very few situations permit the permanent deferral of taxes, the law permits temporary deferral of tax payments in certain situations. Such tax deferral has these benefits:

- Deferring taxes lowers a company's cash flow commitment to the government. This means more cash will be available for withdrawal and use for profit-making opportunities.
- If taxes can be deferred long enough, there is a chance that the federal government will change the tax code to make the payment of taxes more favorable or eliminate some tax liability

entirely. In effect, the deferred taxes may be less when paid after the law changes instead of before. The rate, or the method of calculation of liability, could change. Of course, the reverse may also be true.

- A tax deferral is, in effect, an interest-free loan from the federal government. It can be recognized as a valid financing source because there can be no more favorable rate than a zero interest rate for a loan.
- Many tax options are under the company's control. When one option fails to be favorable, it can change to another.

Tax planning can have significant advantages. It can help conserve cash flow by deferring the payment of taxes. It can make available interest-free capital for the financing and purchase of new fixed assets or expansion. It can free up additional cash and make more disposable cash available for payout.

Controlling Tax Liabilities

When planning for treatment of tax expenses, consider these accounting methods and choices of accounting periods for controlling the amount of tax liabilities that may be incurred.

Deferred Installment Sales

A company may be able to defer income if it makes sales of personal property on an installment sales basis. An installment sale is defined for tax purposes as requiring two or more payments. Therefore, a company that sells personal property on a credit basis requiring only one payment in a certain period would not qualify for use of this deferral method. This deferral is permitted even if the overall method of accounting used is an accrual method. The company realizes a cash flow improvement by not having to prepay the tax on profits until they have been realized in cash payments. If you sell on installment sales contracts, do not fail to utilize this deferral method.

Another consideration is the company's credit policy. In establishing a credit policy, the firm should consider the tax advantages of certain installment sales. This deferral gets particularly beneficial if the company is experiencing an increase in accounts receivable. Typically, big-ticket-item retail stores, such as furniture and appliance dealers, can take significant advantage of installment sales deferment. By looking to the installment sales method of tax deferments, the company may not only have the benefit of deferring income taxes, but it may also provide an opportunity to charge slow-paying customers interest in consideration for extended payment terms.

Bad Debt Method

One company may choose to recognize its bad debts for tax purposes at the point where these debts actually become known to be worthless. Another company may set up a reserve and obtain a tax deduction based on an estimate of the debts that will be bad. The reserve method simply accelerates the tax deduction for bad debt, because the deduction is allowed in the year the reserve is established, based on the probability of some accounts going bad, rather than when the specific debt is determined to be bad.

Accounting for Inventory

Sometimes, by changing accounting methods, a company can eliminate short-term profits associated with inflation and the cost of inventory. In other words, if the company has significant inventory levels that were produced at lower costs and it is currently producing inventory at much higher expenses, by selling off the most recently made or purchased inventory items, the company will realize a profit only between the current selling price and the current higher costs. In doing so, the company retains, as a matter of bookkeeping, only old inventory at lower costs. This is a change from a first-in, first-out (FIFO) accounting system to a last-in, first-out (LIFO) system.

State Tax Considerations

When locating offices and plants, a company with multistate operations should take into consideration the states in which legislation has been passed giving lower taxes for business. Lower state taxes can substantially reduce tax liability and will not inhibit the business from engaging in interstate commerce.

Another important consideration is whether the state has a tangible personal property tax. In some states, on particular days of the year, tangible personal property located within the state will be subject to taxation. Many large companies (particularly airlines and railroads) ensure that the majority of their movable assets are not in states that levy tangible personal property taxes on the day of levy.

Consideration of the Taxable Entity

In planning the creation of a business, the principals should consider discussing tax liabilities associated with the various forms of business entities available. Consideration of whether to incorporate or enter partnerships, subchapter S corporations, or domestic/international sales corporations should be reviewed. Each of these has particular tax liabilities. Some of them are associated with particular types of businesses and may not be applicable to the business in which you engage.

Partnerships and subchapter S corporations can be useful to avoid double taxation, which arises because the corporation is taxed on its profits and again when the profits are distributed in the form of dividends. Again, there is an income tax liability associated with a receipt of the dividends by the owners.

Partnerships and subchapter S entities, however, shift income from the entity to the shareholders' or partners' tax return. Tax losses, as well, flow directly through to the owners or partners.

One of the criteria that should be considered when setting up the business entity is the relative tax rate for the individuals as compared to the corporate rate. The corporate rate may be higher than the rate at which the principals are taxed.

The qualifications for subchapter S status change periodically. The Internal Revenue Service (IRS) can provide up-to-date information on revisions.

Financing Considerations for Fixed Assets

Rapid Depreciation Methods. When a fixed asset is purchased, accelerated cost recovery systems can be used, which at the same time increase cash flow. The law in this area changes frequently, and consultation with a good tax advisor will help you to understand how the depreciation deductions work and what is currently available.

Investment Tax Credits. The laws regarding investment tax credits (ITCs) also change frequently. Congress permits and withdraws such credits as a means of altering tax revenue and/or stimulating the economy. A description of the normal situation when an ITC is available follows.

An ITC affords the taxpayer an opportunity to reduce income tax liability by buying or constructing equipment or other qualifying properties. Property that qualifies for ITC normally includes tangible depreciable property, which typically must have a useful life of at least three years. Due regard must be given to the fact that usually no ITC is permitted for buildings or permanent structural components.

In the case of leased property, a lessor for a qualifying piece of property may be able to pass the credit on to the lessee. The ITC or any portion may be carried back for 3 years or carried forward for 15 years. Unused credit for the current year generally is carried back for the earliest carryback year, and any other remaining unused credit is applied to each succeeding year in chronological order.

Again, serious consideration should be given to consulting with a tax advisor in this area. The tax laws change on a regular basis, and before you make any capital decision, you should consider an ITC.

Leasing

There are certain tax benefits to leasing, although the controversy surrounding these benefits still exists. Leasing may have these advantages:

- The cash needed to purchase the property is available for other uses.
- The lessor may pass through the ITC, if any, to the lessee for his or her use. This benefit probably will not be passed on without a corresponding payment to the lessor.
- The lessor bears the risk of obsolescence or loss.
- Lease payments may exceed depreciation and interest. In this respect, it may give the lessee a higher deduction in the form of immediate expense dollars.

Cash Management through Tax Planning

Compensation Plans. There are three types of compensation plans: basic, deferred, and pension- and profit-sharing funds. Funded and unfunded deferred compensation plans offer numerous advantages. For example, in the funded pension plan, the employer's contribution to the fund is currently deductible as an expense. Any earnings generated internally by the trust fund are tax exempt. Finally, the employees are not taxed on an individual basis until after retirement. After retirement, the employee's income should be less than he or she is receiving as an active employee. The employee gets the benefit of a lower tax rate at a later date. This is an income-deferred plan available to employees through the cooperation of their employer. There are firms and businesses that plan compensation packages, which can be very helpful in demonstrating different ways in which a company may save cash flow through the design of compensation plans.

Employees' Stock Ownership. Like compensation plans, many firms offer their employees participatory ownership plans. These plans offer two advantages.

1. By giving the employees some participatory ownership in the firm, there is greater loyalty and greater concern for the firm's well-being. Each employee has a vested interest in the success of the firm. As the firm grows and succeeds, so does the personal worth of the individual.
2. An employee stock ownership plan offers an employer a deduction without the payment of cash. However, when a stock purchase plan causes significant dilution of the ownership, the company may become subject to a suit called a derivative lawsuit by those owners who have had their percentage ownership decreased by sale of additional stock. This is generally associated with the issuance of new stock and is discussed more fully in Chapter 5.

An employee stock ownership plan may use a profit-sharing or stock bonus format. There is a major advantage to a profit-sharing format: It allows distribution of benefits to employees in the form of cash or securities as well as employer stock. This may be an important consideration if the employer's stock is not publicly traded or does not otherwise have a ready market. In a profit-sharing format, there are two basic limitations.

1. The employees' contributions to the stock ownership plan trust may come only from current or accumulated profits.
2. The plan may not borrow funds on the basis of corporate majority stockholder guarantees to purchase employee stock.

Risk Management

A company may have the best business plan on Earth, execute it with precision, and end up with extraordinary profitability—only to lose it all because it failed to consider and guard against the risks to which every business is subject. This risk can range from the effects of weather, such as floods or earthquakes, to lawsuits, such as by competitors for patent infringement or employees for sexual harassment. In this section, we review the policies and procedures that a company should adopt and follow to ensure that it has identified and protected itself against a wide range of risks.

The first step in developing a risk management system is to have the board of directors formally review and approve a set of risk management policies, such as the one shown in Figure 8.1. These policies predominantly address the types and minimum amounts of required insurance coverage, although there should also be a policy regarding the completion and periodic review of a risk management plan.

This policy forces the management team to not only obtain insurance from qualified independent insurance providers, but also (and more important) to create a risk management plan. This plan is designed to identify the major risks to which a company is subject, as well as specify how those risks may be mitigated. A very important point is that, when determining forms of risk mitigation, insurance should be considered the last resort. This is because insurance is designed to pay a company compensation for damages that have already been incurred, whereas a true risk mitigation strategy will prevent losses from ever occurring, so there would be no loss for an insurance company to cover. Accordingly, the steps outlined in this section to develop a risk management plan address only the need for insurance at the end of the process.

Figure 8.1

Risk Management Policies

1. The company will obtain insurance only from companies with an A. M. Best rating of at least B++.
2. The company will create a comprehensive risk management plan, which will be reviewed by the board of directors at least once a year.
3. No insurance may be obtained from captive insurance companies.
4. The company must always have current insurance for the following categories, using the following minimum amounts:
   - $5 million for director's and officer's insurance
   - $10 million for general liability insurance
   - Commercial property insurance, matching the replacement cost of all structures and inventory
   Business interruption insurance, sufficient to support four months of operations

Source: James Willson, Jan Roehl, and Steven M. Bragg, *Controllership* (New York: John Wiley & Sons, 1999), p. 1317. Reprinted with permission.

A management team should use these 12 steps to create a risk management plan.

1. *Appoint a risk manager.* There should be one person in charge of a company's entire risk management program. The reason for this is that, if too many people are involved, it is possible that some high-risk areas will not be addressed, simply because everyone involved thinks that someone else is addressing the problem. Also, this position should be a full-time one in a larger company and occupy a significant proportion of one person's time in a smaller company, which ensures that a sufficient amount of attention is paid to the subject area. The risk manager's job description should include the review of all corporate risks, estimating the probability of loss for each one, selecting and implementing the best methods for reducing the highest-probability risks, ensuring compliance with all governmental insurance requirements, supervising the work of the company's designated insurance broker, maintaining loss records, and periodically reviewing the company's performance under its loss prevention program.

2. *Determine risk areas.* This step involves a detailed review of all possible risk areas in a company. A considerable aid in completing this step is to use a checklist of insurable hazards, which is available from most insurers. Another approach is to review the past history of insurance claims that the company has filed, although this method will not cover any risks that have not yet been realized. If neither of these approaches is available, then at least review the company's risks based on four key areas: facilities and equipment, business interruption, liabilities, and other assets. The review of facilities and equipment should include a detailed assessment of the risks to which each facility is subject (e.g., flooding, fire); the equipment review should take note of explosion and damage risks for each piece of major equipment. The business interruption review should focus on the amount of cash required to keep the business from going bankrupt during a business shutdown. A crucial review is that of liabilities to other parties that are caused by the company's products, employees, or operations.

This review must include an examination of a company's sales and purchase orders, contracts, and leases to see if there are any additional liabilities that the company has undertaken. Finally, there must be a review of a company's cash, accounts receivable, and inventory to see if they are subject to an inordinate risk of loss for any reason. When the review is complete, all of these data should be summarized in preparation for the next step.

3. *Identify risk reduction methods.* Once the key risks have been outlined, they can be reduced. There are three ways to do so. The first is to use *duplication*, which means that a company can make copies of records to avoid the loss of original documents, or duplicate key phone or computer systems to ensure that there is an operational backup, or even set up duplicate fire suppression systems to reduce the risk of fire damage. The second way is to institute *prevention* measures. These can include safety inspections and safety training for employees, as well as the use of mandatory safety equipment, such as hearing protection, to ensure that identifiable risks are eliminated to the greatest extent possible. Finally, a company can *segregate* its assets, spreading them through numerous facilities, to ensure that losses will be minimized if damage occurs to a single location. All of these risk reduction methods must be documented for use in the next step, which involves their implementation.

4. *Implement risk reduction methods.* Implementing the risk reduction methods just outlined is not simple, because they usually involve either a capital expenditure (i.e., for a fire suppression system) that requires prior approval by senior management or some kind of training or inspection that requires the participation of multiple departments. Because of the additional time needed to complete some of these items, it is best to divide them into two groups—those that can be implemented at once without any further approval by anyone, and those requiring approval. The risk manager should implement the first group right away. The second group should be laid out on a project timeline, including expected completion dates, so the risk manager can methodically obtain approvals prior to implementing

them. This approach will ensure that risk mitigation steps are completed in as efficient a manner as possible.

5. *Schedule periodic risk reviews.* Initially setting up a risk management plan is not enough. Although initially it may provide an adequate degree of risk mitigation, the types of risk will change over time, while the types of risk reduction activities being followed may fall into disuse. To keep these problems from occurring, it is important to schedule recurring risk reviews that delve into any changes in risks, as well as the degree to which current risk reduction systems are being used. The result of these reviews should be a report to management and the board of directors regarding any deficiencies in the risk reduction system, as well as recommendations for improvements.

6. *Require insurance from third parties.* We have just outlined a plan for reducing the level of risk in a company's activities without the use of insurance. To take the concept one step further but without going to the expense of purchasing insurance as a form of risk coverage, it may be possible to force customers to *pay* for insurance coverage. A good example of this is in the rental business, where the renting company can require a customer to provide a certificate of insurance from the customer's insurance agency, proving that the customer's insurer will provide coverage for the specific equipment being rented. This approach allows a company to avoid paying for the same coverage itself, although there is some administrative hassle involved in obtaining the certificate of insurance.

7. *Select a broker.* Most insurance companies operate through brokers who are either their sole representatives or independent, and therefore represent numerous insurance companies to their clients. It is generally best to use an independent agent, since this person will work on the company's behalf to search for the best insurance deals from among the most financially stable insurance companies. This person should be thoroughly conversant in the particular insurance needs of the company's industry and be willing to provide in-depth advice regarding the company's insurance needs. The brokers to avoid are those who overemphasize the need for additional insurance coverage when

the apparent risks do not warrant the extra insurance expense. These people are more concerned with earning a few extra commission dollars than with giving a company only the insurance it needs and no more.

8. *Specify types of insurance to acquire.* Review the risk management plan to determine the types and extent of risk that require extra mitigation through the purchase of insurance. For reference, go to the list of standard insurance types listed in the next section. It is important to identify not only the types of insurance needed, but also the amounts. For example, coverage for business interruption insurance should cover all reasonable ongoing expenses during the time period you would reasonably expect a company to require before the business is once again fully operational. Most insurance brokers have standard forms that assist in determining the correct amount of insurance coverage needed.

9. *Acquire insurance.* It is the job of the company's insurance broker to find insurance coverage. This will usually result in a flurry of forms from interested insurance companies that want more data about the organization and the level of risk to be covered. The risk manager must fill out and return these documents in a timely manner to facilitate the insurance acquisition process. In addition, there will likely be inspections by the potential insurers for some types of insurance, such as boiler and machinery insurance, since they must evaluate the condition of the equipment and facility. The risk manager should be on hand to facilitate these tours and provide any additional information needed by the insurance company representatives. The insurers will then submit their bids to the broker, who will evaluate them with the risk manager, resulting in the selection of a group of insurance policies, possibly from a number of insurance companies, that will comprise the company's insurance coverage for the upcoming year.

10. *Create a claims administration process.* Once insurance has been acquired, the risk manager must set up a standard process for claims filings. It is best to have a standard process already in place before the first claim incident occurs. This will speed up

the filing process, thereby improving the company's chances of receiving rapid and full payment from the insurer. The first step in this procedure should be instructions regarding the mitigation of further damages beyond those that have already occurred, because an insurer can rightfully claim that it will provide compensation only for damages that occurred before company personnel were aware of the problem; after that time, the company is responsible for reducing further damages as much as is within its power to do so. The procedure should also include instructions for compiling a complete list of damaged items, including their book values and replacement costs. This procedure should also include the contact name and phone number of an appraiser, in case a quick outside appraisal of damages is needed. The procedure should also include the contact names and phone numbers for insurers, so the correct insurer representatives can be contacted as quickly as possible. Further, the procedure should note the names of all internal personnel who are responsible for investigating damages and filing claims, as well as the employees who fill in for them during their absences. In addition to this basic filing procedure, the risk manager should have a standard investigation form, which is used to inquire into the reasons why damage occurred; although this information may not be requested by an insurer, it is of great value to the risk manager, who can use it to determine the most common causes of damage and then work to reduce those causes.

11. *Create an insurance documentation filing process.* There must be a well-organized filing system in place that will assist the claims administration staff in storing and retrieving insurance documentation. For each insurance claim, there should be a separate file that is indexed by type of insurance. Within each claim file, there should be a complete description of each incident, as well as a sequential record of all events and outcomes, plus the reserves established against each one and its current status. There should also be a tickler file regarding the expiration dates of all insurance policies, so the risk manager will be warned well in advance that renewals must be negotiated. If a policy requires a report to the insurer at regular intervals, this tickler

file should include that information. Finally, there should be a fully updated insurance policy summary containing the key information about each current policy, such as the name of the insurer and broker, contact names and phone numbers, the effective dates of each policy, insurance premiums and surcharge information, plus an abstract of the coverage, listing all inclusions and exclusions. These files are not difficult to create or maintain, but make a great difference to the risk manager in running a tightly organized function that has all relevant information immediately at hand.

12. *Schedule periodic insurance reviews.* In addition to the risk review noted earlier, there should also be an insurance review. This is a review, with the insurance broker present to provide additional clarification, of all risk coverage provided by insurance, as well as a discussion of all risks not covered and that may require insurance. This step should follow every risk review immediately, so that management can custom-tailor its insurance portfolio to more closely match its current risk situation. The normal outcome of this review should be slight adjustments to the types of insurance coverage, the amount of coverage for each type of insurance, and the size of deductibles.

The key document that a risk manager uses is the risk management report. This document summarizes a company's full range of potential risks, analyzes their probability of occurrence, and itemizes the exact ways to mitigate those risks, which may include the use of insurance. It is the result of the work done in the second and third steps of the risk mitigation process noted in this section. An example of a risk management report is shown in Figure 8.2, which includes a short extract from the report for a rock-climbing school (an endeavor in which the control of risk is a major and continuing concern).

The risk management report can be expanded to include a set of policies and procedures that support the actions of the risk manager, as well as a calendar of report and insurance review dates. When complete, this report should be the governing text that the risk manager uses to administer the primary aspects of the risk management function.

FIGURE **8.2**

Example of a Risk Management Report

Section I: Review of Risks
- Risks related to climbing education:
  1. Risk of school equipment failing.
  2. Risk of accidents due to improper instruction.

Section II: Ways to Mitigate Risks
- *Risk of school equipment failing.* School equipment is reviewed and replaced by the school governing body on a regular basis. Instructors are also authorized to immediately remove equipment from use if they spot unusual damage that may result in equipment failure.
- *Risk of accidents due to improper instruction.* School instructors must first serve as assistant instructors under the supervision of a more experienced instructor, who evaluates their skills and recommends advancement to full instructor status. The typical instructor has previously completed all prerequisite courses and has considerable outdoor experience. All instructors must have taken a mountain-oriented first aid class within the last 12 months.

Section III: Supplemental Insurance Coverage
- *Risk of school equipment failing.* The general liability policy covers this risk for the first $500,000 of payments to a claimant. The umbrella policy covers this risk for an additional $5 million after the coverage provided by the general liability policy is exhausted.
- *Risk of accidents due to improper instruction.* This risk is covered by the same insurance coverage as for the risk of school equipment failing.

Source: James Willson, Jan Roehl, and Steven M. Bragg, *Controllership* (New York: John Wiley & Sons, 1999), p. 1325. Reprinted with permission.

Insurance

The last section focused on the checklist of activities that a company should pursue to ensure that it has an adequate risk management system in place. Part of that process included the acquisition of a sufficient amount of insurance to cover a company's risks that cannot be mitigated in any other way. In this section, we describe the types of insurance that provide coverage for most situations. The most common types of insurance are:

- *Boiler and machinery.* This is particularly valuable insurance, because the most reputable insurance providers not only provide coverage for damage to boilers and machinery, and payments for injuries caused by them, but also a complete on-site review of the condition of the equipment, which includes recommendations regarding maintenance and repairs. This extra advice is consistent with the reasoning behind having a risk management plan, which is to keep potential risks from becoming a reality.

- *Business interruption.* This coverage pays for a company's continuing business expenses, and sometimes even the profits it would otherwise have achieved, during a shutdown period. For example, a company would claim payments under this insurance coverage if its facility had burned down, thereby forcing the insurance provider to cover the cost of the company's operations while it rebuilds the facility.
- *Commercial property.* This insurance is sold in two varieties. One is the "basic form," which covers losses due to vandalism, explosions, windstorms, fires, and hail. The "broad form" is an expanded version of the same coverage, which also includes water and snow damage, falling object damage, and some causes for the collapse of buildings.
- *Comprehensive auto liability.* There is usually no choice with this insurance—state law requires it in most locations. States require specific minimum amounts of coverage for losses due to property damage and bodily injury that is caused by company vehicles, or employees driving their own vehicles while on company business.
- *Comprehensive crime.* This policy covers losses due to burglary, robbery, and theft from employees or company premises.
- *Directors and officers.* This is a type of insurance that the board of directors will be adamant about obtaining, especially if a company is publicly held. This insurance protects officers and directors from personal liability for actions they take in association with a company. This is extremely important in today's increasingly litigious environment, where directors and officers can be sued for almost any actual or perceived transgression.
- *Fidelity bond.* A company purchases a fidelity bond to cover either a specific person or job position, or a group of employees. In

either case, the insurer will pay the company for losses brought about by the dishonesty of the person(s) covered under the bond. This bond is used most commonly for people in the accounting and finance areas.

- *General liability.* Although not mandatory, you should strongly consider obtaining general liability insurance, since this provides coverage against incidents that can have such large payouts that they will ruin a company. The incidents covered are liability arising from accidents at any company facility, as well as ones caused by its products, services, or agents. The dollar amount of the coverage can be greatly increased with an umbrella policy, which provides extra coverage after the first round of coverage is used to settle claims. This umbrella coverage is relatively inexpensive in comparison to the initial general liability policy on which it is based, since it is so rarely used.

- *Group life, health, and disability.* These types of coverage are offered separately and are intended to be a benefit to employees, rather than a form of risk management. Group life insurance typically is offered to employees either for free or at a nominal charge, with the possible option of added coverage at each employee's expense. Health insurance coverage usually is offered to all employees after a short trial period, such as 90 days of employment; a company may offer this insurance at the full price charged by the insurer, or discount it to varying degrees as an added benefit. Finally, a company can offer its staff both long-term and short-term disability insurance, either at full price or at a discounted rate. For all these types of insurance, the primary benefit to the employee is that the coverage simply is being made available to them, because many would otherwise be unable to obtain coverage at any price due to preexisting medical conditions.

- *Inland marine.* A better name for this coverage is "transportation insurance," because it covers damage to company products that are being transported, such as marketing displays or finished goods.

- *Ocean marine and air cargo.* This covers damage to or loss of transportation equipment, such as a freight-hauling truck, plus its cargo and liability claims against the owner of the vehicle. This coverage is obtained most commonly by freight hauling companies and is of little concern to organizations that contract out their freight hauling to third parties.

- *Split-Dollar Life Insurance.* A split-dollar life insurance plan is a way in which a company can create significant cash reserves through the payment of employee life insurance while at the same time offering the employee a benefit in the form of a term life insurance policy. The insurance policy is not actually a term insurance policy except as it appears to the employee. The employee is sold life insurance protection at low cost, but the company owns the cash surrender value of the policy. Under such an agreement, the employee has the benefit of the insurance and the company has a significant portion of the cash surrender value. Under most policy provisions, the cash surrender value can be borrowed against. This offers a low-cost source of additional capital.

- *Workers' compensation.* This coverage is required by government. It pays employees for medical and disability expenses for injuries sustained on the job. Its main advantage from the employer's perspective is that having the insurance legally keeps a company from being liable for additional payments to employees. However, the allowability of negligence lawsuits varies in accordance with the statutes of individual states. This can be very expensive insurance for those companies in high-risk fields, such as manufacturing. A company can greatly reduce the cost of this insurance by working with the insurance provider to reclassify some employees into insurance classifications that are perceived to be less risky, and therefore less expensive, such as office workers and sales staff.

For other types of specialty insurance that are not listed here, a company should work with a broker to obtain them through specialty insurance providers. Examples of this type of coverage include damage to an actor's voice, a dancer's legs, or a pianist's fingers. However, most companies can obtain adequate coverage with the more common types of insurance noted in this section.

Types of Insurance Companies

There are several types of insurance companies. Each one may serve a company's insurance needs very well, but there are significant differences between them that a company should be aware of before purchasing an insurance contract. The types of insurance companies include:

- *Captive insurance company.* This is a stock insurance company that is formed to underwrite the risks of its parent company or in some cases a sponsoring group or association.
- *Lloyds of London.* This is an underwriter operating under the special authority of the English Parliament. It may write insurance coverage of a nature that other insurance companies will not underwrite, usually because of high risks or special needs not covered by a standard insurance form. It also provides the usual types of insurance coverage.
- *Mutual.* This is a company in which each policyholder is an owner and where earnings are distributed as dividends. If a net loss results, policyholders may be subject to extra assessments. In most cases, however, nonassessable policies are issued.
- *Reciprocal organization.* This is an association of insured companies that is independently operated by a manager. Advance deposits are made, against which are charged the proportionate costs of operations.
- *Stock company.* This is an insurance company that behaves like a normal corporation—earnings not retained in the business are distributed to shareholders as dividends and not to policyholders.

Another way to categorize insurance companies is by the type of service offered. For example, a *monoline* company provides only one type of insurance coverage, while a *multiple-line* company provides more than one kind of insurance. A *financial services company* provides not only insurance but also financial services to customers.

A company can also use *self-insurance* when it deliberately plans to cover losses from its own resources rather than through those of an insurer. Self-insurance can be appropriate in any of these cases:

- When the administrative loss of using an insurer exceeds the amount of the loss
- When a company has sufficient excess resources available to cover even the largest claim
- When excessive premium payments are the only alternative
- When insurance is not available at any price

A form of partial self-insurance is to use large deductibles on insurance policies, so that a company pays for all but the very largest claims.

In some states, a company can become a self-insurer for workers' compensation. To do this, a company must qualify under state law as a self-insurer, purchase umbrella coverage to guard against catastrophic claims, post a surety bond, and create a claims administration department to handle claims. The advantages of doing this are lower costs (by eliminating the insurer's profit) and better cash flow (because there are no up-front insurance payments). The disadvantages of this approach are extra administrative costs as well as the cost of qualifying the company in each state in which the company operates.

These are some of the variations that a company can consider when purchasing insurance, either through a third party, a controlled subsidiary, or by providing its own coverage.

Claims Administration

Some insurance companies take an extremely long time to respond to claims and may reject them if they are not reported in a specific format. To avoid these problems and receive the full amount of claims as quickly as possible, consider implementing a strict claims administration process.

Claims administration involves assembling a summary of information to review whenever a claim is filed. By having this information in one place, you can avoid missing any steps that might interfere with the prompt settlement of a claim. The summary should include:

- *Instructions for itemizing damaged items.* Be sure to compile a complete list of all damaged items, including their inventory values, estimates, appraisals, and replacement costs. This assists the claims adjusters in determining the price they will pay to compensate for any claims.
- *Claims representatives.* There should be a list of the names, addresses, and phone numbers of the claims adjusters who handle each line of insurance. Such a list usually requires a fair amount of updating, because there may be a number of changes to this information every year, especially if a company uses a large number of insurance companies for its various types of risk coverage.
- *Key internal personnel.* Company policy may require that key personnel be notified if claims have been filed or payments received on those claims. For example, the accountant may want to know if payment for a large claim has been received, so that an entry can be made in the accounting records.
- *Underlying problems.* Have a standard group of follow-up steps available to review whenever a claim occurs, so that there is a clear understanding of why a claim occurred as well as how the underlying problem that caused the claim can be avoided in the future. Without these instructions, a company may repeat the problem over and over again, resulting in many claims and a vastly increased insurance premium.
- *Instructions for safeguarding damaged items.* If material has been damaged, it is the responsibility of the company to ensure that it is not damaged further, which would result in a larger claim. For example, a company must protect the materials in a warehouse from further damage as soon as it discovers that the roof has leaked and destroyed some items. If it does not take this action, the insurer can rightly claim that it will pay for only the damage that occurred up to the point when the company could have taken corrective action.

All this information is necessary for the filing of every insurance claim. In addition, there are two steps related to claims administration to attend to on an ongoing basis.

1. *Accounting techniques.* Work with the accountant to develop a standard set of accounting entries that are used for insurance claims as well as summarizing the cost of risk management. These relate to accumulating cost information for each claim, so you can easily summarize the appropriate information related to each claim and use it to file for reimbursement. This information should include the costs of claims preparation, security and property protection, cleanup, repair costs, property identification, and storage costs.
2. *Audit program.* No matter how good the procedures may be for the claims administration process, it is common for the claims administration staff to forget or sidestep some procedures. This is especially common when there is frequent employee turnover in this area, with poor training of the replacement staff. To identify procedural problems, it is useful to conduct a periodic review of the claims administration process. To ensure consistency in this audit, there should be a standard audit program that forms the minimum set of audit instructions (to be expanded on as needed) for use in conducting each audit.

It can be cost effective to have some claims administered by outside service companies, quite often by the insurance carrier itself. Usually high-volume, low-cost-per-unit items such as medical claims are in this category. When outside services are used, establish with the provider the controls to be followed and the reports to be prepared. Periodic audits of the outside claims processing operation should be made by the company to ensure that claims are being handled in a controlled and effective manner.

Summary

A company should plan for the tax effect of its decisions on a daily basis. Certainly each financial decision and most operational decisions have direct, if not immediate, tax consequences. Knowing what the tax effects are may enable the company to defer the payment of taxes. Many large firms use tax deferral methods to postpone the payment of some taxes indefinitely.

The form of the business—whether a corporation, an S corporation, a partnership, or a sole proprietorship—changes the form of reporting and the nature of the tax liability. You should look at the tax rates applicable to the entities at various income levels.

Liabilities should be calculated using various scenarios dealing with both the level of income and the payment of that income under various business formats. As income grows and the business prospers, changing the business form may be an integral part of the business plan. Methods of financing capital assets have tax consequences that should be part of the acquisition plan.

Overall, the business should integrate tax planning as part of the operating budget and capital budgeting functions of the business. When taxes cannot be reduced, sometimes they can be deferred, which in some cases can be almost as good as nonpayment.

Finally, develop a risk management plan and review the company's insurance coverage on a regular basis. Often opportunities to reduce costs are available through the development of a comprehensive risk management plan. As a result, policies may be changed, consolidated, discontinued, or altered.

Chapter 9

Reporting

Every business organization has numerous reporting responsibilities. In this chapter, we discuss some of the reporting requirements of the federal, state, and local governments; creditors; and equity owners. In view of the variety of responsibilities that governmental units place on various types of businesses, you are advised to use the services of a competent accountant and/or attorney to ensure compliance with all reporting requirements.

Federal Government Requirements

Federal Employer Identification Number

Every new business must file for and obtain a proper federal employer identification (FEI) number from the federal government. This number identifies the business and is the key for filing and reporting taxes. All federal taxes paid or filed by a business use the FEI as a reference. It is obtained on request by filling out Federal Form SS-4. Some states also use an employer identification number of their own. Information concerning this requirement may be obtained by contacting your state's department of revenue or taxation.

The FEI number is used to identify the business entity for more than tax purposes. Other federal agencies reference the number for compilation of other information relative to business activities such as employment statistics. It is comparable to an individual's Social Security number.

Employment Reports

When a business employs and pays wages to even one employee, it becomes subject to the reporting provisions dealing with payroll taxes. As an employer, the company is responsible for the state and federal income taxes and Social Security taxes withheld from its employees' paychecks and for the taxes assessed directly against it, such as Social Security and unemployment. Payroll taxes must be deposited by specific dates, which vary according to the amounts payable. Contact the Internal Revenue Service for booklets providing this information. Key employment reporting issues follow.

- *New employees.* Employers are required to have each new employee fill out a W-4 form. This form requires the employee to produce a Social Security number. On the W-4 form, the employee specifies the number of withholding allowances claimed. With that number, and the marital status and salary of the individual, withholding tax amounts can be computed. The I-9 form also is required as proof of an employee's right to work and citizenship.
- *Social Security taxes.* Social Security taxes are calculated at rates that vary almost annually. This tax is paid by both the employer and the employee. The employer not only has to withhold appropriate amounts, but also contributes to this fund.
- *FUTA (Federal Unemployment Tax).* This tax is deposited, reported, and paid by the employer only. The tax applies to wages paid to each employee during the calendar year up to a maximum. Once an employee reaches this cap, no additional tax is due.

The income tax and the Social Security tax must be withheld, deposited, reported, and paid by employers to the government. The Social Security tax withheld from the employee is matched by the employer when deposited.

What Wages Are Subject to Taxes? The Internal Revenue Service (IRS) makes available publications on what constitutes wages for the purpose of tax liabilities. Essentially, wages subject to taxes include all compensation given to an employee for services performed. The pay may be in cash, vacation allowances, bonuses, and commissions. Other special considerations to be checked in current IRS publications include:

- Partially exempt employment
- Moving expenses
- Fringe benefits
- Taxable tips

Depositing Taxes. Federal deposit coupon books (Form 8109) are used to deposit paid and withheld taxes. The preprinted coupons are basically a form with boxes for the amount of each tax paid, the FEI number, and the tax period against which the payment is being made. The coupon is mailed or delivered along with a single payment covering the taxes to a federal reserve bank (serving the employer's area) or, more likely, to an authorized financial institution. The frequency of payment depends on the amount due at the end of the month; you should determine the required deposit periods in consultation with an accountant.

Filing Returns and Reporting Taxes. FUTA taxes are reported quarterly, using Form 940. The deposit is due by the last day of the first month after the quarter. If the amount due for any quarter is less than $100, it may be carried over and paid in the next quarter's report.

For income taxes withheld and for Social Security (FICA) taxes, the employer files a quarterly report on federal Form 941. There are some exceptions to this rule related to agricultural employers, household employers, state and local governments, and some others.

Willful failure to file returns and pay taxes when due will result in criminal and civil penalties. The same is true for willful filing of false or fraudulent returns. In some cases in which income and Social Security taxes are not withheld and not paid to the IRS, individuals of the corporation or partnership may be held individually liable for the payment of these taxes along with a penalty of up to 100 percent of the taxes wrongfully uncollected.

Wages and Tax Statement. By January 31 of each year, an employer must provide each employee a statement of wages and taxes. This report, form W-2, includes all wages, tips, other compensations, and withheld income and Social Security taxes. Other payments may be included when applicable: bonuses, vacation allowances, severance pay, moving expenses, taxable fringe benefits, some kinds of travel expenses, and others.

Income Tax Return

Tax rules vary according to whether the operation of the business is as a sole proprietorship, a partnership, a regular C corporation, or an S corporation. These tax rules may affect how the firm carries out its business activities.

Sole Proprietorships. In order to qualify as a sole proprietorship, you must be self-employed and the sole owner of an unincorporated business. Schedule C is filed with a federal Form 1040 (personal tax return) by April 15 of the year following the fiscal year reported.

In a sole proprietorship, there is no tax effect for taking money out of the business for personal use or transferring personal money to the business. However, you should set up and keep separate accounts to keep track of identifiable business expenses and personal withdrawals. Failure to keep adequate business records has been the downfall of many sole proprietorships.

Partnerships. A partnership is the relationship between two or more persons for the purpose of carrying out a trade or business for a profit. Each person contributes money, property, labor, or skill, expecting to share in the profits or losses of the enterprise.

If a husband and wife carry on a business together and expect to share in the profits and losses, they may come under the definition of a partnership for the purposes of taxes. This may occur even by operation of law, where the husband and wife have not executed a form of partnership agreement.

Income from a partnership is reported on Form 1065, U.S. Partnership Return of Income. Also included will be a separate schedule SE, Computation of Social Security Self-Employment Tax. These are "information only" returns. Taxes will be paid in quarterly estimates as a part of the partners' personal (1040) tax reporting.

But for a few exceptions, a partnership determines its income in much the same way that an individual determines his or her income. In determining their income tax liability for the year on their own income tax returns, partners must take into account, separately, each partner's *distributive share*. This consideration must be made whether these items are distributed or not:

- Gains or losses associated with the sale of capital assets
- Gains or losses from sale or exchange of certain property used by the business
- Charitable contributions
- Dividends or interest for which there is an exclusion or deduction
- Other items of income, gains, or losses, as explained in Schedule K, Form 1065

Corporations. Many areas of corporate taxation are quite complex and cannot adequately be dealt with here. For a more complete discussion of corporate tax consequences, the IRS publication 542, Tax Information on Corporations, may be helpful to you.

Every corporation must file a tax return, even if it had no taxable income for the year and regardless of the amount of its gross income for the year. The income tax return for the regular corporation is Form 1120. As in the case of individual taxpayers, the federal government has a short-form application for taxes of small U.S. corporations: Form 1120-A, U.S. Short-Form Corporation Income Tax Return. In order to qualify to use the short form, the business must meet certain requirements, which have usually been:

- Gross receipts do not exceed $500,000.
- Total income does not exceed $500,000.
- Total assets do not exceed $500,000.

- No foreign owners, direct or indirect, of 50 percent or more of its stock.
- It is not a member of a controlled group or a personal holding company.
- It is not a consolidated corporation return filer.
- It is not undergoing liquidation or dissolution.
- It does not owe alternative minimum tax.
- It is not an S corporation, life or mutual insurance company, or other company filing a specialized form. For more information, use the instructions for Forms 1120 and 1120-A.

If the corporation files a return on a calendar-year basis, then the return is to be filed by March 15 following the calendar year. If the corporation uses a fiscal year other than a calendar year, then the report must be filed by the fifteenth day of the third month after the fiscal year. The return is filed with the Internal Revenue Office serving the area where the corporation maintains its principal office—that is, where it maintains its principal books and records.

A corporation will receive an automatic six-month extension for filing a return by submitting an application for an extension on Form 7004. The IRS can terminate this extension at any time prior to the expiration of the six-month period. Interest is charged on the difference between the tentative tax reported on Form 7004 and the actual tax the corporation must pay when it files its Form 1120.

Failure to file on the date required without good cause shown may result in the imposition of a delinquency penalty of 5 percent of the tax due. This penalty will apply to the first month due and may be increased by 5 percent per month for each subsequent month, up to a cap of 25 percent. To avoid penalties, you will have to give an explanation of good cause; that statement will be made under penalty of perjury.

If after filing Form 1120 or 1120-A you wish to correct an error on the return, you may do so by filing a Form 1120X, Amended U.S. Corporation Income Tax Return. You can use this method when you discover that you may have misstated income or failed to claim a deduction or credit.

Estimated Income Tax. Many, if not most, corporations are required to file and pay an estimated tax. A corporation's estimated tax is the amount of its expected tax liability less its allowable tax credits. This estimated tax must be deposited with an authorized financial institution or a federal reserve bank. Each tax payment must be accompanied by a federal tax deposit coupon, according to the instructions in the coupon book.

S Corporations. Some business owners prefer not to be subject to federal corporate income tax liability. If the corporation qualifies, its income will be taxed to the shareholders individually, like a partnership, rather than the corporation. For a complete discussion of the tax liabilities and calculations, the Internal Revenue Service provides publication 589, *Tax Information on S Corporations.*

To qualify as an S corporation, these requirements normally have been applicable:

- All shareholders must elect to be an S corporation.
- The corporation must have a permitted tax year.
- The corporation must file Form 2553, *Election by a Small Business Corporation,* indicating the choice to be treated as an S corporation.
- It must be a domestic corporation.
- It must have only one class of stock.
- It must not have more than 35 stockholders.
- It must have only individuals or their estates as stockholders.
- It must not have a nonresident alien as a shareholder.
- It must not be a member of an affiliated group of corporations.
- It must not be:
  - A domestic international sales corporation.
  - A company that serves as a financial institution, taking deposits and making loans.
  - An insurance company taxed under Subchapter L.

The permitted tax year is generally a calendar year ending December 31. Other years may be requested but require approval from the IRS.

Other Specialized Reporting Areas

Specialized Business. Businesses such as those dealing in firearms sales and transportation, tobacco sales, liquors and spirits, ethanol production, travel agencies, and others have special reports. Most have some relation to the health, safety, morals, and welfare of citizens. These reporting requirements vary for different businesses. For example, dealers in firearms require federal licenses depending on whether the dealer sells rifles and shotguns or handguns, or transports weapons in interstate commerce. In addition, sales have to be reported on various forms prepared and submitted by the dealer.

Special Agencies. Many federal agencies require periodic and regular reporting of various business functions. Examples of agencies requiring reporting are the Environmental Protection Agency (EPA)—air and water quality; Occupational Safety and Health Administration (OSHA)—workplace safety and employee health; Federal Energy Regulatory Commission—utility fuel costs; Interstate Commerce Commission (ICC)—motor and rail carrier rates and charges; Federal Communications Commission: depreciation rates, service charges, and terms and conditions of service.

The discussion of federal reporting requirements has been, by necessity, brief and general. An accountant and/or attorney should be consulted to assure compliance with all reporting requirements. Also, it is a good idea to make use of the publications provided by the various agencies.

State Government Requirements

Unemployment Insurance

Unemployment insurance provides a temporary source of income to make up a part of the wages lost by workers who lose their jobs through no fault of their own and who are willing and able to work. Although the programs may vary from state to state, this description is representative.

The employer generally pays for unemployment insurance as

one of its businesses expenses. Typically, workers pay no part of the premium. The premiums go into a reserve fund to pay claims as they arise. Many states consider the stability of an employer's employment history when establishing a tax rate.

New employers are required to report initial employment in the month following the calendar quarter in which employment begins. The regulating agency then determines whether the employer is liable for taxes. Typical state eligibility requirements include:

- That in a calendar year a business has a $1,500 quarterly payroll or one or more employees
- Liability for federal unemployment tax
- Purchase of a liable business

If the employer is liable for the payment of unemployment insurance, it will be required to make periodic reports and payments of taxes. It may be required to report:

- Total wages paid to covered workers, excess wages, taxable wages, and taxes due
- Individual wage listings with each employee's Social Security number, name, weeks worked, and total wages paid

This report usually is required to be filed along with the proper amount of taxes one month after the quarter in which the qualifying employment occurred. Timely filing is necessary in order to:

- Receive the maximum amount of credit against the federal unemployment tax for the state unemployment taxes paid
- Get proper credit for calculating the experience rating
- Avoid penalty and interest charges established by law for late payment and late reports

Sales and Use Taxes

Sales and use taxes vary greatly from state to state. Their applicability, rates, and exemptions from taxation are dissimilar across state boundaries. In addition, many countries and cities have local option sales and special use taxes. Information relative to the employer's state and local government should be obtained from the offices of the state department of revenue or taxation *and* from the county or city government. This discussion will serve as an example but may not be typical of your state.

Registration. Every person, partnership, corporation, or S corporation desiring to engage in business in the state generally will be required to secure a certificate of registration for each place of business within the state. A business may not have to comply with this requirement if it is engaging in an enterprise not subject to sales and use tax. There is usually a nominal fee ($5–$25) associated with the filing for a certificate. Sales tax of about 4 to 8 percent is levied on qualifying sales made within a state. A use tax is generally the same rate, but the tax is paid on qualifying items brought into the state to be used, consumed, distributed, rented, or stored for use or consumption.

Exemptions in Some States Include:

- Groceries and produce, except those prepared within a premise for consumption
- Medical—prescription and household medicines
- Telephone and utility service (other taxes, however, may apply to these transactions)
- Sale of livestock, poultry, and produce if the sales are made by the producers
- Professional services
- Subscriptions
- Rentals

Payments. Sales taxes are usually payable to the state by a certain date, for example, the twentieth day of the month following the collection of the tax. Some states offer quarterly filing of the tax if the tax remittance is sufficiently low, though monthly filing is more common. Some states allow the business or person collecting the tax to retain a portion of the collection as a fee for the collection process itself. Finally, items purchased for resale may be exempt from the tax, in order to avoid double taxation of an item.

State Corporate Income Taxes

Many states have a form of corporate income taxes. These taxes are imposed on all domestic and foreign corporations for the privilege of doing business or earning or receiving income within the state. Generally, individuals, partnerships, and estates or trusts are not liable for this tax.

Reporting.   A return is generally required by a state if (1) a federal income tax return is filed or (2) the taxpayer is liable for payment of taxes. The return is usually filed on the first day of the fourth month after the close of the taxable year or the fifteenth day after the due date for the filing of the related federal returns for the taxable year. Some states allow for automatic extensions. However, they usually require payment of estimated taxes. Any underpayment of estimated taxes usually will be assessed both penalty and interest. These can be as much as 12 to 15 percent on the amount of underpayment. Remittance of the tax is due at the same time the return is filed. Some states have provisions related to the federal penalty provisions for nonfiling without just cause. Interest generally is applicable at a fixed rate, and the state may even penalize a company for fraudulent returns. Some states assess a penalty for failure to file a return even when no taxes are due.

Tax Basis and Rates.   The tax generally is applicable to all forms of income, including capital gains at (usually) a uniform rate. States typically model their code provisions so as to be consistent with applicable federal code provisions.

Individual Income Tax

If the business operates as a sole proprietorship, a partnership, or an S corporation, the profits may be subject to individual state income taxes. One of the initial considerations that should be made in setting up the form of business is the tax considerations of the entity and the individuals involved. Therefore, the state's individual personal income tax (if it has one) may be a valid consideration in the operation of the business and the policy for the distribution of profits.

Other Possible Tax Returns

Intangible Tax.   Intangible taxes are levied on the ownership, control, or custody of taxable intangibles, such as notes, bonds, and other obligations to pay money that are secured by a mortgage, deed of trust, or other lien on real property within the state. In addition, the state generally levies this tax on shares of stock in incorporated businesses, bonds, notes, accounts receivable, and other obligations for payment.

Ad Valorem Tax.   Ad valorem tax is a tax on the value of real estate as assessed by a duly authorized appraiser appointed or elected to serve in that capacity. The rate of taxation—the millage—usually is expressed in one-thousandths of a dollar. For example, 23 mils means $.0023. Various states and even counties within a state apply various rates (and even various values) for tax purposes. This tax applies to land, buildings, fixtures, and all other improvements to real estate physically located within a jurisdiction.

Some states may have special taxing districts that assess an ad valorem tax on the property for special services (water management, flood control, fire, school, and many others).

Documentary Stamp Taxes.   Documentary stamp taxes are taxes assessed against the execution of certain documents. Although varying in rates across states, this tax generally is applicable on promissory notes, mortgages, trust deeds, security agreements, and other written promises to pay money. Typically not a significant tax (usually being about $.15–$.20 per $100 face value), it is an obligation that must be met in the consummation of certain financial transactions.

Tangible Personal Property Tax.   Tangible personal property taxes, like ad valorem (real property) taxes, generally are assessed by counties at a rate sometimes equal to the ad valorem tax. This tax is based on the assessed value or the value declared by the owner, for business supplies, fixtures, furnishings, and so on. Some states extend this tax to motor vehicles, rail cars, trucks, buses, aircraft, and even ships and boats. Often states that exempt these items from this tax collect a like amount through licenses. Some states include inventories and work-in-process in this class of taxable property.

Others. States may have enacted various other miscellaneous taxes and fees that may impose both a reporting and filing requirement. For example:

- *Charter tax:* A fee or tax associated with the filing of articles of incorporation, amendment to the articles, merger, consolidation, or dissolution
- *Excise tax:* Tax usually collected directly from the ultimate consumer on the sale of utility services

Local Government Requirements

Local governments—cities and counties—have varying amounts of licensing and taxing authority. These powers arise as a result of constitutional provisions, state statutes, county ordinances, special acts of state legislatures, and charters and municipal code provisions. Some of these requirements may include:

- *Occupational licenses.* Counties and incorporated municipalities may be authorized to levy a tax for the privilege of engaging in or managing a business, profession, or occupation within the jurisdiction. The basis and rates for license payments vary considerably. Inquiries concerning these restrictions usually can be handled by individual county or city clerks.
- *Zoning restrictions.* Land use restrictions and limitations may be governed by a local zoning board. This may be under the authority of city or county governments. Zoning restrictions usually are established for an area or a parcel. Variances to restrictions may be petitioned for on an exceptional basis. Often the nature, character, and use of parcels will change over time, bringing about updating and change to land use plans. For example, with the growth of suburbs, land previously zoned agricultural may be changed to residential; some may change to commercial to accommodate malls, shopping areas, and business activities.

- *Sales taxes.* Sometimes counties or cities impose local option sales taxes. These may be ongoing taxes or may have limited durations designed to meet specific needs (e.g., construction of a jail or courthouse, road improvement, modernizing a hospital or school). These taxes may be collected by the state and remitted back to the city or county.
- *Gasoline and special fuels taxes.* Generally all gasoline and diesel fuel used for on-road vehicles is taxed by the state and federal governments. However, counties may have an additional local option tax. Sometimes special fuels sold for residential, agricultural, or commercial marine purposes are exempt from this tax.
- *Local income taxes.* Some large cities (notably New York) have local income taxes. These are levied in addition to federal and state income taxes. There is often a credit or deduction applicable for state and local income taxes against federal income tax.

Creditors

Companies that have advanced credit to a business or that have invested money in the enterprise want to know how their investment is faring. Generally they will insist on some form of status report on a timely basis—weekly, monthly, quarterly, or other regular period. The frequency of the necessary reporting will depend on various factors: risk, volatility of the market, past performances, solvency, and others.

Often several documents must be prepared (balance sheet, income statement, cash flow statement) to inform creditors of the business status and financial conditions.

Together these reports afford a comprehensive model of the operations, liquidity, and the past and current operations of the business. Creditors may also request pro forma or forward-looking financial statements to create an educated future forecast of the business operations of the enterprise.

When loaning money to a business, creditors may require notes and mortgages to carry conditions or covenants. In Chapter 5, we explained how the investors of debt capital probably will condition the loans on a showing of certain ratios. We also discussed how you can and should, to the extent practicable, negotiate these covenants. Covenants are conditions or assurances. They may include:

- Maintenance of specified current ratios or quick ratios
- Limitations on payments or salaries to officers or directors
- Ratios of debt to equity
- Restrictions on dividend payments
- Restrictions on additional debt obligations

Equity Holders

Equity holders are not dissimilar to creditors in their interest in the business results. Secured debt holders have a lien against the property superior in claim to equity holders in the case of default. Debt holders have a superior claim to the equity holder's claim. Equity holders have claims to dividends in after-tax dollars (if any). Therefore, the risk to equity holders is higher and, with luck, so is the expected return.

Management Reports

Chapter 1 discussed how a business generates a budget for operations including targets for materials, and labor and overhead by product and/or by operation. These operating budgets are monthly projections and targets against which actual performance can and should be measured. An overall report against the business plan should be prepared to ensure that the objectives set are being approached. These reports can be generated based on standards showing variances from plan. Variance reporting permits you to address variances with reports of performance and exception reports, which identify reasons for the various and curative steps taken.

Thus far, we have concentrated on reporting requirements to entities outside of a company. There are also a wide range of reports that a management team will want to see that clearly outline its internal performance. We review some of the more useful internal management reports in this section.

In any operation, there are a number of statistics that management wants to review every day. These will vary by type of company, because every business operates in a unique manner that requires a tight focus on different performance measurements. Some information will be common to all such reports, such as the daily cash balance or sales from the previous day. Others, such as the production scrap percentage, will be useful only to a manufacturing company, whereas the number of meals served will be of more consequence to a restaurant. The key underlying reason for adding any measurement to a daily management report is that excluding it could harm operations. This criterion should keep the number of measures on the daily report quite low, usually in the range of two to six measures. Because there are so few of them, they are generally disseminated to management in an informal manner—not in a paper-based report, but rather by voice mail or e-mail. An example of the daily management report, if sent by e-mail, follows.

> Here is the daily management statistics report. Sales yesterday were $120,000, and month-to-date sales were $1,320,000. The cash balance is $275,000. Yesterday's average machine utilization was 72 percent, scrap was 4 percent, and employee overtime was 14 percent.

By keeping the amount of information in the report to just the few key items that management needs to run the business on a daily basis, the report avoids bogging down the recipient in excessive detail. The report should be issued as early in the day as possible, so that the management team has the bulk of the day in which to follow up on the information.

In addition to the daily report, there should be a more comprehensive weekly report that summarizes a business's main operating statistics, as well as a few key financial figures. It is best to cluster the statistics within the report by department, so that department managers can spot all of the measures that pertain to them without any searching. Also, the report format should include the average measures for each of the last three months, plus the previous weekly measures for the current month; this format presents the reader with a trend line of information from previous periods that reveals any significant changes in the statistics. Finally, every effort should be made to keep the report to one page. The intent is not to overwhelm management with too much data, but rather to focus its attention on only the most important statistics. Very few businesses require more than one page to convey this information. An example of such a weekly management statistics report is shown in Figure 9.1.

Note that Figure 9.1 contains the key statistics for five departments and working capital, which is recorded as if it were a separate department. This is because working capital is an extremely important use of cash that must be kept clearly in front of the management team.

A few variations can be included in the weekly management statistics report. One is to add a column listing the goal for each statistic. For example, the inventory accuracy goal may be set at 95 percent, the backlog goal at $3 million, and the machine utilization percentage at 75 percent. This is a useful tool if the management team appears complacent in accepting performance levels that are lower than the goals. You can also add comments to the report. The simplest kind is to list unusual statistics in bold, to make them more prominent. For example, an unusually low cash balance can be highlighted in bold. Also, if the report is maintained on an electronic spreadsheet, such as Excel, you can include comment fields for any cell in the worksheet. These comments are most useful for describing the calculation methods used for each statistic, which readers can access if they have the file (which can be distributed to them each week by e-mail). A spreadsheet containing the goals column and field comments is shown in Figure 9.2. All of these changes improve the informational content and clarity of the weekly management statistics report.

This weekly report is the primary one that management will use to ascertain the condition of a business. However, the information presented in it does not give management a sufficient level of detail to determine the exact causes of problems that are affecting the statistics. To resolve this issue, additional reports are needed. For example, if a company is plagued with high overtime costs, then

FIGURE 9.1

Weekly Management Statistics Report

	Current Month					March	February	January
	Week 5	Week 4	Week 3	Week 2	Week 1			
Engineering								
Bill of Material Accuracy	92%	90%	87%	85%	80%	72%	68%	64%
Finance								
Cash Balance (000s)	$172	$198	$154	$123	$191	$208	$175	$163
Loans Available	$1,071	$1,203	$1,541	$1,678	$1,400	$1,378	$1,205	$1,556
Logistics								
Inventory Accuracy	99%	91%	83%	80%	89%	85%	79%	76%
On-Time Shipping	81%	90%	85%	84%	79%	75%	74%	73%
Customer Returns (000s)	$27	$25	$21	$36	$29	$78	$102	$139
Production								
Machine Utilization	65%	64%	60%	78%	81%	75%	70%	71%
Overtime	8%	10%	12%	7%	11%	10%	9%	12%
Production Schedule Completed	94%	92%	99%	100%	79%	81%	85%	83%
Scrap	4%	3%	4%	2%	1%	5%	4%	3%
Sales								
Backlog (000s)	$2,806	$2,809	$2,819	$2,876	$2,901	$2,904	$2,611	$2,605
Lost Customers	0	−2	−3	−1	0	−2	−7	−11
New Customers	2	3	1	4	0	0	5	8
Period Sales (000s)	$317	$289	$309	$321	$350	$1,251	$1,279	$1,321
Working Capital								
+ Accounts Receivable (000s)	$1,218	$1,327	$1,287	$1,285	$1,270	$1,300	$1,325	$1,330
+ Inventory (000s)	$1,707	$1,754	$1,732	$1,702	$1,659	$1,654	$1,632	$1,607
− Accounts Payable (000s)	$1,100	$1,103	$1,145	$1,307	$1,245	$1,301	$1,247	$1,225
Total Working Capital (000s)	$1,825	$1,978	$1,874	$1,680	$1,684	$1,653	$1,710	$1,712

FIGURE 9.2

Weekly Management Statistics Report with Enhancements

	Goal	Week 5	Week 4	Week 3	Week 2	Week 1	March	February	January
Weekly Management Statistics Report									
			Current Month						
Logistics									
Inventory Accuracy	95%	Total number from a random			80%	89%	85%	79%	76%
On-Time Shipping	99%	sample of 100 counts that have			84%	79%	75%	74%	73%
Customer Returns (000s)	$0	accurate locations, quantities, and descriptions.			$36	$29	$78	$102	$139
Production									
Machine Utilization	75%	Total hours used on actual			78%	81%	75%	70%	71%
Overtime	5%	production during the period.			7%	11%	10%	9%	12%
Production Schedule Completed	98%	Does not include scheduled down time for preventive			100%	79%	81%	85%	83%
Scrap	2%	maintenance.			2%	1%	5%	4%	3%
Sales									
Backlog (000s)	$3,000	$2,806	$2,809	$2,819	$2,876	$2,901	$2,904	$2,611	$2,605
Lost Customers	N/A			3	-1	0	-2	-7	-11
New Customers	N/A	Number of new customers who have applied for credit		1	4	0	0	5	8
Period Sales (000s)	N/A	and who have placed firm orders exceeding $10,000.		9	$321	$350	$1,251	$1,279	$1,321
Working Capital									
+ Accounts Receivable (000s)	$1,100	$1,218	$1,327	$1,287	$1,285	$1,270	$1,300	$1,325	$1,330
+ Inventory (000s)	$1,500	$1,707	$1,754	$1,732	$1,702	$1,659	$1,654	$1,632	$1,607
- Accounts Payable (000s)	$1,300	$1,100	$1,103	$1,145	$1,307	$1,245	$1,301	$1,247	$1,225
Total Working Capital (000s)	$1,300	$1,825	$1,978	$1,874	$1,680	$1,684	$1,653	$1,710	$1,712

managers need to know which departments, as well as which people within those departments, are incurring the overtime. Armed with this information, managers can determine the exact causes of the overtime and correct them. An example of such a report is shown in Figure 9.3. The example is sorted by department and lists every hourly employee within each one. The report lists the percentage of overtime for every pay period (the example assumes two periods per month), so that you can quickly scan the report and see if there are consistently high overtime figures for particular departments or individuals.

Another measure on the weekly report that will result in a request for more detailed analysis is the on-time shipping statistic. If the percentage is low, managers have no way of knowing what shipments were delayed or why, so they can correct similar problems

FIGURE 9.3

Employee and Departmental Overtime Report

	1/15	1/30	2/15	2/28	3/15	3/31	4/15	4/30
Accounting								
Banuelos, Abel	15%	12%	13%	14%	0%	5%	10%	8%
Errett, Cynthia	18%	15%	16%	17%	3%	8%	13%	8%
Hick, Maggie	10%	7%	8%	9%	0%	0%	2%	4%
Knopf, Tom	14%	12%	12%	14%	2%	4%	9%	6%
Departmental Total	14%	12%	12%	14%	1%	4%	9%	7%
Engineering								
Belval, Tom	0%	1%	2%	6%	5%	4%	3%	8%
Fine, David	8%	8%	8%	8%	8%	8%	8%	8%
Holland, Drew	4%	3%	8%	5%	6%	7%	9%	2%
Kramer, Ted	10%	14%	12%	16%	20%	18%	14%	11%
Department Total	6%	7%	8%	9%	10%	9%	9%	7%
Logistics								
Bowker, Abby	14%	14%	16%	16%	16%	18%	14%	15%
Galleher, Patti	12%	13%	11%	10%	9%	8%	12%	15%
Jimenez, Brenda	3%	5%	4%	2%	1%	6%	16%	0%
Laramie, Connie	4%	7%	9%	2%	4%	6%	8%	2%
Department Total	8%	10%	10%	8%	8%	10%	13%	8%
Production								
Castaneda, Jerry	16%	15%	14%	25%	2%	5%	8%	1%
Goick, Gina	11%	15%	12%	20%	8%	8%	8%	8%
Josephson, Mike	4%	0%	3%	21%	6%	6%	4%	3%
Lomheim, Louis	9%	2%	4%	24%	4%	20%	6%	14%
Department Total	10%	8%	8%	23%	5%	10%	7%	7%
Sales								
Drexler, Tom	2%	0%	5%	12%	20%	25%	12%	6%
Gordon, Frank	8%	3%	8%	10%	15%	20%	10%	5%
Kennedy, Dennis	6%	0%	0%	8%	16%	21%	8%	4%
Mansfield, George	4%	2%	4%	6%	19%	24%	6%	3%
Department Total	5%	1%	4%	9%	18%	23%	9%	5%
Company Total	9%	7%	8%	12%	8%	11%	9%	7%

in the future. To remedy this issue, distribute a listing of all customer orders that were not shipped on time, which should include the reason for the problem. There are generally a standard number of reasons, so the problem section of the report can be a simple matrix that lists the standard error at the top and a check mark in the underlying grid for each delayed shipment. This is a sufficiently detailed amount of information for managers to use in conducting their own investigations. An example of the report is shown in Figure 9.4.

Similarly, an additional report is needed if management wants to know more detail about the reasons for changes in the level of machine utilization. An example of such a report is shown in Figure 9.5. This report groups machines by type, so that you can determine the overall usage of each group. If the usage level for an entire group is low, and there is a consistent trend line of results at that level, then management can eliminate some of the machines in that group in order to raise the average utilization level. The reverse decision, that of buying more machinery, may also result if a group utilization number is consistently tracking at a very high level. Also, if utilization suddenly drops to zero for a specific machine, there may be a maintenance problem that is bringing it down. This level of detail is generally sufficient for management to obtain a clear understanding of the reasons for changes in machine utilization.

In the machine utilization example, we are tracking the usage of machines that are employed in the production of candy. Three utilization issues arise in the report. The first is in the candy extruder machine group, in which the total machine usage approximates 50 percent in most months. Assuming that this trend will continue, management could consider selling one of these machines, which would bring the utilization of the remaining machines to approximately 75 percent. The second issue is in the candy wrapper machine group, in which a new machine (CW-01) was added in the beginning of the year and gradually ramped up to full production by April; however, utilization in this area is extremely high, so the purchase of yet another machine for this group appears to be justified, especially if the breakdown of any machine in this group

FIGURE 9.4

Delayed Shipment Report

					Problem Matrix						
Customer Name	Customer Order No.	Part Description	Part Number	Due Date	Freight Carrier Was Late	Insufficient Production Capacity	Machine Breakdown	Missing Materials	Missing Packaging	Scrapped Parts	Tools Broken/ Missing
Avery Arials Inc.	00348	Ski Carrier	SK-412	05/02/200X	X						
Bufford Bump Co.	01982	Snowboard Rack	SN-023	05/03/200X			X	X	X	X	
Chameleon Co.	7701	Ski Edging Tool	SK-401	05/01/200X				X	X	X	
Duffy Mogul Co.	3278	Boot Heater	BT-213	05/04/200X			X				
Entry Designs	1195A	Boot Rack	BT-214	05/03/200X	X	X		X		X	X
Force Powertrain	5004C	Hand Warmer	HA-003	05/02/200X		X					
Gander Aviation	65481	Ski Locks	SK-410	05/03/200X		X			X		
High Fliers	AB-021	Ski Wax	SK-409	05/01/200X			X				X
Itchty Skier	5562	Ski Tuning Kit	SK-413	05/04/200X	X				X		
Jump Ski Co.	905	Ski Decals	SK-423	05/05/200X			X				X

FIGURE 9.5

Machine Utilization Report

Machine Description	January	February	March	April	May	June	July	August	September	October	November	December
Candy Mixer												
CM-01	70%	68%	63%	75%	80%	77%	71%	70%	69%	80%	75%	76%
CM-02	67%	65%	69%	75%	73%	70%	65%	64%	66%	68%	69%	71%
CM-03	69%	67%	65%	76%	75%	73%	68%	67%	68%	72%	72%	73%
Group Subtotal	69%	67%	66%	75%	76%	73%	68%	67%	68%	73%	72%	73%
Candy Extruder												
CE-01	52%	59%	60%	59%	58%	54%	59%	52%	54%	55%	54%	50%
CE-02	51%	52%	54%	55%	51%	52%	57%	58%	52%	53%	55%	60%
CE-03	43%	44%	51%	40%	43%	45%	41%	40%	39%	38%	37%	35%
Group Subtotal	49%	52%	55%	51%	51%	50%	52%	50%	48%	49%	49%	48%
Candy Wrapper												
CW-01	15%	20%	50%	100%	90%	95%	88%	93%	90%	91%	95%	99%
CW-02	100%	98%	99%	97%	98%	100%	99%	93%	98%	95%	98%	99%
CW-03	100%	100%	100%	90%	100%	100%	100%	90%	100%	100%	100%	90%
Group Subtotal	72%	73%	83%	96%	96%	98%	96%	92%	96%	95%	98%	96%
Candy Packager												
CP-01	80%	85%	90%	92%	89%	87%	83%	81%	85%	86%	87%	85%
CP-02	78%	76%	75%	74%	70%	78%	72%	76%	75%	73%	71%	75%
CP-03	79%	79%	81%	82%	81%	79%	75%	79%	79%	75%	83%	78%
Group Subtotal	79%	80%	82%	83%	80%	81%	77%	79%	80%	78%	80%	79%
Candy Cane Twister												
CCT-01	0%	0%	0%	0%	0%	100%	100%	100%	100%	0%	0%	0%
CCT-02	0%	0%	0%	0%	0%	100%	100%	100%	100%	0%	0%	0%
CCT-03	0%	0%	0%	0%	0%	100%	100%	100%	100%	0%	0%	0%
Group Subtotal	0%	0%	0%	0%	0%	100%	100%	100%	100%	0%	0%	0%
Total for All Groups	54%	54%	57%	61%	61%	81%	79%	78%	78%	59%	60%	59%

would result in a bottleneck that could cut into total facility sales levels. Finally, the candy cane twister machine group, located at the bottom of the report, produces a seasonal item. Because of its seasonality, there is no cause for alarm when seeing utilization jump from 0 percent to 100 percent and then back to 0 percent—this is just the nature of the manufacturing process for a seasonal product. These are some of the issues that will be revealed by a machine utilization report.

The "Lost Customers" statistic on the weekly management statistics report yields only the number of lost customers, not who they are or why they left. This information can be included in another report, such as the one shown in Figure 9.6. This is a more free-form document, since there may be lengthy explanations for losing a customer that cannot be readily included in a problem matrix format, such as the one shown in Figure 9.4. The standard information to include in this report is the name of the customer, the date on which the company first learned of the lost business, the names of the salesperson and customer service person who were responsible for the customer, and the reason given by the customer for leaving. The names of the two contact people are important to track, in case one or more of them have a history of losing customers. The information in this report should be stored for at least a year, so that managers can review the historical data to see if there are repeated problems that are consistently causing the company to lose customers. This report can also be modified slightly to track lost quotes. The only difference is that the identifying quote number should be listed on the report. All other fields remain the same.

The lost customers report in Figure 9.6 reveals a consistent problem with a single customer service person, about whom three customers complained at the time they dropped the company as a supplier. By using this report format to discover continuing problems, such as the one with the customer service person, a company can identify and correct ongoing problems that irritate its customers.

The preceding sample reports were all connected to the statistics shown in the weekly management statistics report. The next report is not, because it focuses on a variety of errors that are not easily summarized. It is intended to put the spotlight on repeated transactional errors, so that the management team can focus on correcting

FIGURE 9.6

Lost Customers Report

Customer Name	Notification Date	Name of Salesperson	Name of Customer Service Person	Reason for Losing Customer
Parrot Graphics, Inc.	2/15/200X	O. Harmsen	M. Pierce	Consistently late deliveries.
Little Designs	2/19/200X	H. Davidson	R. Kontmann	Damage to shipping carton for the last three deliveries.
Central Label	3/14/200X	H. Davidson	M. Pierce	Incorrect shipment quantities for four of the last seven deliveries.
Country Art	3/21/200X	O. Harmsen	R. Kontmann	Incorrect bar code labels on shipments, despite repeated requests to change them.
Cloud Designs	4/1/200X	F. Anderson	M. Pierce	Part quantities in boxes were lower than the amounts listed on the box labels. Had to repeatedly request credits for short quantities.
Graphic Industries	4/5/200X	O. Harmsen	B. Zeltmann	Customer service person did not call back in a timely manner, and did not call back at all on three occasions.
Graphical Overlay Company	4/19/200X	D. Schwandt	R. Kontmann	Shipments sent to wrong company location for approximately one-half of all orders.
Water Based Paints, Inc.	4/30/200X	F. Anderson	R. Kontmann	Products sent were correct, but the color was wrong.
Honey Color Graphics Co.	5/11/200X	O. Harmsen	B. Zeltmann	Had repeated problems with overpricing on invoices, because customer service person set prices based on incorrectly low purchase quantities.
Interior Design Associates	5/17/200X	H. Davidson	M. Pierce	Shipments were an average of two days late in arriving, which stopped the production line in which those parts were used.
Candy Stripe Artists Co.	5/19/200X	D. Schwandt	B. Zeltmann	Low-quality parts. Rejected an average of 12% of parts in each order delivered.
Paint by Color Company	5/25/200X	F. Anderson	B. Zeltmann	Had great difficulty in obtaining credits from the customer service person, who did not return phone calls.
Coordinated Label Company	5/29/200X	O. Harmsen	R. Kontmann	Too many extra shipping charges tacked on to invoices. Customer considers these charges to be two times higher than normal.

corporate systems before they cause errors. To create this report, which is shown in Figure 9.7, you must extract all error correction transactions from the computer system. These are, for example, credits given to customers to adjust originally invoiced amounts, or cycle counting adjustments to correct inaccurate inventories, or scrap transactions for discarded materials. This information can be gleaned from the computer system by extracting the detail on these transactions—credits, adjustments, or scrap entries—and summarizing them into a report that notes the type of error, the date on which it occurred, the amount of the error in dollars, and the reason for the error. When the information in this report is summarized for a number of months, the summary-level report reveals where the bulk of a company's problems are occurring, so that management can focus its attention on these areas.

The main problem with a system errors report, such as the one in Figure 9.7, is that it can be used for a "witch hunt" by management, since it is possible to target the people who are repeatedly involved with errors, rather than the systemic problems that cause errors to arise. When employees realize that management is targeting employees instead of the system as a result of this report, a common response is to not make any adjusting entries in the computer system, so that the number of reported errors drops to zero, even though the errors are still occurring. This is a very detrimental result, for the accuracy of the data in the company database will decline rapidly when the staff stops correcting the information contained in it. Consequently, it is very important for the management team to use this report for systemic improvements, or else it will rapidly lose the trust of employees as well as database accuracy.

The reports in this section give management a comprehensive view of company operations. There are daily reports for the small number of crucial daily activities, as well as a more all-encompassing weekly report for which there are a number of supporting detailed reports that give management a thorough view of why there are problems with specific measurements. This type of interlocked internal reporting system is a good way to ensure that the management team is thoroughly apprised of company performance and the reasons for changes in it.

FIGURE 9.7

System Errors Report

Error Type	Error Date	Error Amount	Reason for Error
Customer Credit	7/01/200X	$278	Incorrect pricing that was based on a smaller order quantity than the order the customer actually placed.
Inventory Adjustment	7/12/200X	$1,204	Adjusted item was consumer product that may have been stolen by an employee.
Scrap	7/17/200X	$4,009	Caused by an incorrect setup with improper horizontal dimensions on large jig.
Scrap	7/22/200X	$57	Caused by damage to packaging, allowing welding materials to fall and be damaged.
Inventory Adjustment	7/29/200X	$12,471	Ran job with incorrect specifications for two days before noticed the problem. Had to scrap all completed parts.
Customer Credit	8/03/200X	$710	Shipped wrong product to customer by transposing part number in the order.
Customer Credit	8/14/200X	$654	Shipped too late to meet customer deadline, so product was returned for credit.
Scrap	8/15/200X	$98	Parts were painted the wrong color, due to color being labeled incorrectly.
Inventory Adjustment	8/23/200X	$170	Item was incorrectly counted during the year-end physical count. This entry adjusts back to actual quantity.
Scrap	8/23/200X	$249	Caused by excess sheet metal on sheet after required parts were punched out of it.
Customer Credit	9/05/200X	$1,298	We billed the customer for a larger quantity than was actually in the box.
Inventory Adjustment	9/06/200X	$2,500	Cannot find finished product, part number ABK-5402. Still investigating possible issues.
Inventory Adjustment	9/16/200X	$6,500	Incorrect unit of measure used for tape. Engineers changed it to rolls, which greatly increased the on-hand value, since the quantity had been recorded in inches.
Scrap	9/20/200X	$3,207	Extra wood scrap due to operator error. The machine operator was not well trained in how to use the equipment, and cut 142 planks too short.
Scrap	10/03/200X	$578	Product is missing, may have been stolen during the weekend.
Customer Credit	10/19/200X	$540	Incorrect pricing on product. Used standard pricing on the invoice, but this was a special deal with the sales staff that was not forwarded to the accounting department.
Customer Credit	10/24/200X	$821	Invoice could not be collected because customer went into bankruptcy. Wrote off as bad debt expense.

Profit Center Reporting

The last section was concerned primarily with reporting on operational issues, such as machine utilization and scrap rates. However, these are of no import if a company cannot consistently create a profit or spin off enough cash flow to keep those operations running. In this section, we review the concept of profit centers, and how one should report their results.

Every company creates and issues an income statement that reveals the financial performance of the entire company. For smaller organizations that deal with just a single line of business, such as a plumbing service company, this is sufficient. However, if there are several lines of business, such as a plumbing service group, a plumbing hardware store, and an air conditioning repair staff, then the revenues and costs of each one should be recorded separately, so that management can see if some areas are less profitable than others. An example of this report is shown in Figure 9.8, where we list a separate income statement for each profit center, which summarizes into the summary-level income statement for the entire company, as shown at the far right side of the report. Also in the report is a separate column for corporate overhead. These are costs that cannot be specifically allocated to a profit center. The basic rule for making the allocation determination is whether an overhead cost will disappear if a profit center is eliminated; if not, then do not allocate the overhead cost to the profit center. Also, there is an interest expense charged to each profit center, based on the amount of fixed assets and working capital that each one uses. Finally, after the profit figures at the bottom of the report, we add back the depreciation expense for each profit center (since this is a noncash expense), which yields the actual cash inflow or outflow to or from each profit center. The report reveals that the plumbing hardware store is making very little money, partially because of the interest expense charged to it that covers the cost of funds for the store facility and inventory (as pointed out by the arrows in the figure). Both service groups, having no significant assets, have a much lower interest expense and so earn a larger profit. Based on this analysis, it is evident that the hardware store is a drag on the overall corporate earnings percentage.

FIGURE **9.8**

Profit Center Income Statement (000s)

Description	Plumbing Service	Plumbing Hardware	Air Conditioning Repair	Corporate Overhead	Summary Income Statement
Revenue	$1,400	$1,750	$972	$0	$4,122
Direct Expenses:					
Material	625	1,115	410	0	2,150
Direct Labor	450	250	350	0	1,050
Total Direct Cost	1,075	1,365	760	0	3,200
Total Direct Margin	325	385	212	0	922
Direct Margin Percentage	23%	22%	22%	0%	22%
Overhead Allocation	14	57	14	375	460
Gross Margin	311	328	198	−375	462
Gross Margin Percentage	22%	19%	20%	—	11%
General & Administrative	25	85	25	175	310
Interest Expense	42	193	29	0	264
Net Profit (Loss)	244	50	144	−550	−112
Net Profit Percentage	17%	3%	15%	—	−3%
+ Depreciation Expense	21	81	21	37	159
Cash Inflow (Outflow)	264	131	165	−513	47
Capital Usage:					
Working Capital	325	1,578	175	0	2,078
Fixed Assets	145	565	145	258	1,113
Total Capital Usage	470	2,143	320	258	3,191

To create a profit center analysis, the accounting staff must track billings and expenses by specific profit center, rather than recording them all in a single set of account numbers, which is a slightly more complicated accounting transaction. Also, all assets should be recorded in accounts that are specifically assigned to profit centers, so that interest expenses can be charged based on these amounts. The most difficult item to track is working capital for each profit center, because this requires the identification of all accounts receivable, inventory, and accounts payable by profit center. To record working capital accurately, it may be necessary to either maintain a separate set of accounting records for each profit center or manually compile this information whenever the accounting staff creates a profit center financial statement. Given the amount of detailed information that results from this report, the added work is well worth the effort.

Customer Margin Reporting

If a company creates an income statement report by profit center and the management group still feels that it does not have enough information, the next logical step is to create a customer margin matrix, because it reveals an additional level of detail by showing profits by customer for each profit center. This method results in a matrix, as shown in Figure 9.9, that segregates all company customers into one of four quadrants on a profitability and volume chart. The quadrant in the lower left corner contains those customers that are marginally profitable and also have minimal sales volume. The quadrant in the lower right corner is the worst one, for it contains those customers with low profit margins and high volume (e.g., the company is expending much effort for little result). The company's objective for the customers located in these first two quadrants is to either eliminate them or raise their prices to improve profits. The quadrant in the upper left corner contains customers with high margins but low sales volume. The objective here is to improve their purchasing volume. The final quadrant, which is in the upper right corner, is for high-volume, high-profit customers, and contains all the prized customers that a company absolutely does not want to lose. This report format is extremely revealing in terms of which customers should be dropped and which given special treatment, and, with some deft customer management, can result in a much more profitable mix of customers. The cutoff figures for margin and volume, as noted in the example, will change depending on the business. The dividing line for high and low margins may not be 25 percent, as shown in the example, nor may the volume demarcation be $100,000. A company can set

FIGURE 9.9

Customer Margin Matrix

No. of Customers = 8		**No. of Customers = 5**	
Total Sales = $450K		Total Sales = $800K	
Average Margin = 41%	**Margin**	Average Margin = 38%	**Margin**
All Day Fitness	52%	Central City Gym	41%
Better Body Fitness	38%	Fitter Bodies Co.	47%
Body Builder Warehouse	41%	Nationwide Gyms	33%
Custom Bodies Co.	43%	Powerbuilder Plus	35%
Fitness Designs	45%	Runner's Palace	34%
Jump Higher Aerobics	39%		
Weights by Design	62%		
Weights Warehouse	29%		

No. of Customers = 7		**No. of Customers = 4**	
Total Sales = $325K		Total Sales = $1,417K	
Average Margin = 1%	**Margin**	Average Margin = 11%	**Margin**
All Round Fitness	−3%	Barbells Plus	13%
Dumbells Only	0%	Fitness Distribution Co.	7%
Fit by Night Inc.	3%	Kids Gyms and Day Care	11%
Ladies Workout Co.	7%	Southern Fitness	10%
Midwest Fitness	5%		
Powerhouse Bodies	0%		
Pumped Workouts Co.	−14%		

Margin axis (vertical); 25% and 100K markers; Revenue Volume (horizontal axis)

its own boundaries with different figures. Also, the margins on which this information is based can be calculated in several ways. One is to use direct costing (i.e., price minus direct labor and material costs), because of its simplicity. Alternatively, the margin calculation can include fully burdened costs, although this approach may result in overhead costs being assigned that have little real basis in fact. Accordingly, if margins are to include overhead costs, use activity-based costing to ensure that there is a justifiable reason for assigning costs to a customer.

With the operations reports, profit center analysis, and customer margin matrix, a management team will have a plethora of information on which to base its decisions to improve company profitability.

285

Summary

Businesses have varying reporting responsibilities to federal, state, and local jurisdictions. They have other external reporting requirements to creditors and investors. Finally, they have internal reporting functions used for planning and control.

The federal reporting requirements include employment reports on wage-earning employees, tax reports, and Social Security taxes. Employers pay unemployment taxes for their employees. The federal government has arranged for banks and federal depositories to receive taxes collected from employees and those paid by the employer. The employer withholds federal income tax and Social Security taxes and pays those into the federal depository pursuant to IRS guidelines. Annually, the IRS requires employers to report to their employees the wages and taxes paid and withheld.

Depending on the form of the business organization, there are various reporting requirements for federal tax liabilities. Sole proprietorships, S corporations, and partnerships pay income taxes for the business entity. However, S corporations and partnerships file information returns. Corporations are taxed as a separate legal entity.

Other reporting requirements arise out of the nature of the business. For example, dealers in firearms are strictly licensed and regulated by the United States Treasury Department. Other businesses are regulated as to rates, charges, and services offered. Utilities, transportation companies, banks, and other such industries are closely regulated. Some, because of the dangers associated with working conditions, are closely scrutinized. Coal mining, toxic chemical companies, and airlines are just a few such activities.

State governments also regulate and tax many businesses and activities. States generally tax the real property of businesses and the structures attached to the property through their ad valorem taxing authority. A business's equipment, fixtures, appliances, and inventories might be taxed using tangible personal property taxes. Intangible items of ownership, such as stocks, bonds, and notes, are taxed through intangible personal property taxes. In some cases, sales and purchases made in other states are taxed. Some products, such as groceries, medicines, and telephone services, are exempt in some states.

Local governments may impose taxes, licensing requirements, and zoning restrictions on the operations of some businesses. Some county or city governments may have franchise requirements for the provision of services; these may be exclusive rights to provide services, such as cable television.

Creditors have or seek certain information to ensure the likelihood of payment. Balance sheets, income statements, and statements of cash flow may be prepared and distributed. Investors, likewise, are concerned with these reports.

Finally, businesses have internal reporting requirements for planning and control. These needs vary with the size and type of business and with the style of management used.

Index